Doing Disability Diff

This ground-breaking book aims to take a new and innovative view on how disability and architecture might be connected. Rather than putting disability at the end of the design process, centred mainly on compliance, it sees disability – and ability – as creative starting points. It asks the intriguing question: can working from dis/ability actually generate an alternative kind of architectural avant-garde?

To do this, *Doing Disability Differently*:

- explores how thinking about dis/ability opens up to critical and creative investigation our everyday social attitudes and practices about people, objects and space;
- argues that design can help resist and transform underlying and unnoticed inequalities;
- introduces architects to the emerging and important field of disability studies and considers what different kinds of design thinking and doing this can enable;
- asks how designing for everyday life – in all its diversity – can be better embedded within contemporary architecture as a discipline;
- offers examples of what doing disability differently can mean for architectural theory, education and professional practice;
- aims to embed into architectural practice attitudes and approaches that creatively and constructively refuse to perpetuate body 'norms' or the resulting inequalities in access to, and support from, built space.

Ultimately, this book suggests that re-addressing architecture and disability involves nothing less than re-thinking how to design for the everyday occupation of space more generally.

Jos Boys is a Teaching Fellow in the Faculty of Arts, Design and Social Sciences at the University of Northumbria. She brings together a background in architecture with a research interest in the relationships between space and its occupation, and an involvement in many disability related projects. She is co-founder of Architecture-InsideOut (AIO) which brings together disabled artists and architects in collaborative explorations of building and urban design.

In Memoriam
Georgie Wise

Doing Disability Differently

An alternative handbook on architecture, dis/ability and designing for everyday life

Jos Boys

Routledge
Taylor & Francis Group
LONDON AND NEW YORK

First published 2014
by Routledge
2 Park Square, Milton Park, Abingdon, Oxon, OX14 4RN

and by Routledge
711 Third Avenue, New York, NY 10017

Routledge is an imprint of the Taylor & Francis Group, an informa business

British Library Cataloguing in Publication Data
A catalogue record for this book is available from the British Library

Library of Congress Cataloging-in-Publication Data
Boys, Jos.
Doing disability differently : an architect's alternative manual / Jos Boys.
pages cm
Includes bibliographical references and index.
1. Barrier-free design. Architecture—Human factors.
3. Architecture and society. I. Title.
NA2545.A1B69 2014
725'.54—dc23
2013043300

ISBN13: 978-0-415-82493-4 (hbk)
ISBN13: 978-0-415-82495-8 (pbk)
ISBN13: 978-1-315-77755-9 (ebk)

Typeset in Bembo
by Swales & Willis Ltd, Exeter, Devon

MIX
Paper from responsible sources
FSC® C013056
www.fsc.org

Printed and bound in Great Britain by
TJ International Ltd, Padstow, Cornwall

Contents

Figures

Plates

(The plate section can be found between pages 114 and 115)

Acknowledgements

This book developed out a series of projects – mainly working with disabled artists – to explore critical and creative new ways of doing disability and architecture that started from disability. *Making Discursive Spaces*, funded by Arts Council South East, brought together artists with interior architecture students at the University of Brighton. *So What is Normal?* was a project which prototyped online educational resources about disability and architecture, funded by the Centre for Excellence in Teaching and Learning in Design (CETLD), a partnership between the University of Brighton, Royal College of Art, Victoria and Albert Museum and the RIBA which ran from 2005 to 2010. Architecture-InsideOut was also funded by Arts Council South East to create new kinds of collaborative events between architects and disabled artists. *Doing Disability Differently* could not have happened without this support. In particular I would like to thank David Watson, Katie Lloyd-Thomas and Pam Shakespeare, who all contributed sections to this book, out of this earlier work.

I would also like to especially thank Professor Anne Boddington and Anne Asha from CETLD, at the University of Brighton; Stephanie Fuller and Sarah Pickthall at Arts Council South East; and Zoe Partington-Sollinger, co-founder of AIO. I cannot even begin to express my appreciation for the artists who have been involved at different stages – Noëmi Lakmaier, Rachel Gadsden, Caroline Cardus, Jon Adams, Aaron Williamson, Barbara Lisicki, David Dixon, Sue Austin, Tony Heaton, Chris Ankin, Rubbena Aurangzeb-Tariq, Lynn Cox, Stephanie Fuller, Sabine Gruhn, Joolz Cave Berry, Miles Thomas, Mellisa Mostyn, Tanya Raabe, Mandy Legg, Sarah Pickthall, Zoe Partington-Sollinger and Damian Toal. Architects who participated with such enthusiasm in AIO events were from Architype, Ash Sakula, Fluid Architects, Agents of Change (AOC), Anne Thorne Architects, Sarah Wigglesworth Architects, Avanti Architects, HLM Architects, Robert Barnes Architects and Matthew Lloyd Architects. Additional support came from Marcus Dickey Horley at Tate Modern, Gwen Webber and Mandy Legg for AIO, capture artists Rachel Gadsden, Joseph Young and Abigail Norris, and Chris Higgins and Martin Gent from Map Consortium. The Interior Architecture students who participated in the design project at the University of Brighton were Kerry Alford, Charlotte Brisley, Matt Everest, Laia Martin

Marqueda, Lettie McCall, Alex Paduano, Rohini Pophale, Dominie Shelley, Vasiliki Stylianou, Ellie Taplin and Rebecca Whythe, with Teresa Hoskyns as co-tutor.

Finally, there are many others who have contributed in other large and small ways to the production of *Doing Disability Differently*, all of them incredibly supportive. They include Aaron Williamson, Katherine Araniello, Damian Toal, Sue Austin, Cassie Herschel-Shorland, Georgie Wise, Katie Lloyd-Thomas, David Bonnett, Pauline Nee, Rachel Marshall, Julie Fleck, Mark Lumley, Marcos Cruz, Robert Mull, Revital Cohen, Henry Frank, Sophie Handler, John Walker, Thea McMillan, Colin Hambrook, Liz Crow, David Gissen, Masashi Kajita, Alex Doodle, Hamish Roberts, Paul Redfern, Nicholas Vogelpoel, David Dixon, Ben Cove, Iia Beka and Louise Lemoine, Rob Imrie, Aimi Hamraie, Rachel Luck, Tobin Siebers, Robert Adams, Kerry Boys, Ian Kerr, Isobel Creed, Fran Ford, Emma Gadsden, Ian Howe and Jennifer Schmidt. To everyone, for all your help, my deepest thanks.

Introduction

Why do disability differently?

In an ongoing project called *The Disabled Avant-Garde Today!* artists Katherine Araniello and Aaron Williamson respond to, and re-make artwork based on, some seminal creative practitioners including Jake and Dinos Chapman, Leigh Bowery, Simon and Garfunkel, Martin Kippenberger, Tom and Jerry and Busby Berkeley. Through a series of videos the artists (re-)perform their various artistic and cultural (non-disabled) heroes and are by turns hilarious, absurd and sarcastic commentators, as shown in Plate 1 of the colour section. Though humorous, their point is a savage one – nobody will, of course, ever believe that disabled people could actually form a creative and artistic avant-garde.

Here, though, I want to suggest that *starting* from disability – rather than treating it as an afterthought to building design – does have the potential to generate some truly radical, avant-garde and creative architectural practices. This is because architecture is centrally concerned with both peoples' needs and desires (in all their diversity), and is one of the means through which our everyday social and spatial practices[1] are orchestrated. Thinking more explicitly about disability and being more attentive to disabled and Deaf[2] people themselves, can split open our commonsense assumptions about how the world 'normally' works, and make new opportunities for creating different kinds of designed spaces.

1 'Social and spatial practices' is a phrase that will be used a lot in this book. It is a shorthand way of describing the relationships between material space and the activities that go on in it as a continual process of enacting the 'normality' of our everyday, un-thought-about routines. Spaces, objects and encounters with others are seen as the (partial, complex and uneven) mechanisms through which particular ways of understanding the world are perpetuated over others, but also contested and adapted.

2 Many Deaf people, particularly those who use BSL (British Sign Language), argue that they are a linguistic minority with their own language and culture, and therefore do not define themselves as disabled. For this reason, in some disability writing the term disabled and Deaf people is used. The use of a capital D for Deaf recognises this differentiation; acknowledging that many people who use sign language have a strongly developed sense of their own cultural identity (see glossary). In this book, I use deaf when talking about people in general, and Deaf when referring to the cultural and political movement.

As disabled people, we are forced to constantly evaluate form and function and engage creatively with practical problems around negotiating space.

(Damian Toal, Making Discursive Spaces Project, University of Brighton: blog 8 April 2007)

Why, then, does the idea of disability being creative and avant-garde seem so absurd? Is it because of taken-for-granted assumptions about disabled people: that they are in need of the help of others, are passive consumers of services, constitute a minority of individuals in society who (unfortunately) must bear the brunt of their own medical problems? Is it because creativity slips sideways into 'art therapy' when undertaken by disabled people, and into functional and clinical solutions when undertaken by architects? What if, instead, we see that re-thinking disability enables us to explore critically and creatively assumptions about, and relationships between, disability *and* ability, which, in turn, can offer better ways of understanding the architectural implications of both bodily diversity and everyday socio-spatial practices? What if we actually engage with what Partington-Sollinger calls disabled peoples' 'particular prowess for "reading space"' (2008), or as Tobin Siebers says:

> . . . disabled people have to be ingenious to live in societies that are by their design inaccessible and by their inclination prejudiced against disability. It requires a great deal of artfulness and creativity to figure out how to make it through the day when you are disabled, given the condition of our society.
>
> (Siebers 2010b online)

Disabled people then are not just passive users of services and buildings, but can offer something powerful back to architects and other built environment professionals. Crucially, however, this is about much more that just better defining diverse individual needs and desires so as to better inform architectural design. It is also about disentangling how 'commonsense' stereotypes of disability actually *prevent* our better understanding of the inter-relationships between material space and its occupancies[3] – not just for disabled people, but for everyone. This is because properly engaging with disabled peoples' experiences starts to

3 I have chosen to mainly use the term 'occupancies' as a way of describing the entangled relationships between people, buildings, objects and spaces. Other common terms, such as use or inhabitation, seem quite problematic, because they remain connected to older cause–effect, stimuli–response, man–environment, subject–object framings, which persistently separate out the person from space. Meanwhile the 'newer' terms being introduced to grapple with this difficulty – choreography, enactments, performance – all also have their limitations in focusing on describing the dynamic qualities of our engagements with space, rather than on social practices. In fact, what is most interesting is how lacking language is in being able to express our ordinary (and diverse) inter-weavings of social and spatial experiences.

challenge simplistic and unspoken divisions between disability *and* ability, to expose the many assumptions and problems in architectural framings of the 'user' more generally, and to open up other kinds of creativity through refusing to perpetuate assumptions about disabled people (Figure 0.1).

Re-thinking practices

Despite many years of campaigning and design effort, the built environment continues to be often inaccessible to disabled people. However, this book aims to show that this is *not* because architects are too egotistical to take disabled people seriously – often what they are accused of – but instead the result of the underlying commonsense conceptual frameworks we *all* use to think about disability, ability, occupancies and material space. This affects not only the assumptions abled[4] people make in their everyday lives about what being

Figure 0.1 *Balls!* One of a series of performances exploring disability through playfulness, Turbine Hall, Tate Modern, London by architects Architype and disabled artists Caroline Cardus and Joolz Cave Berry, as part of Arts Council South East funded Architecture-InsideOut event (AIO), 10 May 2008. Photography: Jos Boys.

4 In the UK words like 'cripple' and 'handicapped' are no longer commonly used to describe disabled people (or people with disabilities, or 'physically challenged' people or any of the other terms that circulate in different places and periods). At the same time, disabled people have not only come up with subversive terms for themselves (such as crips and misfits) but also for the 'able-bodied'. Many use the term non-disabled whilst, for example, for Asperger's and autistic activists, 'normal' people are often known – disparagingly – as normo-typicals. Here I use 'abled', because it *names* the specific, usually unspoken characteristics by which the non-disabled assume their own experiences to be obvious and unproblematic.

disabled 'is like' but also the underlying beliefs of architectural theory and practice. So, despite the centrality of architectural design and the built environment to the lives of most disabled people, there remains little serious critical theoretical work in this area. It is important to ask why architecture does not yet have a body of work around disability equivalent to that exploring gender and sexuality, or race and post-colonialism (Matrix 1984, Colomina 1996, Borden *et al.* 1999, Lokko 1999, McCorquadale *et al.* 2001). That this invisibility is reflected across other academic and professional disciplines is an indictment of cultural and critical theory and practice more generally, and illustrates just how deeply disability remains avoided, compared to other disadvantaged identities. Yet this is at a time when disability studies is emerging as an important and creative field, challenging both 'medical' and 'social' models of disability; and critically engaging with key contemporary ideas around post-modernism, feminism, post-colonialism, post-structuralism and post-humanism. Over the last 40 years disability studies has become an energetic and relevant – if highly contested – field, yet it remains largely ignored by architects, including many of its accessibility and inclusive design specialists, and by architectural theorists and critics.

At the same time, there has been within the disability field a tendency, reflecting more general popular beliefs, to assume that the design professions ignore the demands of disabled people because of architects' over-powering egos and creative arrogance. When it comes to critiquing the built environment, debate seems to be restricted by the assumption that designing for people in general, and for the disabled in particular, is obvious and easy; that all that is required is the right kind of effort by architects and then everything will be 'all right'. Here, I take a different position, arguing that starting from disability does *not* lead to universal or simple design solutions but instead opens up to creative engagement the complex, messy and often contradictory intersections of our diverse lives with others, artefacts and material space; an approach that has ramifications for the very shape of architecture's knowledge base across theory, practice and education. This position aims to expose how disability is persistently framed, both by 'normal' social and spatial practices and by architecture's own internal discourses, as only affecting architecture *sometimes*, making disabled people what Tanya Titchkosky calls 'included as excludable' (2011). It explores the disabling effects this has on disabled peoples' lives, on our understandings of disability *and* ability, on the shaping of material space and on architecture as a discipline. What I aim to offer architects instead are some ideas, strategies and tactics for thinking and doing building design that can go beyond the frustrating limitations of the current relationship of architecture to disability, structured through *compliance* – regulations and design guidance – underpinned by an (unnoticed) conceptual framework that keeps disability in its 'place'. This means also unravelling the effects of architects continuing to treat disability in a stereotypical and mechanical way, as an add-on to the 'proper' design process. And it means asking why disabled people seem marooned as marginal and invisible in architectural discourse and practice, despite the wider contemporary turn in the subject towards concepts centred around the body, such as embodiment, affect, difference and hybridity.

In *Doing Disability Differently*, disability *and* ability are understood as ambiguous, complex, inter-related and often contradictory categories. Design for disability is not simple, but demands a careful unpicking of how we frame such categories in the first place. This requires taking attentive notice of the many diverse disabled narratives and strategies for creatively surviving in our unequal world, as well as critically analysing commonsense assumptions about both disability and ability and the ways these become embodied in existing 'ordinary' social and spatial practices, such that disabled people are persistently left out. It proposes that architecture can challenge and shift ideas about, and practices around, disability and ability, that is around diverse occupancies, by designing *from* these complexities and contradictions; by opening up its own internal design discourses to critical investigation; and by creatively exploiting the gaps and openings in architectural theories and practices towards a better understanding of difference. Ultimately, this suggests that re-addressing architecture and disability involves nothing less than re-thinking how we articulate the inhabitation of designed space more generally.

Finally, it should be noted that many of the issues raised here are not just specific to architecture. Contemporary cultural theorists in many fields are exploring how to break out of a commonsense framing of the world through binary oppositions – whether disabled/abled, mind/body, art/science or ideas/practicalities – challenging the very structure of language, imbued with such divisions (Stengers 2000, Thrift 2007, Latour 2007a, Ingold 2011). Critical theory across the arts and humanities is currently examining how to better conceptualize and articulate the intersections of individuals, society and space as situated, embodied, specific, partial and dynamic rather than framed within simplistic binary relationships. It is shifting away from concerns with representation and cultural meaning (what things 'say') to the non-representational, to how life is performed (what things 'do'). Starting from disability, I suggest, also enables critical and creative engagement with these wider concerns, informing how we work towards making better sense of the world, so that we can act towards improving it.

Using this handbook

Doing Disability Differently has been written with many audiences in mind – architectural theorists and practitioners, educators and architectural students, other built environment professionals and those in related academic fields, disabled writers, artists and activists, and all those interested in ways of improving the built environment for disabled people. Whilst it can be read chronologically, readers are also welcome to 'dip' into the sections they find most relevant. The book ranges across theories and examples, personal interpretations and sustained analysis, underpinned by diverse voices rather than a single authorial viewpoint. The overall argument is, of course, ultimately mine, and does not speak for the many other people who have contributed. In covering a lot of ground the work also fails to do full justice to the depth, variation and value of disability studies, to the already existing and important work in accessible and inclusive design, or to the range and concerns of architectural practice and theories more widely. Writing as a non-disabled person, the claim is not to speak for disabled people, but to take responsibility for how abled people perpetuate the marginalization of the disabled, to refuse to ignore that situation and to be part of a movement for change.

Doing Disability Differently had its genesis in, and is deeply informed by, both a series of collaborations with disabled artists and the richness of work coming out of disability studies. It also follows one of the central tenets of disability studies – research and practice must be more than an academic endeavour, also aiming to improve the position of disabled people in society. Whilst architecture as it is taught and practised also has a strong underlying social commitment, this usually remains too vague and generalized to have any recognizable mainstream impact. This is particularly true of dis/ability[5] which remains under-theorized and under-developed, even in radical and community-based practice. Disability fails to be properly embedded in the way architects are trained to think about the world, or to 'do' design; for, as I have already suggested, it is the very shape of the discipline's own knowledge base that can *mitigate against* making any real changes for disabled people. This is because, to paraphrase Mark Wigley:

> The active production of (*disabled/non-disabled*) distinctions can be found at every level of architectural discourse: in its rituals of legitimation, hiring practices, classification systems, lecture techniques, publicity images, canon formation, division of labour, bibliographies, design conventions, legal codes, salary structures, publishing practices, language, professional ethics, editing protocols, project credits, etc.
>
> (Wigley 1996: 329, italics added)

Part of the intention in this book, then, is to expose just when and how slippages occur in design thinking and doing, which ultimately act to make disability disappear (or to appear only sometimes). It is to argue for a renewed social responsibility by architects that accepts and responds to such critiques, not only in specific cases, but also in the very structure of its disciplinary frameworks (Wigley 1991).

5 A final point on terminology. Whilst I use the terms disabled and abled to 'name' people differently depending on their bodily and mental capacities, I also argue that the boundaries between disability and ability are ambiguous and porous; and that disability and ability need to be explored together, not separately. The term dis/ability is therefore used to express such complex entanglements between and across all our many bodies, and to remind us of the endless overlaps and slippages between being abled and disabled.

Our role in society can be likened to that of the satirist . . .

(Paul Hunt, 'A Critical Condition' in Hunt, P. (ed.) 1966: *Stigma: The Experience of Disability*, London: Geoffrey Chapman, p.14)

But focusing on the gaps in architectural theory, education and practice through which disability falls, and arguing for a different kind of socially responsive practice, is not to insist on a form of architectural practice that is merely well meaning, 'politically correct' and (therefore 'inherently') dull. I started this chapter by imagining the possibility of an intertwining of a different kind of architecture with a disabled avant-garde. As Williamson writes, the aim of his work is:

> a politicised, yet humorous sensibility towards disability. Mostly, I devise unique artworks that are created on-site immediately prior to their public presentation. These consider the situation I encounter and represent, in part, my response to it. A constant theme is to challenge and subvert the romantic valorisation of social 'outsiderness' and thus I portray myself in performances and videos in the guise of sham-shamans, pretend-primitives, hoax-hermits, fake feral children, charlatan saints and dubious monsters. With these figures I explore and devise humorous or absurd actions that reference and pay homage to the 'classic' period of performance art in the 1960s and 70s.
>
> (Williamson 2013 online)

Other writers and artists have dealt with issues that speak from disability but go far beyond its limited medical definition. These include the fragility of bodies, the powerful and powerless qualities of being an outsider, strangeness and normality, diversity and difference, communalities and interdependencies, isolation and independence (Figure 0.2), all of which offer potential new forms of architectural thinking and doing at the intersections of bodies, artefacts, encounters and material spaces. In this book I will return to this work often, as a means of generating creative and constructive engagements with dis/ability. It is such inventive spaces, I suggest, that can form the basis for an alternative – even avant-garde – architecture in which disabled bodies become central, not peripheral.

Figure 0.2 *Experiment in Happiness*, 2008, Noëmi Lakmaier. Photography: Hannah Facey.

> **Because my body is visibly disabled that body will always be read into my work, so it is probably worth considering from the start rather than ignoring it. But my work is really about taking the risk of being out of control.**
>
> (Noemi Lakmaier, 2013 interview with Jos Boys)

Section I

Starting from disability

1 Challenging commonsense

Human beings are not stereotypes. We are not defined by everyday assumptions, about what it is to be disabled/abled, old/young, female/male, black/white or fat/thin. But we do live our *relationships* to these (and other) stereotypes, and to our own and other people's commonsense[1] beliefs about how the world works, what is normal behaviour, what is an 'unsatisfactory' life and so on. The underlying argument of this book is that both commonsense assumptions and everyday social and spatial practices are performed, re-produced and challenged through continual processes of negotiation; and that this is a form of *work* that is both very important and goes mainly unrecognized.

> **[L]anguage recommends that we conceive of the able-body as something that just comes along 'naturally' as people go about their daily existence.**
>
> (Titchkosky 2002: 103)

Crucially, this work – which is endlessly and creatively managed by both disabled and abled people – is dominantly framed from a position of *ability*, tending to go by on a daily basis, as completely ordinary, unnoticed and unproblematic. This work is an entangled mixture of the practical (dressing, washing, cooking, cleaning, journeying) and of our personal, emotional and social interactions with each other, artefacts and spaces; that is, it is integral to the making

1 'Commonsense' is often seen as an obvious and unproblematic view of the world that is shared by most people, so straightforward as not to require any discussion. Here, on the contrary, it is taken as crucially important that we take more careful notice of, and critically unpack, our commonsense beliefs, as a means of exposing how the everyday world, and people's assumed different places within it, come to be shaped in particular ways rather than others. In this book commonsense notions of the world are always treated as problematic. This is because 'commonsense' is built from the ideas, assumptions and stereotypes we think with, rather than think about. To better understand how disability comes to be described in particular ways rather than others, we need to critically analyse just how dis/ability is constructed and perpetuated in everyday beliefs, feelings and actions. Using commonsense will never help us do that.

and re-making of what I have already called everyday social and spatial practices. Opening up the differential effects around how easy or hard that work is, and how enabling or disabling the situations in which it takes place are, is thus centrally important to better understanding relationships between disabled people and the design of the material landscape (an issue that will be returned to throughout this book). But before we can explore some of the specific intersections between dis/abled people, artefacts and material space, we must first expose how disability is located in a particular and difficult place by the 'taken for granted' commonsense assumptions about what disability is 'like'.

Handling the abled

Many disabled people will say that their biggest problem is not so much the fact of impairment itself, as the disabling attitudes and barriers that come from other people only seeing that impairment:

> Disabled people have to work continually against destructive forces which see us as powerless, passive and unattractive. It seems that no matter how cheerfully and positively we attempt to go out in the world, we are bound to be confronted by someone whose response to our lack of ordinariness, and difference from the norm leaves us feeling powerless and angry. Trying to understand the complicated feelings which arise out of our everyday encounters with the world is central to the lives of disabled people.
>
> In fact, if you bring any group of disabled people together, before very long we'll be swopping stories about the annoying, appalling, patronising, insensitive, unhelpful and sometimes just plain funny encounters that we have on an almost daily basis.
>
> (Keith 1996: 70)

Impairment, then, is not a neutral or objective fact; it is made and remade through everyday feelings, experiences and encounters. Lois Keith, writing about the impact of becoming disabled and 'the difference between how I wanted to see myself, as a now visibly different but still competent and private person, and how others saw me and would continue to see me' (Keith 1996: 70), highlights the disabling effects of abled attitudes:

> We are not supposed to understand that non-disabled people feel uncomfortable at our presence in the world and that what they sometimes feel is more than discomfort, it is revulsion. The central confusion of the relationship between us is that on the one hand they are disconcerted by our presence, and are confused about how to behave towards us or even what words they should use to describe us, but on the other hand they have a clear idea that they should be helpful and kind. Our part of the bargain is to ignore their unease and confusion and accept the 'help'. Our gratefulness is part of the lie that everything is really alright between us.
>
> (Keith 1996: 81)

Keith notes that – particularly where a disability is visible – the most immediate problem is that non-disabled people cease to see other 'normal' markers of social position and identity (class, gender, social status) that we are routinely able to read from each other's bodies when we first meet. All that is seen is the disability, making initial encounters awkward, and framing disabled people in ways that they themselves do not recognize. Only seeing the disability dehumanizes disabled people; they are voided of any 'normal' characteristics or personality traits. At the same time, conventional frameworks for what constitutes 'proper' social responses are also altered where there is the appearance of (or assumption of) a disability. As Keith goes on:

> All social encounters are governed by rules of behaviour. There are things that it is normally acceptable for strangers to say to each other and things that are not. For example, in the particular section of British society in which I usually mix, it is considered okay, indeed complimentary, to remark that people are thin, but rude to say that they are fat. It is acceptable to tell people that they are tall, but impolite to remark on the fact that they are unusually short. And there are things that people feel that they can say to disabled people which they wouldn't dream of saying to anyone else.
>
> (Keith 1996: 72)

This includes asking complete strangers, 'How did you get like that then?' or treating disabled people as if they are childlike, passive and incompetent. Here, disability is assumed to be negative, not whole, a lack and 'less than' normal; even worse, commenting on it is not regarded as an intrusion of privacy (who would ask someone bald how long they had had that condition?). Unfortunately this 'conventional' abled response is also understood as about being kind and charitable, for which disabled people should feel gratitude. Encounters therefore start out already skewed and unequal. As Sandy Slack writes:

> They have made some judgments already because they are privy to visual information about me which they then feel at liberty to comment on. The opening to the conversation will mostly be 'how long have you been in a wheelchair?' or 'what happened to you?' . . . The effect is to block the possibility of opening the conversation with equal information sharing about each other . . . I wish I could say I have dealt with this dilemma but alas I have not. My responses are as varied as the colours of the rainbow and depend on so many other factors. I am not consistent. It depends on who the person is, the occasion, the importance, my mood, my energy, my quickness of mind and my desire not to sound rude on the first meeting.
>
> (Slack 1999: 33)

This framing of the encounter from the position of the 'normal' person also acts to invisibly police what is considered acceptable behaviour by disabled people, particularly the display of anger and frustration:

> I always feel alone with my frustration. Here a complex set of emotions comes into play. Most friends deny me my justified anger, and because of their embarrassment I am drawn into a game which on the one hand wants to protect them, and on the other wants to scream at them for not seeing the oppression for what it is . . . From day one I have been fed a diet of goodwill, well meaning, persuasion, steady debate, until I feel obese with it all. Overflowing with too much trying, bloated with patronage, engorged with the rigidity of the world around me. In the early days it felt easier to let people do what they needed to do in order to feel good about themselves and confirm my disability. I colluded with this script for a while in an attempt to keep the peace and conserve energy. Until one day with almost thundering recognition it dawned on me that this compliance had little to do with my legs not working or the pain I experience but everything to do with denying my rights. My right to move freely and choose a variety of life experiences.
>
> (Slack 1999: 31–2)

Here is an ugly and inconvenient truth: it is not abled people who 'look after' the disabled, but disabled people who *protect* the abled from their own fears and confusions. Keith also describes some of the strategies she uses for coping with these attitudes, such as avoidance, politeness, anticipating difficulties, getting in first, taking an educator role, humour and anger (Keith 1996: 85–7). As she says:

> People offering help or asking questions is not in itself dis-empowering, but it is when we know that behind these questions are a whole set of assumptions about how awful the quality of our life must be and how fortunate they are not to be us. Just as difficult is the other side of the coin – the 'I think you are so wonderful, I don't know how you do it' kind of approach. Disabled people rarely, if ever, experience this as praise, unless it is said when we are doing something wonderful, rather than getting on with the business of living.
>
> (Keith 1996: 87)

Like many other disabled people, Sally French has had to 'manage' situations where assistance is offered or requested. As she says:

> Most people I approach are willing to help in any way they can and many volunteer. Mostly I am treated with respect. Taking control by stating with assurance exactly what help is needed seems to discourage condescension and patronage and induce relaxation and confidence in those from whom help is sought.
>
> (French 1999: 24)

Lois Keith is more forthright. Many other authors have noted the important differences between 'care' and 'help' (Shakespeare 2000, Mol 2008, Mol *et al.*

2010). Care implies a passivity – that disabled people cannot look after themselves or after others – while help suggests a more equal sharing:

> The cultural message that you must be kind to 'the handicapped' is a very powerful one. It acts as a mechanism which both distances the 'giver' of kindness from the recipient and allows them permission to patronise. The idea about caring for and caring about people who are less fortunate than ourselves is important . . . but unfortunately this state of goodwill and generosity often works to dis-empower disabled people . . . As Jenny Morris argues, 'our gratitude is an essential part of the relationship; charity is actually about making the non-disabled person feel good about themselves . . .'
>
> What harm is there in being grateful for the help that others give you? Well none if that help is freely offered on equal terms with nothing required in return except a simple thank you. All the wheelchair users I know say an awful lot of thank yous each day and we do so quite happily when people open heavy doors for us, see us sitting looking at a steep ramp and ask if we'd like a push, offer to take a tray of cups of tea to the nearest table for us, remove a chair so we can sit at the table and drink it or make any of the other thoughtful gestures which many people do each day. This is non-threatening, non-invasive assistance which makes both parties feel good about the other. It works on the basis that people will stop and look at us, ask if we would like a hand and move on if we say no. The problems come when people's motives for offering to help are not so straightforward.
>
> (Keith 1996: 79–80)

(Mis)reading devices

One of the odder aspects of these disabling stereotypes is that abled people tend to view the devices that support disabled people as problematic rather than valuable. Sobchack, for example, notes the differences between how non-disabled people 'see' her artificial leg, and how she 'feels' it for herself:

> The experience or use of a prosthetic does not determine whether a user feels that his or her body is disrupted. Indeed, in common use, as Kurtzman writes, 'artificial limbs do not *disrupt* amputees' bodies, but rather reinforce our publically perceived normalcy and humanity . . . artificial limbs and prostheses only disrupt . . . what is commonly considered to be the naturally whole and abled Body.
>
> (Sobchack 2006: 23, quoting Kurtzman, 2001: 380–1)

As another example, abled people often tend to see wheelchairs as an additional impediment, something that gets in the way and adds complications to 'normal' mobility. But wheelchairs are an enabling device, not a negative metaphor of lack – not 'a symbol of need and dependency' (Keith 1996: 71) (Figure 1.1, Plate 3). Rather, 'people like myself who rely on a wheelchair, for

Figure 1.1 Sue Austin, *Creating the Spectacle*, Unlimited commission as part of the 2012 Cultural Olympiad, co-curated with Trish Wheatley. Copyright: www.wearefreewheeling.org.uk. Photography: Norman Lomax. See also www.pushmeplease.co.uk/artists/sue-austin; www.susanaustin.co.uk

mobility and independence, see it as a piece of liberating equipment' (Keith 1996: 75–6). Or as Slack writes: 'My wheelchair is my best friend – I wheel it with pride and confidence. It takes me into the world' (Slack 1999: 35). Or for Peter Anderberg:

> The feeling of freedom and independence was enormous. With three wheels and a motor under me, I set off into the world again. First with my friend as a guide and for security, later on my own. Me and my machine. The machine that obeyed me. Just me. Up the hills and into buildings. Down the backstreets and over kerbs. Strong, quiet, obedient, without a fuss, without exhorting. No questions and no negotiations.
>
> (Anderberg 2006a: 114)

Yet wheelchairs (and other 'disabled' mobility aids and assistive technologies) are interpreted differently to other, ability-supporting, devices:

> I have noticed that most people who are in work live some distance from their workplace. They are not able to walk the long distance, so they usually look for some form of transport for their mobility needs. It may be a private car or public transport. This is considered the norm and in no way would it

> ever be described as a special need. Disabled people who require a wheelchair or a car for their mobility needs are described as having a special need.
>
> To disabled people this is neither a need nor special, it is an essential norm. Why, then, is it so difficult to obtain the mobility which is appropriate to that person's life?
>
> (Slack 1999: 34)

In fact, wheelchairs only get in the way of abled assumptions about what constitutes individual mobility rights by demanding space in the wrong places (entrances, interiors, etc.) where unencumbered walking is assumed to be the norm and anything else a problem. Cars, another mobility aid, also take up space, but making space for car parking is just another 'normal', unnoticed spatial practice (except, interestingly, disabled parking, which is often seen as problematic by abled people as giving an unfair advantage to the disabled). Sally French experiences these ambiguities of 'normal' interpretation when she uses her white cane – both as a mobility aid and, on occasions, as a device to signal to the non-disabled:

> White sticks can be used to supplement communication. I use a white stick intermittently as a symbol of visual disability. I use it to influence people's behaviour, for example, to attract their help or to alert them to take care . . . Despite this, I do not feel that people will believe it if, having used the white stick to cross a busy road, I fold it up and read a book. The feeling of discomfort to which this gives rise in the presence of others is very strong . . .
>
> My feelings about using my white stick are mixed. I regard it as a symbol of independence rather than a symbol of dependency. It is understood throughout the world and has assisted me in travelling with confidence in unfamiliar countries on my own. I constantly feel, however, that others are judging me and thinking I am a fraud.
>
> (French 1999: 24)

I will return later (in Chapter 6) to this issue of why devices for extending the body's abilities are – in the case of disabled equipment – seen as problematic markers rather than valued mechanisms of bodily augmentation. Like many blind and partially sighted people, Sally French has some vision, which affects how she engages with different contexts (close-up, complex visual situations, crowds). Here, though, the assumptions of the non-disabled that people are *either* blind *or* sighted affects her self-confidence in her own strategies, through the worry that she will be 'read' as fraudulent in her particular form of partial sightedness.

The ambiguous 'divide' between disability and ability

As Keith says, disabled people are just like everyone else, simply trying to get on with the business of living 'to move freely and choose a variety of life experiences'. But as well as dealing with abled responses to that one component of your personal situation that is an impairment – as French shows – disabled people must also develop strategies for dealing with simplistic stereotypes about what disability *should* look like, and how it *should* be enacted. This tends to demand a clear – preferably visible – division between being disabled and being able-bodied, in ways that appear to reinforce assumptions that disability is a lack, and tends to incapacity and passivity.

As well as assuming that the world divides non-problematically into the able-bodied and the disabled, many people also assume that having a disability is obvious, that it can be 'read' from the bodies of those who are 'different' through either their appearance or their actions. In fact, the diversity of our bodies makes this much more partial, difficult and shifting. People may be born with an impairment, or develop one later in life; it might be chronic, variable, or short-term. Many people may show no obvious physical symptoms, or can keep their exhaustion or medication 'hidden' from others. Liz Crow, in her series of performance installations, *Bedding in, Bedding Out* (Figure 1.2, Plate 5) expresses the complexity and ambiguity of being labelled disabled (here in direct response to recent English changes in disability benefits payment processes, which have required disabled people to 'fit' particular categories of impairment):

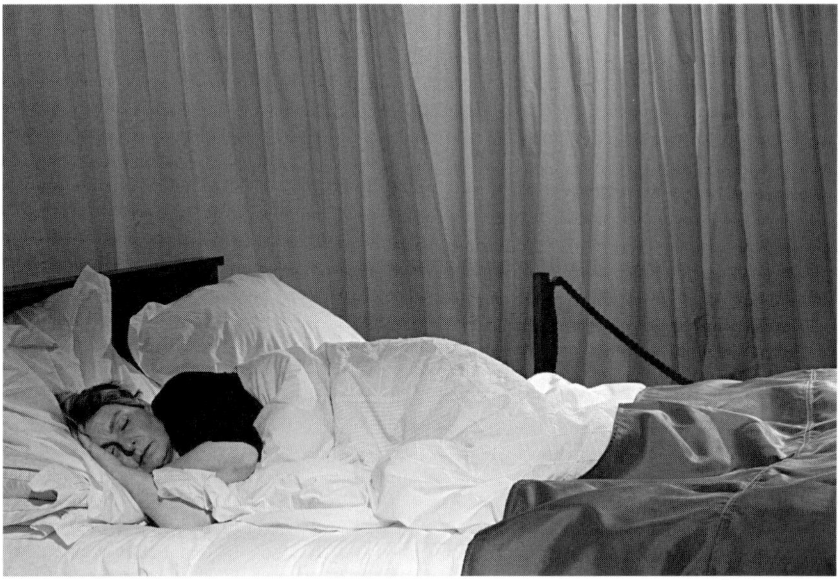

Figure 1.2 Liz Crow, *Bedding Out*, 48-hour durational performance at Salisbury Arts Centre, April 2013. Photography: Mathew Fessey/Roaring Girl Productions. www.roaring-girl.com

> I wear a public self that is energetic, dynamic and happening. I am also ill and spend much of life in bed. The private self is neither beautiful nor grownup, it does not win friends or accolades and I conceal it carefully.
>
> . . . *Bedding Out* is a performance in which I take my private self and make it public, something I have not done in over 30 years. On this stage, for a period of 48 hours, I am performing the other side of my fractured self, my bed-life. Since the public me is so carefully constructed, this will be a kind of un-performing of my self.
>
> I want to show that what many people see as contradiction – what they call 'fraud' – is only the complexity of real life. This is not a work of tragedy, but of in/visibility and complication; a chance to perform my self without façade.
>
> (Excerpt from Liz Crow interview: http://dpac.uk.net/2013/03/bedding-out-liz-crow-10-12-april-2013)

This gap between the personal experiences of a particular impairment or illness and the commonsense labels attached to disability produces ambiguity, where disabled people make choices about the extent to which they decide to 'pass' as abled. Precisely because the dominant social narrative of disability is about overcoming it, about approximating as much as possible to the 'normal', and because disabled people just want to get on with the business of living, many play down the extent of the additional work and effort demanded by this 'passing':

> I was born without a left hand, an impairment which I began to conceal at some point in my childhood (probably around 9 or 10 years of age). This childhood concealment strategy has left a long legacy: I still struggle with the 'reveal or not to reveal' dilemma, and more often than not will hide my 'hand' and 'pass' as normal. But concealment carries, and continues to carry, considerable psychological and emotional costs and has real social consequences. This hiding strategy was partly bound up with school life, but looking back I think a key influence was my association with the 'Roehampton Limb Fitting Hospital' . . .
>
> The main 'prize' of these visits was a series of artificial, or 'cosmetic' hands. These were ghastly, heavy and uncomfortable objects which I invariably relegated to the drawer soon after receipt . . . You could count the number of times I wore these on the fingers of one hand! However, they did their work indirectly because the underlying message was clear. The 'experts' were saying that my hand was something to be hidden, disguised. I had to appear as normal as possible. I found the easiest solution was to keep my 'hand' in a pocket, and I became very skilled at this concealment. Thereafter, I always had to have clothes with a strategically placed pocket. So it was, and so it is.
>
> (Thomas 1999a: 54)

Vivian Sobchack, by comparison, enjoys a creative tension between 'passing' as abled with a prosthetic leg, and wanting to display its virtues:

> My objective description of the prosthetic as technology doesn't begin to touch on the great pride that I've felt in my physical accomplishments or the great delight that I take both in the way my prosthetic leg can pass as real and the desire I have to show it off. This paradoxical delight and desire have led me to strangely unself-conscious and exuberant exhibitionism that always catches me by surprise.
>
> (Sobchack 2006: 33)

Disabled people, then, are always negotiating commonsense assumptions that refuse the ambiguity, overlaps and complications across being disabled or abled. This can involve a wide range of diverse attitudes and creative strategies, from exploiting invisibility through to 'playing' with exposure. As I said at the beginning of this chapter, it is *not* about living the stereotypes, but relating to, engaging with and living *in response to* these stereotypes.

Re-framing disability

The shift from the medical model, which sees impairment as a personal tragedy, to the social model, which focuses on disability as a socially constructed concept framed by the barriers to everyday life in the external world has been very important in the history of disability activism.[2] However, more recently many disability theorists, writers and activists have been re-exploring how to re-integrate the personal experiences of impairment with the public campaigns demanding improved services and environments for disabled people. The deliberate and political emphasis in the social model, developed by disability activists in the 1970s, was on what *society* should and could do to improve the lives of disabled people, centrally including demands for improvements in the accessibility of the built environment. More recently, this downplaying of the real, and often limiting, effects of impairment is being explored again, for example through the development of an 'affirmation' model.[3] As Liz Crow writes in considering disability campaigning strategies, disability does have (many diverse) effects that need to be considered:

2 Most disabled people differentiate between a medical and a social model of disability. The medical model focuses on the individual and their impairment; perceived as a personal problem that can be improved through medical intervention. The social model of disability argues instead that the problem is not with individuals but that it is the barriers, prejudice and exclusion by society (purposely or inadvertently) which are the ultimate factors in defining who is disabled and who is not in a particular society.

3 Swain and French (2000) explain the affirmation model as 'essentially a non-tragic view of disability and impairment which encompasses positive social identities, both individual and collective, for disabled people grounded in the benefits of lifestyle and life experience of being impaired and disabled' (p. 569).

> We align ourselves with other civil rights movements and we have learnt much from these campaigns. But we have one fundamental difference from other movements, which we cannot afford to ignore. There is nothing inherently unpleasant or difficult about other group's embodiment: sexuality, sex and skin colour are neutral facts. In contrast, impairment means our experience of our bodies can be unpleasant or difficult . . . Yet our insistence that disadvantage and exclusion are the result of discrimination and prejudice, and our criticisms of the medical model of disability, have made us wary of acknowledging our experiences of impairment. Impairment is safer not mentioned at all . . .
>
> What we need to do is to find a way to integrate impairment into our whole experience and sense of ourselves for the sake of our own physical and emotional well-being, and subsequently for our individual and collective capacity to work against disability.
>
> (Crow 1996: 209–10)

We live in a world where individual mobility, autonomy and personal competence are both highly valued and seen as normal. People who are less than fully mobile, are interdependent with others, or seem 'slow' then become the *problem*. This applies to anyone whose movement is restricted, such as mothers with small children, older people, and people with less access to resources, through poverty or social position. There are aspects of not fitting the 'norm' of an abled person that are broadly shared. But it is also important to reclaim the realities of different impairments, of living with issues of pain and exhaustion, whilst not blurring together the diverse experiences of different disabled people:

> [T]he perception of impairment as a personal tragedy is merely a social construction; it is not an inevitable way of thinking about impairment.
>
> Recognising the importance of impairment for us does not mean taking on the non-disabled world's ways of interpreting our experience of our bodies. In fact, impairment, at its most basic level is a purely objective concept which carries no intrinsic meaning. Impairment simply means that aspects of a person's body do not function or they function with difficulty. Frequently this is taken a stage further to imply that the person's body, and ultimately the person, is inferior. However, the first is fact, the second interpretation. If these interpretations are socially created then they are not fixed or inevitable and it is possible to replace them with alternative interpretations based on our own experiences of impairment rather than what our impairments mean to non-disabled people.
>
> (Crow 1996: 211)

Explicitly recognizing the experiences of impairment and illness as a *normal* part of life means that we urgently need to explore how to better engage with dis/ability, that is to simultaneously take notice of the many strategies and narratives of disabled people themselves, and to engage more critically with the unspoken assumptions behind what constitutes being *abled*. This requires seeing disability and ability as a series of overlapping concepts and experiences, with varying and differential effects that are ambiguous and relational. What the people talking here reveal is that disability is an *unstable* category, but one that the abled too often attempt to hold as fixed (and preferably) avoidable. It is only by starting from dis/ability instead, that we can begin to unravel how such processes operate to ignore the inherent vulnerability of bodies, and to continually marginalize disabled people (making them invisible within architectural theory, practice, education and material spaces), and thus begin to challenge and find alternatives to the problematic effects of abled people's thoughtless (that is, without thought) commonsense assumptions about the world.

Figure 1.3 Caroline Cardus, *The Ruby Slippers* (2003). www.carolinecardus.com

2 Beyond accessibility

The previous chapter has shown how stereotypes of disability can distort our understanding of the diversity and complexity of disabled peoples' lives, and make invisible the continuous entanglements between disability and ability. Next I want to critically explore the commonsense assumptions about disability *within* architectural education and practice. Whilst, as already outlined, disability activism and campaigning from the 1970s has had a huge and important impact on building design through both regulatory standards and design guidance, nearly 50 years on there are still many inaccessible buildings, and disability continues to be an afterthought in most architectural design.

Here I want to make a – potentially radical – claim, by proposing that current 'normal' and compliance-centred approaches to designing for disability ultimately work *against* the very aims they are trying to achieve. This happens (unintentionally) because the language of accessibility and inclusive or universal design[1] frames disability and architecture in quite specific and limiting ways, hiding as much as it reveals. This is not to dismiss the many fine built examples that have been designed under these rubrics. It is to propose that the continuing lack of progress towards accessible buildings – and the continuing relative invisibility of disability issues within architecture – is literally built into its current location as a 'separate issue', informed by regulatory and advice-giving guidance, rather than as an integral part of everyday design practices. So, instead of arguing the case for inclusive design (however important), I will concentrate on better understanding *why* accessibility and inclusive design has failed to make a proper purchase in architectural design, education and practice, and begin to explore how this might be creatively and constructively changed. I will suggest

1 The concept of designing for disability comes with many names – universal design, barrier-free design, accessibility, design for all, inclusive design, etc. The overall belief (or hope) is that making buildings accessible for the disabled will also make them work better for everyone. What these tend to share is an approach that starts from general principles, and then develops these through the listing and illustration of concrete detailed design examples. Here, I will be critical both of the assumptions that the 'needs' of the diversity of disabilities can be met unproblematically through building design, and that the principles/examples technique is the best way of re-doing disability in architecture.

that the continuing marginalization both of disabled people and of inclusive design within architecture is perpetuated because disability/accessibility has become stuck in older, rationalist and modernist understandings of architecture, which reinforces its 'unattractiveness' to, and lack of resonance with, contemporary design ideas and practices, even as these become more concerned with the body and difference; and that its predominant mode of argument through facts, principles and problem-solution examples ends up running 'parallel to' how architects actually think and do when they design, putting it always in an 'uncomfortable' position that then becomes the very *justification* for avoidance and exclusion. In fact, its (hard-won) regulatory placing at the end of the design process generates and then perpetuates abled commonsense assumptions that disability *only* needs to be equated with technical and functional requirements. This allows architects to avoid thinking about it very much (except in specific cases), to avoid 'doing' disability as a normal part of their design activities, and to just apply 'ready-made' solutions disconnected from any kind of creative engagement. The result is a dominant form of designing for disability that operates only sometimes and mainly at the *level of appearances*.

Architects design in their own image, often centralize their own experiences of space and marginalize and negate the experiences of others.

(Morrow 2000: 43)

These difficulties around disability/accessibility intersect with problematic understandings of the 'user' more generally, and can open up for critical investigation some of architecture's own assumptions about how to design for diverse occupancies. In particular, this has emphasized making space more 'flexible' to meet different needs, and developing user participation as a method for understanding these needs more precisely in specific cases. I will propose that whilst such alternatives have produced many well-designed and responsive spaces, they still avoid the deeper implications of starting *from* dis/ability. I will end by arguing that we should move beyond the framings of disability within architecture as predominantly about accessibility; looking as well for alternative theories, strategies and tactics that can integrate into the architectural design process *itself* a taking notice of diverse disabled narratives and strategies; and a critical and creative analysis of commonsense assumptions about dis/ability and the ways these get literally embodied into existing 'ordinary' social and spatial practices.

Problems in implementing the social model of disability

Contemporary architectural and educational practices have responded to a wider cultural shift from medical to social models of disability. As Eliza Chandler (2011) put it, the former approach of containing disability – physical, mental, psychiatric, emotional, and intellectual – in asylums positioned disability as 'there', which guaranteed, although impossibly so, that it was 'not here'. This has been replaced by the integration of disabled people in society. Why then, do dis/ability in general, and disabled people in particular, remain an awkward complication for architectural theory, practice and education? Why is it still 'there but not there?' Partly this is just a reflection of more general commonsense abled attitudes to disability, outlined in the previous chapter. Here, though, I want to show some of the problematic and unintended ways in which the social model of disability has intersected with changing architectural theory and practice over the last 40 years. On the one hand, the emergence of disability experts (such as access consultants and specialist designers) has kept this field as a parallel, separate and often oppositional activity which has left it isolated from important changes to mainstream design approaches – most crucially those which have re-thought the limitations of architectural modernism, through, for example, post-modernist, post-structuralist and, more recently, post-humanist ideas. This has caused accessibility guidance (if not its actual built realizations) to be left behind in older and quite limited functional concepts of the user. On the other, as authors such as Rob Imrie (1996) have shown, it has resulted in disabled people being mainly located in marginal positions, such as on access forums, which has severely limited their voices in, and challenges to, architectural design. Disabled people are thus only able to criticize what architects and designers propose on a case-by-case basis, rather than through the creation of any kind of longer-term discursive space. Locating disabled people predominantly within the separate category of accessibility also leaves them over-exposed as a difficulty for designers: people whose needs can be met only through a series of solutions that are problematic to achieve, yet basically technical (thus banal and dull). Here we have what is a recurring pattern of both *invisibility* – all too often either left out as relatively unimportant or undifferentiated from 'normal' people – or *over-exposed* as highly visible, that is as a 'special' case, concerned only with disabled 'needs'. Disabled people are thus somehow simultaneously 'users', just like everyone else, and 'not-users', outside of everyday social and spatial practices, an issue I will return to in the next chapter.

The end result is that much consideration of disability and architecture is still treated resolutely in a functionalist way, at the practical/technical end of architectural considerations, and that disabled people continue to be framed as passive, non-creative users, except in special one-off cases. Where accessible elements are included, they are only infrequently treated with the kind of creative, obsessive detail that other parts of the building design are seen to warrant. Thus, what may be accessible on paper (in its mechanical cutting and pasting from design guidance) often turns out to be problematic in reality (Figure 2.1).

What is more, in both education and practice, this binding of disability to function – which is an unnecessary rather than obvious connection – is all too often perceived as making it marginal to the more central and conceptual ideas

Figure 2.1 Caroline Cardus and Jos Boys, *Toilet Trauma*, demonstrating an inaccessible 'accessible' toilet, Truman's Brewery, London, 2007. Photography: Jos Boys.

or processes, that is, as a drag on or as potentially undermining architectural creativity and design fluency (Morrow 1999, Morrow and Moore 2004, Morrow *et al.* 2004). In fact, the whole language of accessibility and inclusive design[2] tends to be framed around a belief in functional solutions to the problems of a range of specific impairments, which – it is assumed – can be simply, coherently and comprehensively designed so as to meet all the 'needs' of all disabled people. These solutions predominantly aim to make disabled bodies more 'normal' through the addition of designed devices (ramps, platform lifts, grips) which enable them to overcome the physical restraints of different impairments. Thus,

2 There are, of course, examples – perhaps most immediately the Lifetime Homes initiative in the UK – that have developed and implemented effective design principles that are making a real impact on people's lives, which go beyond mechanistic approaches. See Chris Goodman (2011), *Lifetime Homes Design Guide*, Watford: IHS BRE Press. Available for download from www.lifetimehomes.org.uk/pages/lifetime-homes-design-guide.html.

the emphasis within the social model on the importance of physical barriers – to be resolved by their designing out – appears to support architectural solutions, but fails to challenge the underlying assumptions of disability as an 'abnormal' condition, compared with the natural obviousness of able-bodied mobility, autonomy and independence, and cannot therefore effectively criticize the everyday social and spatial practices which perpetuate particular stereotypes of disability.

> **In many cases it is true that what is good for disabled persons is also good for the majority without disabilities, but it is no universal truth. Even less of a universal truth is that what is good for some disabled people is good for others.**
>
> (Anderberg 2006b: 51–2)

In addition, because when disabled people are 'seen', they are treated as non-normal users with special functional needs, their diversity as a group and preferences as individuals also become invisible. A particular disabled person can come to stand for/conform to a whole category of medical impairment, such that the rich experiences, responses and strategies of different disabled people to their material surroundings are flattened out into the single-dimensional, essentialist relationship of physical access. As part of this, impairments are most often articulated as clear, objective and specific categories. Both the concepts of accessibility and of inclusive design can unintentionally imply that disability is a 'fixed' and ahistorical category where all the limitations of different impairments can be listed accurately and completely and then can be resolved 'straightforwardly' through design. The very ambiguous slippages between what is abnormal (cancer? deafness? obesity? baldness?) and what is 'normal' are ignored, as are the considerable conflicts, gaps, complexities – and sheer impossibility – of meeting everyone's needs, everywhere, all the time. Unintentionally, then, access and inclusive design end up focusing on what the social model has tried to avoid – an endless attempt by legislators, planners, designers and other experts to pin down the 'correct' special needs requirements of different impairments so as to provide a 'matching' design solution.

> **Getting re-routed is a common part of the disabled experience. Being asked to do something differently in order to do it in the first place, is problematic. It is these little journeys 'up the goods lift' or 'round the back' that can be so devoid of comfort, creativity and humour.**
>
> (Sarah Pickthall, comments as part of *So What is Normal* project, University of Brighton)

This has also ended up creating a disconnect between the attitudes and methods central to creative building design processes and the language of design guidance, with its precise detailed solutions, linked through 'objective', technical and behaviourist cause and effect, stimuli-response associations. Much committed work in inclusive design is articulated from a rationalist perspective, and it therefore aims to persuade with facts and figures, and support with principles and examples (Figure 2.2).

In fact, this produces several difficulties for architectural education and practice. First, whilst such a framing is both important and well intended, it has little purchase on actual building design activities which tend, on the one hand, to be informed by an attitude developed out of engagement with ideas from within architectural form-making discourses, and on the other to engage through a detailed diagnosis with the specificity of particular sites and situations. Whilst this has the potential to critique the shape of architectural design knowledge itself (for example, in its lack of methods by which ethical and social principles can explicitly intersect with, and be implemented through, design ideas and practices), the separate placing of inclusive design – either in opposition to, or at the end of 'normal' design processes – actually prevents such a challenge from being noticed.

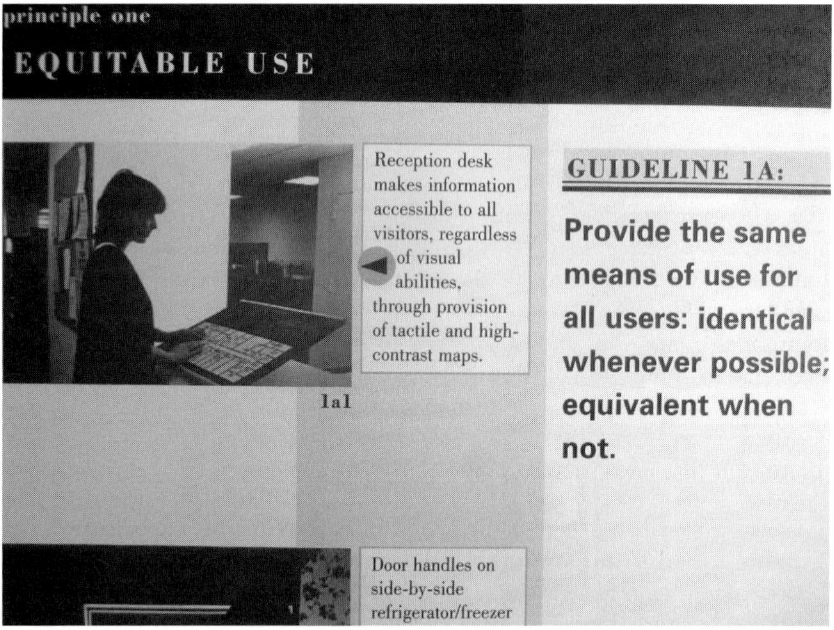

Figure 2.2 Illustrative example from Molly Story, James Mueller and Ronald Mace (1998) *The Universal Design File: Designing for People of all Ages and Abilities*, NC State University Center for Universal Design, p. 39. www.ncsu.edu/ncsu/design/cud/pubs_p/pudfiletoc.htm

Second, even the most straightforward design concerns may not be so easily solved across the whole diversity of disabled people's experiences and requirements. If disability ceases to be viewed as a stable category where various functional needs can be straightforwardly met, then it is possible to admit to the complexities and contradictions in attempting to make physical improvements to the built environment that work for everyone. This is at every level; from differences in impairments, to the differential enabling and disabling effects of various 'accessible' devices, through to the complex design choices architects are making all the time. As just a few examples: sense-based designed environments can offer enjoyable and stimulating spaces for people with severe learning difficulties, but may be deeply unsettling for someone with autism. In the UK, tactile paving at road junctions has become the new (accessible) norm, as a navigational support for blind people who use canes, despite the fact that the bumps actually produce problems for the less mobile, for people using wheelchairs, and may have little relevance for some blind and partially sighted people with severe diabetes and thus little feeling in their feet. And an example from Anderberg, who uses a wheelchair:

> I once had to use a bathroom at a Centre of Independent Living I was visiting. The bathroom held a number of different advanced adaptations; these were not helpful but rather in the way for me, and made the bathroom virtually unusable.
>
> This paradox is of course a well known, but a seldom problematized (at least to any depth) fact within Design for All and Universal Design writings.
>
> (Anderberg 2006b: 51–2)

These are not just 'mistakes' that can be rectified by better design guidance and better adherence to the guidance. They are inherent (potentially creative) tensions in our hopeful attempts to improve the built environment for everyone. In fact, the narrative that accessibility is 'easy', and of benefit to everyone, locates disabled people deeply problematically as simultaneously the 'same' as everyone else and as particular cases, who deserve special treatment. In part, this was (and is) a campaigning 'line', drawn out of the social model and its deliberate focus on the social and external constraints on disabled people. But it has also meant that ideas of accessibility and inclusive design can end up blurring the complexity of designing for impairment and dis/ability as both ambiguous and relational.

'Solving the problem' of the (disabled) user through participation

Whilst the social model of disability was impacting on architecture through design guidance and regulatory changes, the architectural framing of 'users' more generally was also under attack. Throughout the 1970s, popular criticisms of modernist design also set in binary opposition architects as egoists, concerned only with aesthetics, and 'ordinary' people using the resulting spaces, whose needs are obvious if only building designers would take notice (Jacobs 1961, Booker and Lycett Green 1973, Rudosky 1987). Within architectural practice this created a range of responses, most particularly an interest in flexible or 'loose fit' space, for example in the work of British architects such as Richard Rogers and John Weeks; and in the development of more participatory ways of relating to clients and users. As Imrie writes, particularly about disability but with equal relevance to popular attitudes more generally:

> one way of returning knowledge and competence to the wider community is, as O'Neill (1995) argues, to institutionalize the 'transferability and thereby accountability of expert knowledge in order to raise the level of the well informed citizen or the need to create a pedagogy that will subordinate expert knowledge to the needs of political democracy' (p. 170). This, then, is one example of what Oliver (1992) terms reciprocity, or a situation whereby the role of the architect is to be an enabler and educator rather than preacher or provider, with the resources of the design industry being placed at the disposal of local communities. Thus, to empower people with disabilities in the design process is a multi-faceted, multi-dimensional, process which, as a minimum, requires an engagement at the level of values and ideology, as well as the material base of building processes.
>
> (Imrie 1998: 142)

The participatory approach came into regular use through the 1970s and 80s across both radical and some mainstream architectural practices in the UK and America, as a response to the commonly held belief that modernist architects and designers had failed to understand users' needs (Wates 1976, Knevitt and Wates 1987). By involving 'ordinary' users on a case-by-case basis, attempts were/are made to guarantee an 'authentic' understanding of these particular users through some form of direct involvement. Such methods were introduced for a variety of important reasons: so as to move beyond the perceived modernist reduction of users as merely functional entities; so as not to 'speak for others'; and as part of a wider radical shift towards locally based democratic and participatory practices. Such methods have been extremely valuable tools for developing improved understandings of the multiplicity of lived experiences (and have continued to be developed more recently through, for example, co-designing) but – crucially – I want to suggest that the participatory project also has its own gaps and problems in relating disability, difference and architecture. In fact, I will even propose that in some ways the participatory project is as much about architectural anxieties and avoidances over how to engage with users who are 'not-users' – that is, who do not fit within everyday social and spatial practices – as it is about making better buildings. This is because, across architectural practice and education, it is predominantly those groups who are perceived to stand *outside* average users (whose habits and activities we can

Figure 2.3 Architecture-InsideOut (AIO), participatory event between architects and disabled artists, Lightbox, Woking, 21 June 2008. Photography: Jos Boys.

predict in architectural design without encountering any difficulty, precisely because they are deemed 'normal'; that is, 'like us') who are often engaged with through participatory methods (Figure 2.3).

Why is this a problem? Well, first, social design engagement easily became framed as 'giving people what they want', as if this was a transparent, consensual and straightforward process of gathering people's views and producing a proposal in response, with the designer as merely a neutral conduit. The users under consideration are then a special case, so that lessons learnt about developing awareness of difference (which are relevant to all projects, not just ones designed for 'others') are not transferred into other, more 'normal' design projects.

Second, the participatory project works on the assumption that user requirements are best learnt 'from the horse's mouth', that is, are authentic and accurate when offered up by a particular (in this case) disabled person. But this fails to engage with the complexity of difference; by making individuals stand not only for an entire category – of an impairment, or of disability more generally – but also as a cover for the difficulties of prediction, future uncertainties and likely changes of occupancy. Thus, whilst it is essential to attend to diverse disabled narrative and strategies, both forms of engagement, and then the translation of specific disabled experiences into architectural design, need to be made much more explicit and opened up to critique and debate (Figure 2.4).

Figure 2.4 Architects and disabled artists work together at Architecture-InsideOut (AIO) design event, Tate Modern, 10 May 2008. Photography: Jos Boys.

Finally, only putting 'non-normal' categories of users (disabled, poor, working-class, ethnic minorities) into this different and special relationship with designers leaves these groups still located 'on the outside' of mainstream assumptions about what spaces are for 'normally'; that is, it also perpetuates what accessibility and inclusive design do by separating out disability into its own category.

This, again, puts disability in a different place from most architectural educational or design projects. These are not, after all, always such participatory projects. When designing for 'normality' it is assumed that creative professionals will be capable of integrating complex and partial variables – always analysing situations about which they do not know very much and predicting how to instigate social, spatial and aesthetic improvements through the transformation of material space and objects. Conventional learning and teaching design emphasizes this process of iteration and values the ability to creatively and critically empathize with 'other' situations based on limited knowledge, through sensitive understanding and interpretation. Disability continues to remain absent here, an anxiety we don't want to speak about; where the non-disabled hide their insecurities by asking for design 'solutions' from the disabled themselves; where engaging in critical debate/disagreeing with a disabled person (as 'authentic' representation) becomes difficult; and where such a case-specific approach can become a crutch for the abled architect or student to lean on, as they suddenly seem to forget their 'normal' professional design skills (Figure 2.5).

Figure 2.5 Disabled artists working as design tutors: *Making Discursive Spaces* project, School of Architecture and Interior Design, University of Brighton, May 2007. Photography: Jos Boys.

Thus, as with specialist access consultants, access forums and design guidance, such case-by-case participatory projects have made important improvements to the material landscape for disabled people, whilst simultaneously keeping dis/ability issues fragmented to individual good examples, and preventing either disabled people or architects from finding other kinds of gaps and opportunities from which the avoidances in architectural theories, education and practices can be challenged more comprehensively. Just as disability is an add-on to 'normal' architecture, so too are user participation or 'flexibility' add-ons to normal architectural practice. We even have the same patterning of either non-normal users being special cases *or* being part of an 'everyone' who can remain undistinguished by the creation of more flexible space. In the process, the problematic shape of architectural design knowledge itself remains unchallenged.

The public realm and city centres have the potential to be vibrant, buzzing and connecting spaces for everyone to enjoy. My vision as a disabled person, is for a radical change in urban design that places disabled people at the centre alongside designers to define creative, unexpected solutions not yet identified in current inclusive design structures.

(Zoe Partington-Sollinger, CABE Scholar 2008, *Naked Space*, p. 2)

Re-framing users

I have already suggested that shifts in approaches to disability within architecture have also been connected to shifts around the idea of the user more generally.[3] The stereotypical modernist concept of a user is outlined by Imrie:

> The body, in this view, is little more than an object with fixed, measurable parts; it is neutered and neutral, that is, without sex, gender, race or physical difference. It is residual and subordinate to the mind, or that realm of existence that is characterised by what the body is not; such as self, thought and reason.
>
> (Imrie quoted in Hill 2003: 24)

Over the last 40 years many architectural theories and practices have been challenging this simplification and exploring ways of re-framing conceptualizations of, and assumptions about, the user. For example, for Jonathan Hill in *Actions of Architecture* (2003), the central issue here is that the architect–user relationship is framed as a false dualism, in which the concept of user is essentially marked as passive and inferior (Hill 1998, 2003) rather than actively creative and participatory. He suggests that 'the user is an important consideration in the architect's design process. But the user is also a threat to the architect because the user's actions may undermine the architect's claim to be the sole author of the architecture' (Hill 2003: 3). Architects, then, can see the user as an 'intrusion' (Hill 1998: 5). However, users are creative – they construct buildings anew through use. Hill coins the term 'illegal architect' to cover both professionals and users who actively engage with and subvert building design and proposes that:

> Architects can transform their forms of authorship and production once they do not fear the creativity and unpredictability of use. Architecture is a far larger category than the work of architects who are just one group of producers among many . . .
>
> There are two occupations of architecture: the activities of the architect and the actions of the user. The architect and the user both produce architecture, the former by design, the latter by use. As architecture is experienced it is made by the user as much as the architect. Neither are the two terms mutually exclusive. They exist within each other. Just as the architect is also a user, the user can be an illegal architect.
>
> (Hill 1998: 6)

3 Users is another difficult word. The lack of purchase or slipperiness of, and contestation over many of the key terms in this volume is of course itself a strong indication of how anxiously hidden are the difficulties in resonantly articulating human relations with each other, space and artefacts and the inherent flaws and contradictions built into much of our commonsense language.

Hill, then, looks at ways of defining the user that can challenge occupancies as a passive state of distraction ('a state of absent-mindedness enforced by habit and repetition'; Hill 2003: 27) as well as enabling more active participation in the design process itself. Here, though we need to interrogate more carefully just what Hill means by 'user'. In fact, the concept of user itself is not problematicized. Users *already* exist as ordinary, undifferentiated, autonomous and competent subjects, who are questioned only after this moment, at the point at which they interact with the material world. The material world, in turn, does not *already* have enabling or disabling effects on different users. In fact, the problem is only that (all) users are being prevented from, first, being even more independent and engaged as subjects; and second, such potential engagements are not recognized enough as being about intersecting with and/or adapting the designed space itself. In addition, this act of recognizing use as importantly about the interactions between architectural space and its users is itself subversive (it is 'illegal'). I suggest that such an understanding is, in fact, a sideways slippage (even an unintentional diversion) from the much more crucial difficulty of the concept of user itself and its blurring of all users together, thus ignoring the fact that it is *out of* their very diversity that different users experience built space unevenly and unequally.

Is the user a norm?

Work from within disability studies is much more scathing of the idea of a normal 'user' and the underlying assumptions and unspoken hierarchies it both contains and obscures. Lennard Davis (2002), for example, examines the history of how and why bodily differences became constrained to a norm or average, and the implications for disabled people. As he writes:

> the word 'normal' only appeared in English about a hundred and fifty years ago, and in French fifty years earlier. Before the rise of the concept of normalcy, there appears not to have been a concept of the normal, but instead the regnant paradigm was one revolving around the word 'ideal'. If one has a concept of the 'ideal' then all human beings fall below that standard and so exist in varying degrees of imperfection . . . No one *can* have an ideal body, and therefore no one has to have an ideal body.
>
> (Davis 2002: 105)

What Davis shows here is the ways in which aiming for a standard also caused the exclusion of those who failed to fit:

> Around the beginning of the nineteenth century in Europe, we begin to see the development of statistics and of the concept of the bell curve, called early on the 'normal' curve. With the development of statistics comes the idea of the norm. In this paradigm most bodies fall under the main umbrella of the curve. And those that do not are at the extremes – and therefore

> are 'abnormal'. Thus there is an imperative on people to conform, to fit in, under the rubric of normality. Rather than being resigned to a less-than-ideal body in the earlier paradigm, people in the last one hundred and fifty years have been encouraged to strive to be normal, to huddle under the main part of the curve.
>
> (Davis 2002: 105)

It is not unexpected to see that such an aim coincided with the rise of eugenics, and that key figures in the movement such as Francis Galton used statistics to argue for a clear differentiation between the normal and others, through a re-framing of how statistics could be interpreted:

> First, the application of the idea of a norm to a human body creates the idea of deviance or a 'deviant' body. Second, the idea of a norm pushes the normal variation of the body through a stricter template, guiding the way the body 'should' be. Third, the revision of the 'normal curve of distribution' into quartiles, ranked in order, and so on, creates a new kind of 'ideal'.
>
> (Davis 1995: 8)

Thus, the idea of the user (as an average, statistically valid 'typical' person) becomes simultaneously representative of everyone, and excludes the 'non-normals'. For, as Davis also notes:

> An important consequence of the idea of the norm is that it divides the total population into standard and non-standard populations. The next step in conceiving of the population as norm and non-norm is to attempt to norm the non-standard – the aim of eugenics. Of course, such an activity is profoundly paradoxical since the inviolable rule of statistics is that all phenomena will always conform to a bell curve.
>
> (Davis 1995: 7)

Thus we have a problem. An average or norm can only be produced by starting from a whole spectrum of people. It cannot exist without this diversity. But if *normal differences* are reduced to a *single norm*, and – worse – then blurred with an ideal (that is, aligned with a goal of human perfectibility) the realities of our variously vulnerable bodies disappear. This, then, is about more than the problem of the user as passive or active. It is about how our underlying assumptions construct users as particular kinds of 'ordinary person'. It is this paradox that allows us to conceive of disabled people in everyday commonsense as simultaneously within the norm (without any need to acknowledge differences) and as non-normal, as outside of, and different from, 'normal' users. Since these two cases cannot be true at the same time, they are held in different spaces in architectural practice and education, as elsewhere – as either (invisibly) part of all users, or special and different to be dealt with on a case-by-case basis.

At the same time, as I have already said, disabled people overlap with many others, through the everyday commonsense of an oppositional relationship between 'architects' and 'people'. This is maintained through reactive complaints about specific components of a design. The responses from many disabled people to their experiences of material space are very similar to those of most users; that a particular light switch is in the wrong place, or a selected colour is unattractive or lacking contrast. But if the general view of 'everybody' is that architects tend not to meet their needs, then particular interest groups often find themselves demanding attention as a special case. This puts disabled people in a double bind. On the one hand, existing buildings and spaces are often thoughtlessly designed or managed and do not operate well for disabled people. On the other, it is important to get beyond what Davis calls 'oppressed identities or populations understood as docile/wounded' (2002: 31), where disabled people find themselves pleading as a special case in need of particular 'protecting'; caught in having to 'be' a single group, without internal differences, in order to have a unitary and identifiable position in response to discrimination. But it also puts architects into an ambiguous position; it puts them on 'the other side' of an over-simplified (and equally inaccurate) binary power relation of oppressor and victim. In this process both groups are put in stereotypical opposition, where the architect is assumed to have all the power (which, given the complexity of building processes, is simply not true) and the disabled person to be passive, 'difficult' and powerless, which also fails to capture the multiple realities of their lives.

Re-locating difference, shifting design practices

How, then, can we go beyond the 'user' as 'norm', and the disabled person as the problem? How can we re-integrate human difference and diversity into buildings? How does one encompass the full variety of personal preferences, individual needs and desires in the design process, whilst taking notice of, and challenging, its differential, disabling effects? What can one do in the face of the multi-faceted and many-variabled procurement, development, design and delivery of buildings to create spaces that are useful, enjoyable and responsive to diverse occupancies through space and time? Masashi Kajita's research explores how to better model and architecturally embed relationships between accessibility requirements and social inclusion with spatial analysis. He formulates a synthesis of these three variables into a potential new framework that aims 'to integrate accessibility – both as a concept and an instrument – into creative processes of architecture and the built environment' (Text Box 2.1).

I have also already been suggesting that we can move beyond simplistic binary oppositions between disability and ability by seeing both dis/ability and occupancies as ambiguous and relational. In this chapter I am proposing that rather than re-producing that binary opposition in architecture, through the framing of inclusive design as either for 'everyone' and/or to meet the 'special needs' of disabled people, we need to instead explore the interplays between

Text Box 2.1 Masashi Kajita, Spatial Dimensions of Accessibility (2013)

Kajita is interested in how to extend the concept of Accessibility. In his PhD thesis research *Spatial Dimensions of Accessibility* (undertaken at the Institute of Planning, Royal Danish Academy of Fine Arts, Copenhagen) he explores the challenge of how better to integrate accessibility – both as a concept and as an instrument – into the creative processes of architecture and the built environment. Accessibility must be understood not as a concession but as the 'gorgeous norm'. It must advance built environment design by aiming to create spaces that have an equivalence of experience for all.

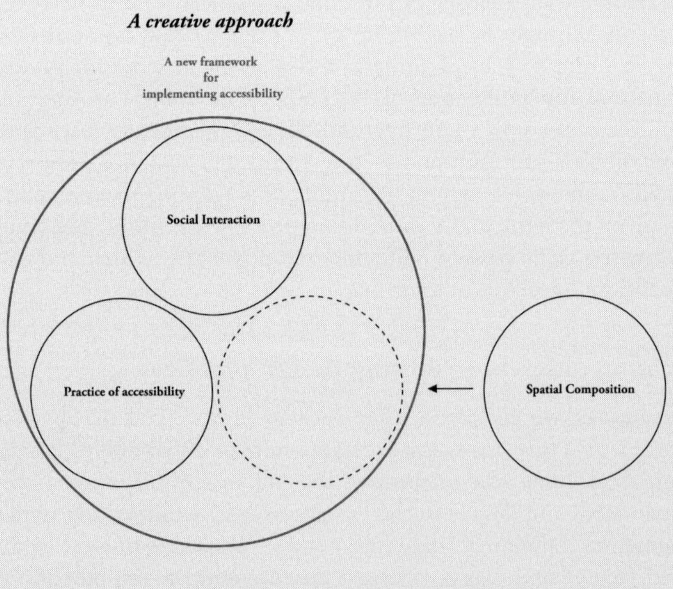

He sees Universal Design as sitting at the intersections of accessibility requirements, social inclusion and spatial composition. As he describes it:

> this new framework consciously includes the perspectives of both architects and users in the process as well as outcome of space making. The spatial analysis contextualises accessibility requirements into spatial discussions: as well as forming the background for social analysis that studies social interactions between users in different social contexts.

Kajita's research explores both how to analyse existing buildings, and how his approach could be used as a method to produce inclusive buildings.

disability and ability, so as to expose the differential effects material spaces have on different kinds of bodies. As Hill writes in *Occupying Architecture*, these effects are also ambiguous, relational, situated and operate at different registers simultaneously:

> [A building] is, primarily, a particular relation between a subject and an object, in which the former occupies the latter, which is not necessarily a building, but can be a space, text, artwork or any other phenomenon that displays, or refers to, the subject–object relations particular to architecture . . . Architecture is experienced in a state of distraction but not a state of unawareness. It is a particular type of awareness that enables a person to perform, at the same time, a series of complex activities that move in and out of focus from a conscious to an unconscious level. In architecture, habit, memory and experience are coupled with the sensual disembodiment of twentieth-century forms of communication to form a complex compound of spatial and temporal layers. Someone talks to you, caresses your back, while you listen to the phone, read the fax and peer out of the window. Architecture is experienced collectively and individually, each facet of a person reacting to a building and other people in distinct and maybe conflicting ways.
>
> (Hill 1998: 5–6)

Here, users are conceptualized as intersecting with built space through multiple registers simultaneously. What disability brings to this kind of understanding is, I suggest, profound. This is because it cannot just be about universal, unproblematic 'users' but must face up to the concrete realities of physical as well as personal, emotional, social and cultural *differences*. What it makes persistently visible (if the abled only stopped to take notice) is the ambiguity of categories, the unevenness and inequality of experience and the work involved in simply living an everyday life.

At the same time, as well as finding better ways to open up such relationships to view (as will be explored further in the next chapter), such a critical engagement beyond accessibility requires that architecture is also much more self-critical of itself as a profession and a discipline. I have proposed here that the 'normal' architecture/inclusive design divide acts unwittingly to perpetuate the marginalization of disability in building design, and to maintain a 'disconnect' between disability and architectural education and practice. Whilst, as already noted, architecture considers itself to be socially responsive and committed to a duty of care, its everyday framings of dis/ability in fact fail to have much purchase on the 'bigger picture' of architectural theory and approaches to form-making, remaining as a generalized principle without strategies or tactics for implementation. We urgently need to have methods for exposing the invisibility of the work we do: both in literally enacting our own lives, and in the ongoing maintenance of (and contest, adaptation, etc.) of the underlying assumptions about what everyday life is about.

When disability and architecture are connected through such a framework, we can go beyond accessibility, and instead put better understanding of everyday social and spatial practices centre-stage; that is, exploring how our various emotional, social, personal and functional registers, and their shifting patterns of attention and distraction, operate at the intersections between people, artefacts and spaces. In turn, dis/ability and architectural theory, practice and education become about analysing how such processes (re-)produce societal patterns of inclusion and exclusion; and how architecture can challenge and shift these patterns. These, then, are the themes for the rest of this book.

3 Unravelling dis/ordinary occupancy

Throughout this book I am aiming to open up architecture to new and interesting approaches by, as Schillmeier says, 'centralizing dis/ability as a major concept of agency that disrupts, questions and alters the common modes of spatial ordering' (2010: 116). As I have already suggested, to do this requires an unravelling of how both 'normal' and 'abnormal' bodies are mapped, maintained and contested through our everyday actions; that is, in the ordinary, unnoticed social and spatial practices that entangle people, language, artefacts and spaces. In this chapter I will explore already existing methods from the social sciences such as ethnography and ethnomethodology[1] that can offer one way to critically navigate such inter-weavings.

> **The body is never a single physical thing so much as a series of attitudes towards it.**
>
> (Davis 2002: 22)

These approaches see the ordinary ways we talk and act as continuously 'performing' what is the normal thing to do. As Titchkosky writes:

> language recommends that we conceive of the able-body as something that just comes along 'naturally' as people go about their daily existence. People just jump into the shower, run to the store, see what others mean while keeping an eye on the kids, or skipping from office to office and, having run through the day whilst managing to keep their noses clean, hop into

1 Ethnomethodology is the study of the everyday methods that people use for the production and perpetuation of social order, and as a means of making sense of the world. It is problematic in some ways, because it has been predominantly used for mapping only 'normal' social and spatial practices, rather than being interested in offering critiques and challenges to those practices. However, it is used here because it is particularly good at unravelling the various mechanisms through which 'ordinariness' is maintained.

> bed. All of this glosses the body that comes along while, at the same time, brings it along metaphorically. Speaking of 'normal bodies' as movement and metaphor maps them as if they are a natural possession, as if they are not mapped at all.
>
> (Titchkosky, 2002: 103)

The abled (or at least the young and fit ones) can act without thinking, and not 'notice' any potential difficulties or disruptions in the design of the built environment, nor have these impinge, or only infrequently, on what they want to do, or the speed at which they wish to do it. But Titchkosky is also making another point here, beyond simple differences in body performance. It is this very invisibility and lack of notice of their own abled-ness that allows 'normal' behaviour to seem nothing much, not worth talking about. At the same time, ordinariness is in fact fiercely maintained through built-in mechanisms for exposing (through social embarrassment, or bodily discomfort, for example) those who do not fit – are not 'ordinary' – and of framing them as a problem. However, these norms are already constructed around patterns of not just inclusion but also exclusion; those 'others' cannot fit, whatever they do or is done 'for them'.

Since the everyday act of occupying built space seems so normal and straightforward that (mostly) abled people don't even think about it, we need to begin to critically unpick what exactly constitutes the ordinary. I have already suggested that this involves *work* – work to 'go to the shops', but also work to maintain, even police, normal social and spatial practices, and work to disrupt, challenge and re-shape those practices. In a seminal article called 'Notes on the Art of Walking' Ryave and Schenkein (1974) proposed a way of studying our everyday encounters with people and places. They explored how people behaved in crowds so as to discover some of the unspoken conventions that enable us to move about without bumping into each other. For them, even the act of walking together or apart requires 'the concerted accomplishment of members of the community involved in its production and recognition'. They suggest we can examine the detail of such ordinary practices (they used video cameras and observational studies) so as to discover the implicit rules that govern 'what is normal' in our encounters . . . the multitude of cues that don't just exist, but have to be recognized and 'must be continually produced . . . in order to make the activity continually available and accountable'. Some disabled artists make work that deliberately aims to disrupt such assumptions (Figure 3.1).

Harvey Sacks, in his paper 'On doing "being ordinary"' (1984), describes the kind of work this involves and how it differentially affects some people:

> So one part of the job [doing 'being ordinary'] is that you have to know what anybody/everybody is doing: doing ordinarily. Further, you have to have that available to do. There are people who do not have that available to do, and who specifically cannot be ordinary.
>
> (Sacks 1984: 415)

Figure 3.1 Caroline Cardus, signs from *The Way Ahead*, 2004, Interaction Milton Keynes and touring exhibition.

By beginning an investigation of occupancy from the narratives and strategies of diverse disabled people in Chapter 1, I have already begun to expose how that 'ordinariness' has consequences for those who specifically 'cannot be ordinary'. Here, I will first explore in more detail some of the underlying patterns of these processes, in order to open up for attention and inspection our unspoken assumptions about what 'anyone' does in the built environment, before going on to outline some specific examples of the effects of making and re-making the dis/ordinary.

Doing dis/ordinary architecture

We can also take from the work of Sacks and others the idea of what is not 'storyable'. Sacks, one of the 'fathers' of ethnomethodology, explored these processes through which people work at being ordinary and, in discussing it, structure their comments so that it appears as if very little happens: 'nothing much'. So when it comes to occupying buildings, how do people accomplish being ordinary? And in what ways is this to be contrasted with the experience of disabled people who inhabit a building with plenty of stories to tell, but for whom achieving 'nothing much' is, in fact, deeply problematic? I will show below, through an important study by Titchkosky (2011), some examples of particular 'narratives of justification' around building design and accessibility, stories that continue to take precedence as stories that are 'heard', and agreed with, rather than the stories told by disabled people themselves. For Titchkosky it is precisely what is storyable that structures both dialogue and material spaces such that disabled people come to be 'included as excludable', an understanding that will be returned to time and again here.

In addition, I want to explore more about the relationships between doing 'being ordinary' and the act of creating built spaces. When buildings and interiors are designed, how are the everyday practices of occupation articulated? What is 'storyable' and what is not? How is what is storyable in architecture passed on from generation to generation? What can we 'read' from building interiors and spaces about the stories they think they are telling, and what are the intersections between designers' narratives, the everyday acts of doing 'being ordinary' in specific spaces and the experiences of the disabled as dis/ordinary people? Most importantly, how might starting from dis/ability open up alternative ways of 'taking notice' of the world?

We can begin with the notion of 'anyone'.[2] In ethnomethodology there is a strong thread that focuses on how societal membership works:

> Members as social actors assume that their everyday and 'normal' work is a factual reality which is there for 'anyone' to see and they regard it as a commonplace, generally taken for granted environment, which no competent member has problems recognizing and acting upon.
>
> (Payne 1976: 33)

Ethnomethodologists are concerned with how this commonplace world is worked by people, by what 'anyone' knows and does. This is really difficult to get at. Not noticing things and making assumptions is often a socially achieved activity. In any environment or situation there are a myriad of behaviours and options that are available to anyone, and are routinely undertaken by anyone and for this reason go unrecognized. One way to focus on this is to use the phrase 'it goes without saying', which is used to draw attention to that which 'we all know'. But there are also circumstances in which some actors are re-assigned – not any longer as 'anyone'. Payne uses a simple example:

> 'Anyone' knows how to sit down. Generally no-one asks permission to sit down. Anyone does it and knows how to do it. However, what anyone also knows is that in some circumstances some people have to wait to be seated, stand in a queue, wait until a table is available, wait until the judge has sat down and so on. In particular cases, people are marked down to acquire an identity, which sets them apart from 'anyone'.
>
> (Payne 1976: 35)

2 This section was written with Pam Shakespeare, previously Professor of Practice Based Open Learning, Faculty of Health and Social Care, Open University, UK. Her expertise in ethnomethodology has been invaluable.

And it is often not until routine behaviours are breached that we understand what they are and how 'anyones' are distinguished. At the same time, because sitting down is something anyone does, someone with a disability for whom sitting down may not be straightforward can find themselves no longer just 'anyone'.

The design of space also assumes an 'anyone', although who this 'anyone' is will vary from context to context. The particular 'anyone' may be explicitly articulated by the designer or just assumed. It may be contested, or ignored, or absent-mindedly transformed through actions by the client, contractor or planner. That 'anyone' will be translated (unevenly) both into predicted patterns of social and spatial practices and into representations of those practices. Designed spaces based on one sort of 'anyone' can also be disrupted through unexpected patterns of engagement. At the same time buildings can mark out who is not 'anyone' by allocating them specific locations or presumed actions, or by simply designing on the basis that everyone will be doing 'being ordinary', without noticing those who specifically cannot be ordinary in this particular space. So the problematic accomplishments of doing 'being ordinary' are related to material space, but this is not a simple or transparently obvious relationship.

Garfinkel has suggested that the most effective way to see what differentiates being 'anyone' from 'not-anyone' is by analysing processes of breaching:

> Procedurally it is my preference to start with familiar scenes and ask what can be done to make trouble. The operations that one would have to perform in order to multiply the senseless features of perceived environments, to produce and sustain bewilderment, consternation and confusion; to produce the socially constructed affects of anxiety, shame, guilt and indignation and to produce disorganised interaction should tell us something about how the structures of everyday activities are ordinarily and routinely produced and maintained.
>
> (Garfinkel 1967: 37–8)

Garfinkel developed a series of breaching experiments where he asked students to deliberately perform in unexpected ways, and monitored the results (Garfinkel 1967: 42). The participants – who were asked to act like visitors in their own homes rather than inhabitants – reported such responses as that they were perceived as being 'too nice' and were obviously 'after something'. When one asked if they could have a bite to eat from the fridge a parent noted that this was behaviour that had been going on for a long time and wondered why they had suddenly decided to ask. One parent thought the student was being hostile to his mother and suggested that he leave the house.

But for disabled people, often already located as not-anyone, as non-members of a community, that is, as inherently breaching (or threatening to breach) normal social and spatial practices, it is the regular moments of being 'marked out' that matter.

As has already been said, this is not merely a matter of the impact of specific impairments, but because disabled people are persistently located as *out* of the ordinary, being, in ethnomethodological terms, less than full societal members. Examples of ways the abled maintain and *police* the boundaries around what it is to be 'anyone' engaged in 'normal' social and spatial practices have already begun to be explored in Chapter 1. These also include staring (Garland Thomson 2009) and 'body-policing' (that is, assessing the social and personal acceptability of particular body shapes and configurations); body language, such as showing awkwardness and exaggerated care; behaviours such as assuming disabled people are stupid, or impatience at being kept waiting by a disabled person; everyday talk such as believing that disabled people make special claims or are getting special treatment (for example by being allocated disabled parking spaces, or wanting ramps on the front of buildings), or are really making a fuss about nothing and taking advantage of abled people; patronizing beliefs that people's stories (anyone) can talk *for* disabled people; and, ultimately, abusive and violent responses, that literally attack disabled people for their presence in society (Davis 2002).

What then, are the implications of this for building design? To what extent do architects as a profession, and architecture as a practice and product, act to justify and perpetuate certain norms through unthinking, unnoticed and continuous acts of both living and designing for particular social and spatial practices rather than others? This, of course, is not just something architects do; it is part of everyday assumptions about, and attitudes to, human bodies; what are 'normal' things to do or say in different situations; and how objects and spaces are assumed to 'work'. However, architects and other built environment professionals – as well as their clients and other procurers of buildings such as developers – do have a particular responsibility here. This is because abled 'commonsense' works twice to disadvantage disabled people when it comes to the design of buildings and spaces. First, the translation of specific social and spatial norms into built form – their literal 'making concrete' – is part of perpetuating the problem. As I have said before, architectural space and form is, after all, one of the mechanisms we use for the everyday reproduction of commonsense assumptions about how the world works.[3] The design of material space (normally if not always) reinforces, through its patterns of enabling and disabling, ordinary social and spatial practices. But in addition, the 'non-noticing' of, or lack of serious critique around, such 'normal' practices in architectural theory and practice, has resulted in a failure to explicitly address the problem, or to work towards alternatives.

3 I worked in Moscow for a few years, where there were no standards for stair heights and depths. In addition, there were fire safety regulations that meant doors open out into circulation spaces. The everyday 'normality' of British building regulations felt 'breached' on a daily basis.

> **The interpretive act of justification is intimately tied to collective understandings of the meaning of what is. As an interpretive social act, justification is not merely second order to the fact of exclusion . . . it is how we *do* exclusion as well as *generate* its everyday sensibility.**
>
> (Titchkoksy 2008: 41)

Including as excludable

The various writings of Tanya Titchkosky and Rod Michalko offer a powerful example of understanding disability as not only always blurring with 'ability', but also as persistently framed by commonsense assumptions of 'what the world is like'. In 'To Pee or Not to Pee?' (2008) and *The Question of Access: Disability, Space, Meaning* (2011) Titchkosky is particularly interested in what it is possible (ordinary, normal) to say about making changes to the built environment that can improve the everyday experiences of disabled people. She examined her own workplace (a Canadian university) and both its intentions around, and implementation of, accessible building design, particularly accessible toilets. She proposes that the commonsense view of many of her colleagues towards disabled people is that whilst 'anyone' will be aware of disability, they are willing to treat it as a marginal issue, and to see failures to provide access as understandable mistakes. This, she suggests, persistently locates disability as 'included as excludable'. She is particularly interested in how such an 'ordinary commonsense' is articulated through everyday conversation; and how it can be critically unravelled and analysed:

> Ordinary talk justifies the shape of daily life by relying on unexamined conceptions of disability. This provides an opportunity to explore how meanings of disability are generated. Taken-for-granted conceptions of disability are one way in which disabled people are viewed as irrelevant and absent. (Thus) the ordinary use of unexamined conceptions of disability reproduces the status-quo even as the material environment changes.
>
> (Titchkosky 2008: 1)

Titchkosky noticed that in her building, which did have accessible entry, there were both no accessible toilets and an inaccessible toilet with incorrect signage claiming it to be accessible for wheelchair users (Text Box 3.1):

> I was disturbed by the lack of access and, in the course of daily life, I talked to many people in the building about the lack of an accessible washroom and the obviously incorrect signage. My intent was not to make this concern into a research project, nor was I covertly collecting data. I was simply attempting to live with, understand, and fix a problem. In drawing attention to these barriers, I also was given a plethora of stories regarding the lack of accessible washrooms as well as stories explaining the

posting of inappropriate access signs. I was struck by the various stories-at-the-ready that are part of this workplace environment and likely part of every Western(ized) work place, judging by the absence of physically disabled people from all of my places of work.

(Titchkosky 2008: 2)

Text Box 3.1 Extract from Damon Rose, 'Is it time for a new wheelchair access icon?' BBC News *Ouch*, 22 September 2013. www.bbc.co.uk/news/blogs-ouch-24149316

Participants spray paint new accessible icons at the Diller Family Volunteer Day, 2 June 2013. Photography: Arianna Dines. http://bostondillerteenfellows.blogspot.co.uk/2013/06/diller-family-volunteer-day.html

Seen on toilet doors, parking bays and practically every public building in the developed world, the International Symbol of Access has been in circulation since 1969. But now a group calling itself the Accessible Icon Project want to give the design a more twenty-first century, even paralympic, feel.

The new icon is based on the old one but shows the figure leaning forward, actively pushing the wheelchair – more David Weir than Ironside. The group's website is critical of the old icon: 'Its arms and legs are drawn like mechanical parts, its posture is unnaturally erect, and its entire look is one that makes the chair, not the person, important and visible.'

Artist Sara Hendron, a lecturer at Rhode Island School Of Design, USA, is one of those behind the project. She says the new icon started as a piece of 'guerrilla art' on the campus of Gordon College near Boston, where she and collaborator Brian Glenney adapted existing access signs by overlaying a transparent sticker of a new active wheelchair user so old and new could both be seen . . .

The designers wanted to get people thinking. Hendron says the new symbol is 'a metaphor for self-direction and self determination', and believes the old one has become politically invisible. She thinks that other similar public information symbols are more dynamic than the classic wheelchair sign and are pictured actively engaging with the world.

There's another issue with the classic symbol, which is not necessarily addressed by the new version – it depicts a wheelchair user, but is also supposed to symbolize access for blindness, autism and many other non-wheelchair related impairments. In fact, although there's an estimated 750,000 wheelchair users in the UK, that's still less than 10% of the disability community.

Visual artist Caroline Cardus doesn't want the symbol to contain a wheelchair at all.

'If no other impairments are included in the sign then there's a subliminal message that if it's all right for wheelchair users then everyone else can just struggle along – and that's massively unhelpful.'

In 2004, Cardus created *The Way Ahead* [Figure 3.1], a travelling exhibition of thought-provoking disability road signs which was very popular and has only recently ended.

'I've thought for a very long time I would love to have a sign with something like a big "A" or whatever letter access starts with in your language, because then you could potentially have some visual shorthand which maybe has different levels . . . The A could perhaps have one dot for physical access and two dots for cognitive awareness,' she says. 'Something that basically says things are completely accessible or things are slightly accessible.'

See also The Accessible Icon Project: www.accessibleicon.org

As she goes on to say, the response from most people was to be genuinely puzzled that nothing was being done:

> All sorts of people are perplexed to find out about the inaccessibility and puzzled that those in authority do not consider the lack of a washroom meeting minimum accessibility standards to be a crisis for those working in the building. This perplexity, verging on incredulity, conditions what it means to work in this building. 'My Department requested those in charge to at least take down the misleading signs. But the signs are still there. What should we do?'
>
> (Titchkosky 2008: 53)

But at the same time, where there was awareness, it did not lead to anger or action. The fact that the lack of an accessible toilet would prevent many disabled people from easily using the building was just something that happened; the problem was not articulated around the unacceptability of disabled people being discriminated against, but as the (unfortunate) result of the many difficulties in achieving such laudable aims. Titchkosky calls these 'narratives of justification':

> Narratives of justification make it ordinary to disregard the absence of an accessible washroom as a noticeable barrier. The washroom is not missing; what is missing is any need to respond to such a barrier to participation. Justification, with its inherent lack of alarm, makes it reasonable not to notice the missing accessible washroom, and keeps the obviously incorrect signage from coming to collective attention. No one is responsible, because there is nothing to respond to – the absence has been made absent, and ordinarily so.
>
> (Titchkoksy 2008: 53)

This, she suggests, is the normal structuring of ordinary talk around disability; that it is adequate to seek, and then give a reason for, the lack of access; that this is enough; 'giving reasons is an acceptable response, and surprises no-one'. She thus shows us two key elements in the framing of disability and architecture generally. First, exclusion from a specific building is 'just one of those things', rather than a shocking or motivating event for most abled people. Second, there is no urgency in redeeming this situation. Since disabled people are often absent, only present in small numbers, or themselves responsible for enforcing their right to access, the abled do not need to face up to their own failure to perceive disabled people as legitimate participants in every building and public space. Here, there is a kind of slippage which would not be acceptable any more for other disadvantaged groups:

> Imagine preventing a woman or a black person from entering a public building where they had legitimate reason to be there (imagine even planning to ask them, or any other able-bodied person if they had a legitimate reason). But, since disabled people can get in some buildings some of the time, there is no need to be immediately horrified by the spatial apartheid this perpetuates or to make an increased effort to challenge such a situation right now. This despite the fact that disabled people have the least access, find it less easy to go somewhere else or to knit together complex journeys across space and time. Inclusion as excludability also means inclusion as assumed substitutability; that other spaces will do 'just as well'.
>
> (Titchkosky 2011: 143)

As I outlined in the previous chapter, similar processes happen within architectural design practice. Because accessibility is *already* assumed to be a difficult addition to normal procedures, it seems too problematic to make much effort over, and any lack of achievement can be framed as a normal – even inevitable – response. This is because it is accessibility (and by extension disabled people themselves) that is seen as the problem, not the exclusion of some of the population from spaces and facilities available to everyone else.

In his book *Disability Theory* Tobin Siebers gives another example (2008: 30–2) of this 'including through excludability'; this time, around assumptions about what constitutes 'normal' design. It concerns the building of a 38-bed lodge high in the Appalachian Mountains in 2000, which was required to comply with the Americans with Disabilities Act (ADA) so as to be accessible to people with disabilities, a requirement that was resisted by 'normal' people. As Siebers writes:

> Its members ridiculed the idea that the building, which could be reached only by a super-rugged 4.6-mile trail, would ever be visited by wheelchair users, and the media tended to take their side.
>
> At this point a group from Northeast Passage, a program at the University of New Hampshire that works with people with disabilities, decided to make a visit to the Galehead hut. Jill Gravink, the director of Northeast Passage, led a group of three hikers in wheelchairs and two on crutches on a twelve-hour climb to the lodge, at the end of which they rolled happily up the ramp to its front door. A local television reporter on the scene asked why, if people in wheelchairs could drag themselves up the trail, they could not drag themselves up the steps into the hut, implying that the ramp was a waste of money. Gravink responded, 'Why bother putting steps on the hut at all? Why not drag yourself in through a window?'
>
> (Siebers 2008: 31)

As Siebers explains, for abled people climbing steps to an entrance is assumed to be so 'normal' as to be completely unnoticed and unworthy of comment, whilst the idea of climbing in through a window rather than using a door is 'obviously' absurd. This offers a perfect example of ordinary social and spatial practices and the surprise generated if breaching them is proposed. What is provided for the abled is taken for granted – 'nothing much' – whilst anything for disabled people is a problematic extra. As he goes on (and as outlined in Chapter 1):

> the built environment is full of technologies that make life easier for those people who possess the physical power to perform tasks without these technologies. Stairs, elevators, escalators, washing machines, leaf and snow blowers, eggbeaters, chainsaws, and other tools help to relax physical standards for performing certain tasks. These tools are nevertheless viewed as natural extensions of the body, and no one thinks twice about using them. The moment that individuals are marked as disabled or diseased, however, the expectation is that they will maintain the maximum standard

> of physical performance at every moment, and the technologies designed to make their life easier are viewed as expensive additions, unnecessary accommodations, and a burden on society.
>
> (Siebers 2008: 31)

Thus, we have two intertwined mechanisms for perpetuating the 'making concrete' of everyday social and spatial practices within architecture. First, ordinary talk makes it normal to not take accessibility seriously, to have shared and often repeated justificatory narratives that make it okay to exclude thinking about disabled people when designing. Simultaneously, the normal elements of design – doors, stairs, corridors, tables, surfaces – just 'naturally' enable the abled and fail to 'fit' (disable) more diverse bodies. While the usual characteristics of these elements are unnoticed as 'nothing much', they may become exposed to view to the abled when they are disrupted by an unexpected alteration in what is 'ordinary', for example by uneven and non-standard treads and risers on a set of stairs, or doors that open out into a corridor rather than inwards, into a room. Of course such elements do change (because of technological innovations and/or manufacturing processes and/or regulatory reasons and/or shifting consumer preferences). So, for example in the UK, standard kitchen units are now 600mm rather than 500mm wide. And part of an architect's job is to actively re-design these elements, as well as their relationships to each other and to space and form. Why then, does re-design which supports diverse bodies not form a normal part of what architects do?

Why don't architects just . . .

- **think about glare, bouncing sound, stuffy rooms – these can make the built environment uncomfortable for most and unusable for many**
- **use high colour contrast for steps or any raised areas as a standard practice**
- **consider how we engage with space and the built environment on a psychological level**
- **stop placing pedal bins in disabled toilets? Am I meant to do a wheelie to get my hand towel into the bin?**
- **explore the simple effect of making doors wider as a standard – 'could' lead to massive impact across the board**
- **design toilet door locks that are big enough to see from a distance, and use big enjoyable graphics to show if the cubicle is vacant or not**

(Responses to a post on Disability Arts Online (DAO) September 2013, www.disabilityartsonline.org.uk)

Why is dis/ability not seen as providing creative potential in these acts of making architectural forms, spaces and components differently, alongside and interwoven with the other variables of designing? I am already suggesting that in the simultaneous processes of (re-)producing ordinary social and spatial practices and of not noticing these practices, architects, like many others, fail to see dis/ability except *sometimes* and to only include it as excludable. But to this must be added the issue of architecture's own internal discourses, the diverse ways the profession approaches the design of buildings and the extent to which dis/ability 'intrudes'. Whilst I have dealt briefly with the modernist stereotypes of the universal user in the last chapter, and will explore in some detail a few specific architectural theories and practices in the next section, here it is important to outline what is generally 'storyable' in architectural discourses about ordinary social and spatial practices. Architecture, after all, is centrally about making new stories, shifting existing ideas, attitudes and practices, generating new kinds of form, and offering up different social and spatial arrangements. But it turns out that only certain alternative 'non-normal' narratives are allowable, and that others – for example, inclusive design – are excluded. How, then, does this come to be the case?

Dis/educating architects

Titchkosky calls learning to perpetuate everyday social and spatial practices without noticing 'dis-education':

> This dis-education teaches that the category of legitimate participant does not [for example] include wheelchair users. The dis-education of the sensorium [the culturally specific ways our senses are hierarchically ordered] includes a way to sense and make sensible the legitimate participants with their legitimated 'normal' accommodation expenses: lighting, chairs, technology, privacy, directional signs, pleasing eye-scapes and, of course, a place to pee. Legitimated participants rarely confront access as a question. They can take for granted the whole massive infrastructure of and for ableist consumption and use, which the sensorium has educated them (us) to consider normal and even natural.
>
> (Titchkoksy 2008: 50)

As I have already noted, architectural education and practice prides itself on its social commitment and duty of care. Whilst this issue will be dealt with in greater depth in the following chapters, here I want to briefly explore what happens to such a social commitment when architectural students are introduced to these potentially parallel universes; that is, what ends up taking precedence through the processes of architectural education. A head of a School of Architecture (that at the time was rightly well-known for its engagement with social issues) was asked about how disability was being taught at his institution, and replied as follows:

> [O]ne cannot cover all aspects of the design of the built environment, but one can set up an ethos in which issues such as inclusion, access, autism, the vernacular, safety (to name just a few of the recent surveys) are inculcated as values to be taken seriously. I would say, but then maybe I would, that this is the ethos (here). We explicitly refer to the user as a core part of our focus, and in this see the user as diverse (including issues of disability). Our 'mission' is specifically about the social and environmental responsibility of the architect. I argue that the development of this ethos and responsibility then can be applied to more specialist areas.
>
> (personal email exchange, 28 September 2007)

Without doubt, many people within architectural education and practice would agree with this response, and see it as perfectly acceptable. Yet simultaneously incorporating disability as one among many important inclusions (users), and then separating it out as something 'specialist' which can be applied later, repeats what has already been critiqued here; that is, it is one of the justificatory narratives through which disabled people disappear, again included as excludable. For architects and design educators, meeting the 'needs' of the disabled can seem to be just another pressure on what is already a highly complex job, with many, often conflicting, stakeholder demands. I know that I have done this myself in my own architectural and interiors teaching, discussing disability in a general way, but not always allowing it to 'intrude' on students' 'more important' learning about how to design material space. In architecture, in addition, the problem of both describing and generalizing users is often an implicit rather than explicit concern. In architectural education students and staff may base their ideas on what they already know (themselves and their peers) or on stereotypical notions of others (disabled = wheelchair) or on an artificially created 'performative' figure (the artist or other creative/eccentric figure) as a deliberately poetic abstraction. It is then assumed that through the practice of repeated design exercises, both whilst studying and in employment, students will learn to listen to their clients and users, and to interpret and translate their various and diverse articulations into built form.

The normative model for first year is to isolate the students from reality in order to allow them 'space to fly'. Students are brought via design briefs to the edges of architecture (design a space for a juggler) in the hope that this 'stretching' will unleash their creative potential.

(Morrow *et al.* 2004: 3)

In fact, research shows that architectural students do *not* learn to engage with dis/ability or occupancy more generally; rather they focus on working out what their tutors want, and quickly imbibe the unspoken assumptions that strong design concepts and methods 'win out' over usability or practicalities. It is the parallel universe of internal architectural discourse that takes priority in shaping their ideas and practices. Two studies, reviewed by Strickfaden *et al.*, illustrate just how embedded this disconnect is in architectural education, moving students away from dis/ability as part of a critical, theoretically informed analysis of occupancy:

> The first study [Strickfaden and Heylighen 2009] involves observation *in situ* of two groups of senior design students, who are focusing on user-centred design principles while designing: 12 third-year BSc students in the UK, and eight MDes students in Canada. Each group is observed from the onset to the completion of one design project. The findings of this study indicate that other people are characterised and defined so generically that they are devoid of gender and age, let alone more specific attributes such as (dis)abilities. Surprisingly across the two groups the students never demonstrate an intimate knowledge of other people in general, nor do they show any understanding of the variances in people's preferences and needs. Many participants even admit explicitly to working from their memory of an age group or a certain experience with the kind of artefact they are designing. Even worse is that the students do not stop to question or even consider that they may be mirroring their own assumptions and creating generalisations about people. The central finding of this work is that students are driven predominantly by what they perceive as their teachers' needs (the major stakeholders in their projects), which seems to impair their ability to perceive other people beyond a superficial level.
>
> (Strickfaden *et al.* 2009: 449)

The other study was of a group specifically interested in inclusive design (three students trained in architecture and one trained in sociology, all post-graduates working towards a PhD degree with various interests in disability studies). These students were collaborating on the re-design of an inclusive office space in a historical building, supported by several books on design, a visual image bank of projects (including inclusive design examples) and a consultant disabled user/expert to provide advice. However, as the researchers note:

> even with heightened awareness towards disabilities, these students consistently default to their own perceptual frameworks and personal capital. Interestingly the sociology student acts as the conscience of the group by interjecting questions and persuasive reminders of how a space may be perceived, interpreted and experienced by other people. Of even more interest is the fact that the students do not investigate the majority of provided resources, i.e., one of four of the students looks through all books, two of four glance through some, none of them looks at the image bank, and none of them consults the user/expert.
>
> (Strickfaden *et al.* 2009: 449)

The authors suggest that the problem lies in designing for an 'absent audience', rather than with participating users, and looks for techniques to enable students to 'empathize' more with diverse users in their absence.[4] Here, though I have already suggested that user participation has only limited value, as it leads to disabled and other disadvantaged groups being included only *sometimes*, and argued that this persistent difficulty instead lies in the commonsense frameworks through which users are conceptualized more generally within architecture. As the authors show, what the students reveal is, first, that other people remain 'positioned at a distance and untouchable – simply "someone" or "*anyone*" else' (Strickfaden and Heylighen 2009: 449, my italics), and second, that they default to their designer-centred approach, as a reflection of how they have been trained, 'suggesting that people from outside are potentially marginalized or even negated' (p. 450).

Thus, what is 'storyable' within normal social and spatial practices is here perpetuated. When that ordinary commonsense intersects with architectural education, then not only does 'anyone' fail to be critically explored (either as a concept or a complex reality), but the unnoticed and unthought-about framings of 'anyone' within design discourse become *the* means through which occupancy gets translated into material space and artefacts. This suggests – following Titchkosky – that we need to urgently begin becoming critically self-aware of designers' own justificatory narratives so as to unpick their effects across both 'normal' and architectural discourses and practices.

Opening up dis/ordinary social and spatial practices

Here, I have given some examples of how thinking about dis/ability can begin to undermine the conventions of ordinary social and spatial practices. I have stressed how important it is to challenge assumptions that disability is an unfortunate breach of 'normal' life but one that does not require action on the part of the abled. I have begun to open up for critical investigation the problematic and non-coherent intersections between everyday social and spatial practices and architecture's own knowledge base and ways of working. Here, finally, I want to show how starting from dis/ability can help reveal the hidden logic behind everyday social and spatial practices, not because it breaches 'norms' but because it exposes, resists and alters the 'ordinary':

> I am in the East Room at Tate Modern in London for a public lecture about disability arts. It is rectilinear, monochrome, modern, minimal with floor to ceiling glazing on three sides, currently curtained, with an even-

4 Ann Heylighen has received a European Research Council (ESC) Proof-of-Concept Grant for her proposal 'Rent-a-Spatialist' which aims to develop the work outlined here, so that she and her team can investigate whether and how disabled people's experiences can impact on architectural education in Belgium. The research runs from November 2013 to October 2014: www.asro.kuleuven.be/aida/index.php?ref=project.

> ness of overhead lighting and with a long table in front of the remaining blank wall. The occupants are settling: time is taken negotiating and sorting the space for a better fit. A woman lies across a large black sofa (out of her wheelchair and in less pain on her back). One of the speakers is of short stature. He rests his chin and arm directly on the speaker's table. Other people position themselves and are positioned – for comfort, for view, for friendship. Sightlines are orchestrated to BSL and SSC interpreters and other bits of useful technology. Signing makes its own, roughly circular, spaces for the deaf participants. The conventional serried ranks of chairs are disrupted, adapted, some shuffled into smaller semi-circles of parallel conversations. Relationships in the space take on a different form, from parallel and active/passive to eddying and contingent.
>
> Throughout the talks, speakers are interrupted where a point is not clear. Tensions open up momentarily between speaker and participant or between participants where their preferences do not align, or where translatory devices are not working properly. A deaf and learning-disabled participant questions the cultural 'jargon'. Signers stop proceedings to check if they have understood properly. All sorts of spaces are endlessly being explicitly and constructively negotiated.
>
> (Jos Boys, unpublished notes, December 2007)

In this lecture room, the long table with few chairs behind, faced by many rows, indicates the 'normal' form of operation. Conventionally this is a space where the 'top table' does the talking and the audience passively listens, except for specifically located moments for verbal exchange, usually after the speakers have finished. This is the 'normal' socio-spatial practice of 'going to a lecture', so ordinary for people who attend such events regularly that we don't even notice the underlying patterns. The space, too, is relatively 'normal', especially for a white-cube kind of art gallery, with the speakers' table deliberately parallel to the longer wall (to make a wider, less hierarchical relationship to the audience), and white undecorated surfaces. The overall conference, then, conforms to such kinds of presentation more generally, as speakers present (with images) one after another.

But such seemingly obvious and commonsense socio-spatial practices are disrupted and rippled when the 'normal' rules of recognition of such a public performance don't fit or are refused. Hitherto unnoticed spaces of interaction reveal themselves as relationships, as acts of translation between bodies, event, artefacts and space, that cannot be merely assumed or distractedly enacted; but which produce a kind of positive stutter – a timely delay – in the space. The participants disentangle themselves from the homogeneous mass of assumed normality and open up processes of (absent-minded) recognition and (instantaneous) translation to disagreement, negotiation, to the taking of time, and the re-adjustment of relationships in the room. At the same time differences in relationships to socio-spatial practices are exposed; both between the different dis/abled people present in the room, and between these diverse people and their stereotypical 'namings'. The everyday assumptions of an 'everyone' fail to have any purchase; there are no (or fewer) hidden assumptions about what is so normal as to be unnoticed; every social and spatial relationship must be negotiated.

This does not produce some alternative 'normal' since the resulting arrangements are equally built on the mixture of consensus, tensions, contradictions, mismatches and unintended consequences that in reality make up abled social and spatial practices. But what it does do is two important things for the arguments being made here. First, it creates a space where dis/ability is *not* the issue (despite the large majority of disabled people attending). Rather, it performs the enabling of encounters and relationships that *constitute* the event for its participants. Second, it reveals, takes time over, and, most importantly, *(re-)designs* the acts of translation, the gaps between an 'ordinary' social and spatial practice and its performance. This gap which is 'normally' nothing much, transparent, obvious or even non-existent, the just jumping on a bus, finding the fifth floor room, going to a lecture, getting home, is revealed as what it really is. As I have said before, what it allows us to notice is the *work* embedded in making and re-making everyday life.

Ultimately, then, an extended ethnomethodology, or a similar method, offers critical and creative engagement with dis/ability and architecture. It enables exploration of how 'normal' everyday social and spatial practices are made and re-made through feelings, actions, encounters, artefacts and spaces. It opens up to view the ways in which ability becomes unnoticed and disability becomes marginalized – included as excluded – through these processes (whether in everyday life, in the shape of material spaces and artefacts or in relation to architecture as discourse and practice). At the same time, it begins to suggest a means of learning from dis/ability, both by starting from how diverse disabled people creatively manage the work of everyday living, in its intersections with the material landscape; and by cracking apart the normal 'forgetfulness' that resides in the ordinary and the abled.

I have also begun to suggest that to do this properly we need more developments in this area that can critically map how disabled people and dis/ability are located within architectural theory, practice and education; and that can build from these into alternative theories, strategies and tactics. Such different approaches need to find ways of capturing the multiple and simultaneous registers through which we experience built space, continually coming in and out of focus and relevance as we go about our everyday lives, and the enabling or disabling effects that are produced. And they need to be able to engage with different 'kinds' of knowledge simultaneously from the personal and anecdotal to the academic and theoretical. Following Sobchack, this is neither to treat disabled peoples stories as 'true', nor to

> privilege . . . autobiographical experience as somehow 'more authentic' than 'less authentic' discursive experience. Experience of any kind requires both bodies and language for its expression, and both autobiographical and

> discursive experiences are real in that they both have material causes and consequences.
>
> Rather [anecdotal moves are] meant to ground and expand the tropological premises [as these] inform the aesthetic and ethical imaginations of the humanities and arts. Perhaps a more embodied 'sense-ability' . . . by cultural critics and artists will lead to a great apprehension of 'response-ability' in its discursive use.
>
> (Sobchack 2006: 18)

It is this inter-relationship between contemporary discourse and practice that *Doing Disability Differently* turns to next, before going on to offer up some alternative kinds of mapping, design strategies and tactics for creatively examining the intersections of dis/ability and architecture, and, finally, making proposals for different kinds of architectural 'doing'. To begin this process, in the next three chapters I will propose that, across contemporary architectural theory, a slippage persistently occurs *away from* the differential and inequitable effects of everyday social and spatial practices. Instead, architects' interests in occupancy assume its subjects to be abled in the normal way: that is, having a readily available ability (mobility, independence, competency) that comes 'naturally' as people go about their daily existence. In turn, this obvious ease in moving through and navigating material space becomes centrally focused in developing design ideas on people's specific relationships to the building or space itself, rather than the building supporting the diverse dis/abilities of people as they go about their everyday lives. In addition, the particular intersections foregrounded through a specific architectural theory become both a means of generating form, and of making the relationship *to* the building more powerful. This may be by intensifying 'normal' practices or by disrupting them.

> **Imagine what would happen if we were to design environments only for wheelchair users, write books mostly in Braille, or communicate in sign language. Who would be disabled those cases?**
>
> (Galis 2011: 831)

What is important here is that the breaching processes of ordinary social and spatial practices and the making dis/ordinary of disability through both exclusion and over-exposure thus disappear from much architectural discourse for an unexpected reason. Social and spatial practices come to be not about the multi-layered relations between people, artefacts and spaces as they go about their everyday lives (which I will return to in the last chapter), but predominantly about people's interactions with buildings *as* architecture. And the enabling and disabling effects of 'normal' practices – as boundaries are maintained and defended in particular forms rather than others – becomes merely about the relative resonance of a particular spatial and aesthetic experience.

Of course, it is true that when we experience buildings our emotions, ideas, personal preferences and practical requirements simultaneously come in and out of focus (are noticed or unnoticed, more intense or distant, more or less comfortable) dependent on the relational context. This is the experience of everyone; a bodily complication or material obstacle or unexpected or unknown situation or deeply beautiful view can bring the inter-relationships between body, space, artefacts and others into jolting consciousness; as the work involved in everyday life surfaces into attention. I have already suggested that these consciously engaged moments are both more often obvious to, and more tellingly felt by, disabled people. Bodily work connected to an impairment may require more attentiveness and time to plan and support. And 'normal' social and spatial practices often produce disorienting, discomforting, frustrating and disruptive effects for disabled people, which they must creatively manage, alongside their impairment. But a building designed out of an interest in generating intense or unexpected *architectural* effects almost seems to be operating in a parallel universe to the one outlined here. It is another way of being in the world, that does not so much 'automatically' reinforce normal social and spatial practices, as intersect *peculiarly* with these practices, with a variety of enabling and disabling consequences, that urgently need to be unravelled. This then, is the stumbling intention of the next three chapters.

Section II

Re-connecting architecture with dis/ability

4 Destabilizing architecture?

In the 1970s and 1980s Rem Koolhaas was one of a large number of architects internationally who set about challenging the underlying assumptions of previous modernist architectural practices. In his book *Delirious New York* (originally published in 1978) he explored an 'alternative modernism' (both real and fictionalized) centred on an architecture of desire rather than on a universal, functional user, and where – taking the standard New York block as an exemplar – architectural form could be allowed to be a simple 'container' in which, nonetheless, unexpected and even outrageous human interactions could be housed (Text Box 4.1).

Text Box 4.1 Rem Koolhaas: excerpt from 'Definitive Instability: The Downtown Athletic Club' in *Delirious New York: A Retrospective Manifesto for Manhattan*, 1994 edition, New York: Monacelli Press, p. 155

The lowest floors are equipped for relatively conventional athletic pursuits: squash and handball courts, poolrooms, etc., all sandwiched between locker rooms. But then ascent through the upper layers of the structure – with its implied approximation of a theoretical 'peak' condition – leads through territories never before tread upon by man.

Emerging from the elevator on the ninth floor, the visitor finds himself in a dark vestibule that leads directly into a locker room that occupies the center of the platform, where there is no daylight. There he undresses, puts on boxing gloves and enters an adjoining space equipped with a multitude of punching bags (occasionally he may even confront a human opponent).

On the southern side, the same locker room is also serviced by an oyster bar with a view over the Hudson River. *Eating oysters with boxing gloves, naked, on the nth floor* – such is the 'plot' of the ninth story, or, the *20th century in action.*

In a further escalation, the tenth floor is devoted to preventive medicine. On one side of a lavish dressing lounge an array of body manipulation facilities is arranged around a Turkish bath: sections for massage and rubbing, an eight-bed station for artificial sunbathing, a ten-bed resting area. On the south face, six barbers are concerned with the mysteries of masculine beauty and how to bring it out. But the southwest corner of the floor is the most explicitly medical: a special facility that can treat five patients at the same time. A doctor here is in charge of the process of '*Colonic Irrigation*': the insertion into the human intestines of synthetic bacterial cultures that rejuvenate man by improving his metabolism.

Since then, through both projects and writings, and together with his practice the Office for Metropolitan Architecture (OMA), Koolhaas has been influential in offering strategies and tactics that can move design beyond a simplistic version of modernist design methods, shaped by functionalism and a belief in universal, comprehensive and coherent solutions. So what are these approaches and how can they be interrogated productively through dis/ability?

Destabilizing architecture

One of the crucial factors of Koolhaas's challenge to the modernist architectural ideal is to show just how relatively powerless architects are; how difficult, partial and uneven the relationship between theory and practice, ideas and realization is. As he writes:

> Architecture is a hazardous mixture of omnipotence and impotence. Ostensibly involved in 'shaping' the world, for their thoughts to be mobilised architects depend on the provocations of others – clients, individual or institutional. Therefore, incoherence, or more precisely, randomness, is the underlying structure of all architects' careers: they are confronted with an arbitrary sequence of demands, with parameters they did not establish, in countries they hardly know, about issues they are only dimly aware of, expected to deal with problems that have proved intractable to brains vastly superior to their own. Architecture is by definition a *chaotic adventure*.
>
> (Koolhaas and Mau 1995: xix)

Since this chaos and randomness of achievement is inherent in the architectural process, Koolhaas wants his fellow practitioners to accept it, to admit to their lack of God-like control, and to explore ways of starting from this resigned self-knowledge, most immediately in no longer attempting to appear neutral and objective in their rationales for building projects. The book

S, M, L, XL (1995), which is in fact more of a manifesto, begins with a series of images detailing in diagrammatic form (overlaid on photographs of the practice's dishevelled design office) staffing, expenditure and global reach. The rest of the volume combines an alphabetically organized vertical band of relatively randomized keywords and their definitions, together with a wide variety of graphic layouts combining images and text. Thus the layout of the book itself reflects Koolhaas's belief that neither overall coherence nor connective tissue exist, that incomplete and/or contradictory actions are inherent in how we think, work and inhabit the world. This is also expressed in how he writes – as a series of stories that attempt to reveal deeper truths than theoretical polemics, factual histories or descriptions of reality; here he is operating not at the level of explicit argument and explanation but in fable and personal interpretation; not a formally coherent grand narrative but a series of resonant fragments, expressed through filmic, graphic and magazine type formats (Figure 4.1).

If architectural narratives (both about themselves and about their projects) are inherently unstable and ambiguous, so too is the actual designing of architectural space. The unachievable, if assumed, direct and transparent

Figure 4.1 Cover illustration to *Content* magazine, Rem Koolhaas, 2004, Cologne: Taschen. Photography: Jos Boys.

correlations between a building's users, function, construction and internal and external appearance in modernist ideology are here re-framed through both a re-reading of modernism's alternative histories and through an explicit political (in the widest sense) engagement with contemporary global architectural and societal contexts. For Koolhaas, this leads to at least two threads, which appear in different ways in various projects. The first is, as with many of his contemporaries such as Bernard Tschumi,[1] to understand design as a form of narrative and sequencing rather than functional plan-making:

> I think the professions of scriptwriting and architecture are very close; for both you have to consider a plot, you have to develop episodes and you have to create a kind of montage that makes it interesting, and a sequence that makes the circulation or the paths or the experience of a building interesting, and gives it a certain suspense.
>
> (Heidingfelder and Tesch 2008)

Second, in envisioning occupancies as event rather than function based, Koolhaas increasingly comes to the view that individuals make their own purposes in the buildings they occupy in ways that cannot be delineated into neat patterns in plan or section. And as buildings get bigger, as these dynamic patterns become more various and complex, they cease to be something that architects can even think about organizing or controlling spatially. As he says:

> I am not interested in scripting exhaustively all the reactions there are . . . design, build, explain – [I am] more and more interested in withdrawing from that situation. . . . I am basically filled with ambiguity about it.
>
> (Heidingfelder and Tesch 2008)

In OMA's more recent works this is most deliberately expressed through a separation out of the compositional manipulations of form, which are treated very much abstractly and 'architecturally' (as 'the box'), and the more free-form opening up of the spaces within and around to not just their supposed activities but to other opportunities, as yet unknown. As Dutton and Mann put it:

> OMA designs 'large envelopes' unprogrammed by differentiated activities. Not simply a romantic pluralist, Koolhaas places this random freedom for activities within an exaggeratedly rigid, inhuman, non-referential

1 Koolhaas is just one of a whole generation of architects such as Bernard Tschumi and Zaha Hadid, who have challenged architectural modernism in innovative and important ways. Koolhaas, in turn, has influenced a considerable number of younger architects, such as Winy Maas of the Dutch firm MVRDV and Bjarke Ingels of the Copenhagen-based BIG, who both worked for him.

> form, something meaningless in which the meanings of activities will evolve.
>
> (Dutton and Mann 1996: 291)

In this OMA deliberately use *different* design methods for creating the overall solidity of the form and structure, and for orchestrating dynamic and relational patterns of occupation. The first works at the level of ideas from 'within' the discipline's own history and theory, by being generated from, commenting on and responding to previous buildings or approaches. The second is based on a belief that occupation is too various and dynamic to be coherently inscribed into a new designed space, but that the design of that space does come from the detailed specifics of a particular situation. Koolhaas outlines this as follows:

> If there is a method to this work, it is a method of systematic *idealisation* – a systematic awareness of what exists, a bombardment of speculation that invests even the most mediocre aspects with retroactive conceptual and ideological charge . . .
>
> The mirror image of this action is the most clinical inventory of the actual conditions of each site, no matter how uninspiring, the most calculating exploitation of its objective potential.
>
> (Koolhaas and Mau 1995: 208, emphasis in original)

This 'clinical' inventory, however, then becomes the basis for what Dunham-Jones (2013) calls 'programmatic instability in order to counteract architectural rigidity'; that is, a means to generate unexpected rather than normative responses. For non-architects, this is further complicated by a third, overlaying, process because Koolhaas and OMA then enjoy deliberately 'playing' with the tensions created by both this separation and the differences between 'formal' and 'functional' procedures. The inter-relationships of these two methods becomes itself a way of expressing architecturally the central idea of ambiguity – of architecture as working at the intersections between the mutually constitutive but separate, contradictory and non-coherent realms of representation and of events, social good and commercial gain. Simultaneously, the potential for unexpected connections and displacements becomes a means to make deliberately transgressive comments about conventional and 'normal' planning and aesthetics, and about the bigger contradictions of an exploding capitalist world, a point to which I will return.

An early design method derived from such thinking was 'cross-programming' (again clearly influenced by the *Delirious New York* work), introducing unexpected functions in room programmes, such as running tracks in skyscrapers. More recently, Koolhaas (unsuccessfully) proposed the inclusion of hospital units for the homeless in the 2003 Seattle Public Library project. This is perhaps the key mechanism through which, at a conceptual level, Koolhaas aims 'to restore a kind of honesty and clarity to the relationship between architecture and public' (Koolhaas and Mau 1995: xix) both in text and designed form. He starts from some of the conventional social and spatial binary divisions between, for example, marginal/important, destroyed/rebuilt, realism/utopianism, permanence/instability, large-scale urban/small-scale individual, western/non-western, relativity/essence and absence/presence. He then brings what are often oppositional concepts back into deliberate and/or unexpected formal and spatial juxtaposition. The resulting intersections remain contradictory and entangled, because – unlike modernism – bringing different ideas together is here not about finding an underlying coherence, but about both expressing and enjoying ambiguity. Such unexpected surprises more often occur, not so much at the level of programme, but as a means of making 'non-normal' events within a building; for example, making the goods vehicle delivery road a visible backdrop to the stage of the lecture hall at the Kunsthal in Rotterdam (Figure 4.2).

The Villa at Bordeaux

> **The husband explained . . .: 'Contrary to what you might expect, I do not want a simple house. I want a complicated house because it will determine my world.'**
>
> (http://storiesofhouses.blogspot.co.uk)

Figure 4.2 Interior of main lecture theatre, Kunsthal Rotterdam by OMA, completed 1992. Photography: Marianne (as part of Wiki Loves Art/NL project) via Wikipedia Creative Commons.

What, then, does such a design attitude and method end up feeling and looking like? Whilst the Villa at Bordeaux in France, begun in 1994, is a small single family house rather than a large corporate or governmental building, we can use it to explore how these ideas are played out in practice, in one specific case. It is one of OMA's most famous projects, built on an isolated countryside plateau for a client who used a wheelchair, and for his family. Architecturally this is a seminal building for contemporary architects, equivalent to the great modernist examples of Le Corbusier's Villa Savoye (1929) and Mies van der Rohe's Farnsworth House (1951), to both of which it makes explicit reference, generating its language of form and structure through a dialogue with these projects. This is achieved by OMA through a series of games and reversals, acknowledging and then subverting modernist architectural assumptions. For example, the building is divided into three horizontal layers (in good modernist fashion). But the top floor, which contains the bedrooms, refuses to respond to the panoramic views (the house overlooks the Garonne river) through the conventionally contextual and modernist technique of large windows and light spaces. Instead this top floor is a deliberately heavy concrete 'bunker' with only slits for windows; and the whole 'weight' of it seems to challenge any 'normal' structural logic (with a shape which 'upends' the implied structural coherence of a typical modernist post and beam structure). The openings in this floating box *do* have a clearly stated contextual logic but one that sets a tension between what would architecturally be seen as an overly heavy form and its internal requirements. As Jacques Lucan writes:

> Rem Koolhaas has opted for a myriad of views that require the eye to occupy a series of precise points in space at the summit of the virtual visual cones generated by the portholes that are perforated in the thick shell of reinforced concrete. Instead of a sweeping and unimpeded view of the horizon, the eye has a choppy vision, never perceiving more than the sum of miniature pictures.
>
> (Koolhaas 1998: 19)

The next layer down, the main living floor, which would 'normally' be expressed and celebrated by modernist architects, is here 'invisible', non-articulated – merely the slot of space between top and bottom which is half inside and half outside. Finally, the lowest level is 'cave-like', what Koolhaas calls 'a series of caverns carved out from the hill for the most intimate life of the family' (Koolhaas 1998: 21). If Le Corbusier's Villa Savoye is – conceptually – a coherent and flowing journey upwards from the ground to the sky, then the Villa at Bordeaux instead deliberately offers visual and compositional mismatches around ideas of transparency and solidity, absence and presence (Figure 4.3).

The compositional device that intersects these more architectural gestures with the realities of everyday occupancies is the 3-metre by 3.5-metre vertical moving floor plate central to the plan, which is both a lift and a 'room' for the

Figure 4.3 Exterior view, OMA, Villa at Bordeaux, France (1998). Photograph courtesy of *Living Architectures*, www.living-architectures.com/Koolhaas_houselife.php

wheelchair-using client. Marked by a wall that integrates all three layers (and contains everything the owner might need: books, wine, office, etc.) the lift platform acts as a resonant metaphor, of the centrality and importance of the owner to the activities of the house. It expresses a 'void' when he is absent on another floor, and architectural form as a continually transitional process between occupation and space, by moving freely between realms 'changing plan and performance' (Koolhaas 1998: 62). Architecturally, this is a play with and against Le Corbusier's use of the ramp at Villa Savoye as a unifying and dynamic element throughout the building. But the gesture is taken even further; by juxtaposing a smooth and easy flow of movement for the wheelchair user with deliberately awkward and challenging elements for the abled participants in the house, most notably a tightly spiralling staircase and a series of difficult-to-see glass edges and unprotected holes in the floor. In the film of the building, *Koolhaas Houselife* (Bêka and Lemoine 2013) the cleaner memorably hauls a vacuum cleaner up the spiral staircase (Figure 4.4). Whilst the disabled man glides friction-free up through the space – and makes that space his by his very arrival – the abled must watch their step and be constantly aware of barriers to easy progress. As one of his colleagues says wryly and only half-jokingly in the film *A Kind of Architect*:

> [This is an] extremely theatrical if not filmic architecture. . . . Breaks are built in, resulting in moments of suspense and irritation, the ground gets

Figure 4.4 Video still from *Koolhaas Houselife* (Bêka and Lemoine 2008) featuring Guadalupe Acedo, the housekeeper, as she looks after the house. Available from www.living-architectures.com/Koolhaas_houselife.php

> swept from under your feet, you lose your footing. A critic once wrote: you rarely leave a building by Koolhaas without bruises.
>
> (Heidingfelder and Tesch 2008)

How then does a project like this, and the theoretical framework through which it has been developed, help us think more critically and creatively about dis/ability and architecture? First, what has been important about the work of architects of both this generation, and those since, is that they have challenged and re-thought many of the assumptions of architectural modernism built on a reductive image of human occupation and its representation in built form. Koolhaas and OMA, by decisively separating out aesthetic and compositional concerns from programmatical ones, as well as by admitting to the partiality of what architects can do in social terms, have opened the way for much more complex and nuanced understandings of relationships between people and built space. At the same time, rather than designing for a mechanical idea of a universal 'user', Koolhaas builds in some idea of the unfixability of human needs, desires and preferences; and of the uncontrollability of events. If his early work around desire, which described detailed, embodied encounters – as in the

New York Downtown Athletic Club – became less relevant to him as building projects got bigger and bigger, it has still enabled the imagining of occupancy as rich and complex.

In addition, Koolhaas and OMA have been at the forefront of radical shifts in how architects think and talk about what they do, and in extending our architectural vocabularies in creative and thought-provoking ways; particularly through their insistence on a conscious discrepancy between the formally designed 'box' – 'the search for form' as a conscious patterning of solid and void – and its contents, 'the process of fitting programme into this form' (Koolhaas 1999: 108). In OMA's buildings the resulting intersections are often clearly visible in the built project's formal, architectural manipulations; partly because Koolhaas deliberately does not attempt to disguise the monotony of many repetitive block-type organizational forms, and partly because his focus on manipulating the building-as-box tends to use the most obviously cinematic components – patterns of movement – as both a formal and a programmatic element, often seeming to literally carve through the other spaces. This has tended to make circulation a kind of 3-D cutting through of the box that, almost accidentally, has generated many buildings that treat floor surfaces as planes and levels, where ramps function as hinges, and floors warp, opening the way to later generations of architects to integrate sloping floors and ramps into their work as a matter of course, and as integral to conceptual thinking, rather than as a specialist, practical and added-on 'disabled' element. I will return to the relevance of this explicit playing with levels in Chapter 5.

At the same time, though, Koolhaas and OMA's work raises big questions about *how* architectural design is or should be generated. This is as much about what gets left out and remains invisible to debate, as what is explicitly said. Next, then, I want to explore how the 'peopling' of architecture in general, and dis/ability in particular, becomes marginalized or invisible in architectural approaches like this.

> **The Bordeaux House engages architectural discourse in a way that conventional accessible buildings do not.**
>
> (Fitzsimons 2012: 9)

Falling down the gaps between composition and programme

Many aspects of Koolhaas's and OMA's development programme in the case-by-case specificity of each project can actually be quite conventional, and similar to architectural practices more generally. For example, almost all of his houses make a programmatic split between spaces for adults and those for children. And, as with many other architects, possible propositions are explored through the organizational 'diagramming'[2] of intended activities and their relationships (through sketching, drawings and models) and the mapping out of routes and relationships around and between these activities. The particular attitude of OMA here, as I have already outlined, is to try to be relaxed about big buildings and 'banal' spaces, that is to only intervene spasmodically and without any co-ordinating intention, but to concentrate on design moves that orchestrate specific unexpected or provocative 'moments' in relation to some aspect of the building. This, then, is not merely a diagramming of 'normal' functions, or organizational or social relationships, but often unexpected or intentionally surreal relationships, such as the height of art spectators at the Guggenheim Grozny (Text Box 4.2), or deliberately discomforting (functionally and/or in terms of 'normal' social and spatial practices). However, despite these deliberate juxtapositions and contradictory relationships I suggest that the primary framing of architecture's relationship to its inhabitants at the level of the specific case remains firmly located in the concepts outlined by Hill – aesthetic contemplation, sequential movement, and/or functional performance – even whilst being a commentary on, and deliberate destabilization of, those concepts' more ordinary and commonsense understandings.

Text Box 4.2 Excerpt from Ann Lewinson, 'At the Guggenheim Grozny', *Hayden's Ferry Review* 2005, Issue 36 (Spring/Summer). Downloadable from www.asu.edu/piper/publications/haydensferryreview/issue36/fiction/pdfs/guggenheim_grozny.pdf.

We arrive exhausted.

But you must see the Guggenheim Grozny, they've told us. Worth the detour. An architectural marvel. Proof that people will travel thousands of miles out of their way just to look at a building.

Functionaries in the newly declared Chechnyan capital of Gudermes had requested a swirling, titanium-clad sprawl of a museum, but Frank Gehry was otherwise engaged designing the Guggenheim Pristina. 'We will commission a visionary architect,' said Thomas Krens, director of the Solomon R. Guggenheim Foundation. 'We can get you Rem Koolhaas. It will be unimaginable, the Guggenheim Grozny.'

2 If modernist architects used the term 'brief' to describe the set of client requirements for a building project, more recently the concept of 'programme' has become dominant. This is perhaps because it aims to articulate activities rather than 'needs' and frames space and what goes on in it as a dynamic and inter-relational process. In addition, the idea of 'diagramming' is taking hold, particularly through the influential work of Peter Eisenman (Vidler 2000, Eisenman 1999). Whilst architects have always used diagrams as a means of analysing situations, and sketching out and testing design ideas, the contemporary interest is in how diagramming can work as a conscious design act, through rigorously intersecting multiple variables, both obvious and unexpected.

Bringing tourism to Grozny is as hazardous as the terrain, secretly pockmarked by undetonated land mines and riddled with so many underground air pockets – scars of random and reckless oil-drilling – that the entire city could collapse into a yawning abyss at any moment. Rem Koolhaas surveyed the land and said, 'Ah, the client as chaos. My Guggenheim, like the brutal landscape on which it rests, will teeter on the verge of implosion.'

The Guggenheim Grozny is built in long, horizontal slabs, like a club sandwich. Each ascending layer is larger than the one below it. It is as if to say, 'Ha, land of Grozny, I dare you to implode!' And what if the Guggenheim Grozny does, indeed, collapse? At a press conference, Rem Koolhaas only shrugs . . .

To reinforce the museum's apparent instability, a highway runs straight through the middle of the ground floor. At the coat check you can breathe deep the regulation-free emissions, deafened by the roar of unmuffled engines. 'All to raise the discomfort level,' says Rem Koolhaas . . .

To calculate exactly how high on the wall each painting must be hung, architects from Koolhaas' Rotterdam firm OMA/AMO have made a scientific study of the average heights of those who favour particular artists. The average James Rosenquist fan is 6'1", while the average Anselm Kiefer devotee is only 4'11". The space is thus 'scripted', to use Koolhaas' term, determining exactly what an individual visitor will see, and lessening the aggravation of the diminutive Lucian Freud enthusiast who will no longer have to confront that irritating R.B. Kitaj.

What, then, are the effects of such an approach on occupancies and dis/ability? Well, first of all, it leaves a gap, both in theorizing and in interacting with, everyday social and spatial practices that, as has been outlined in the previous chapter, percolate through, and are continuously (re-)performed in, our material landscapes. The work is not underpinned by, nor feels the need for, any explicit general theory or method that can better understand 'normal' social and spatial relationships, so as to generate truly critical (that is, socially radical) programmes in different cases. Whilst Koolhaas has been deeply informed by wider theory, particularly the Situationists and Bataille (Dunham-Jones 2013), his re-workings of these ideas have taken them completely into the internal spaces of architectural discourse (that is, becoming centrally engaged with how theory can inform the manipulation of *form*). As a result, the mode of translation from idea to actual space and material through diagramming works ultimately only at the level of poetic commentary. Take the moving room at the Bordeaux villa, for example. This is a fantastically resonant device; it literally makes the owner central to the house, its viability as actual usable space dependent on his intentions and movements. This both reverses the usual, marginalized,

Figure 4.5 Interior view of the Villa at Bordeaux showing unprotected staircase. Photograph courtesy of *Living Architectures*, www.living-architectures.com/Koolhaas_houselife.php

experiences of space for disabled people, and fits with the client's requirements for a 'complicated house'. His personal power is then reinforced by the deliberate relative powerlessness of the other occupants in the house, making their staircase-bound journeys much more tortuous (Figure 4.5). The room (and the house's other circulation mechanisms), then, act both as formal representations and actually map out what can and can't be enacted. But, in making an architectural *commentary* on the stereotypical binary divisions between disability and ability, Koolhaas merely reverses them. He enhances the space for some of its occupants at the expense of others. This makes such an approach a limited mechanism for capturing and responding to how people occupy space differently (and are located differently *in* space). Instead, some aspect of the complexity of, and differences between, desires, needs and 'placing' of people generates a specific architectural component, or set of components, that ultimately prevents something else – the development of an underlying attitude, or set of principles, or socially engaged design process. This also means that the practicalities of occupation continue to be relatively marginalized.

Finally, as I have already mentioned, inhabitation only needs to be analysed comprehensively at the level of individual and specific programmes. In this, like many of his generation, Koolhaas is making an important critique of the all-encompassing logic of rationalist modernism. But it also means that the complexities of analysing occupancy 'on the ground' as a *conceptual* problem underlying *every* design problem continue to be avoided. Instead it remains at the level of case-by-case decisions, where socio-spatial conventions may be happily and unproblematically reproduced or commented on through architectural form (as with the Villa at Bordeaux) and/or disrupted through architectural means to achieve particular effects in relation to some specific facet of those ordinary practices, for example through awkward spatial relationships between what is 'usually' public or private. If the artificial integration of form and function in modernism reduced occupancy to the abstract 'universal user' then the separation *out* of form from function in contemporary architecture means that re-thinking occupancy in general, and dis/ability in particular, just falls down the gap; and the importance of architects being able to model diverse occupancies as part of their repertoire continues to be as invisible in just as much recent work as it was during the period of architectural modernism.

The problem of creative disruption

The OMA partnership uses design not just to create inhabitable space but also to provoke, disrupt or reframe some of our everyday assumptions and actions. I am suggesting that this produces a kind of slippage, where creative disruption moves away from making potentially radical buildings (within the very real constraints that Koolhaas describes) to, as a strategy, commentary on contemporary society, and, as a tactic, to creating a more intense experience of the building itself for its occupants, through elements of suspense and surprise. Koolhaas is particularly renowned for creating a very sophisticated engagement with the first of these positions, as outlined above, in his provocative ability to layer conceptual, professional and societal contradictions, refusing neither to try and make the best of the inherently compromised position of architectural practice nor to stop designing for autocratic regimes or other problematic clients. But for critics such as Dunham-Jones this is not a progressive form of architectural practice:

> Equating capitalism with modernization and change, Koolhaas identified early on how global capitalism created dynamic, highly speculative urban conditions that were transforming the contemporary city. As he pointed out in his acerbic writings of the time, these same forces were destabilizing and liberating architectural thinking from staid preconceptions, providing an audience – and a market – for the kind of radical, iconic buildings being designed by his Rotterdam-based practice OMA. This powerful combination of '60s irreverence and '90s relevance catapulted Koolhaas to star status; it also revealed the inevitable contradictions in trying to marry art and capitalism, radicalism and pragmatism, icon-making and city-making. Nonetheless, over the decade, his writings and designs contributed significantly to shifting design discourse away from critical theory toward post-critical, non-judgmental research, and from autonomy toward engagement

> – albeit engagement largely with the elite beneficiaries of the New Economy, now often described as 'the 1%'.
>
> (Dunham-Jones 2013)

She recognizes that this is a deliberate position that has been very successful 'in navigating the intersection of the pragmatic corporate sector, on the one hand, and the "delirious" and volatile realm of desire and possibility, on the other. Keenly aware of these inherent contradictions, Koolhaas revels in their creative friction.' This, however, Dunham-Jones sees as a negation of his more radical roots (in the counter-cultural politics of 1960s Paris), a joining up with the establishment whilst appearing to criticize it. She berates him for not 'questioning the costs or benefits, the winners or losers, of the forces of modernization and global capitalism'; that instead of trying to 'shape the wave of modernization' and 'trying to fix the damage left in the wake' he just rides one wave and then scans the horizon for the next. She criticizes him for limiting his transgressions to architectural and urban discourse and blames him 'for the proliferation of large, avant-garde iconic buildings which serve to declare the client's participation in the New World Order and the designer's participation in the global economy'.

> **Many architects still see their practices as about the designer providing buildings with critical capacities, so that the architect can engage 'with contemporary problems through formal manipulation'.**
>
> (Ghirardo 1991: 12)

Here, though, I think Koolhaas perfectly understands that there is no 'moral high ground' in commercially grounded architectural practice (a view which itself is a telling criticism of modernist beliefs in the superiority of their own judgements), that there is no place 'outside' the actual society we live in, and that creative and critical engagements must necessarily muddle around in and among the inevitable contradictions and instabilities of making (big) architecture for a living. But whilst one of the most important aspects of this architect is how he positions himself explicitly within wider political, social and economic contexts, I suggest that the *tools* he has developed remain too heavily embedded within the limited confines of architectural discourse. Like many of his contemporaries, he plays at the intersections of socio-spatial concepts and formal architectural vocabularies. For example, when he juxtaposes the concepts of absence/presence, he is interested in how to challenge the assumption of *architecture* as presence, by aiming to celebrate its more absent qualities (rather than, for example, the relative absences and presences involved in occupancy). So in comparing one of his most famous early projects in Berlin with a more recent one in China, he says:

> For me, the Berlin Wall as architecture was the first spectacular revelation in architecture as to how absence can be stronger than presence. For me, it is not necessarily connected to loss in a metaphysical sense, but more connected to an issue of efficiency, where I think that the great thing about Berlin is that for me, it showed (and this is my campaign against architecture) how entirely 'missing' urban presences or entirely erased architectural entities nevertheless generate what could be called an urban condition. It's no coincidence, for example, that the center of Shenzen is not a built substance but a conglomeration of golf courses and theme parks, i.e. basically unbuilt or empty conditions. And that was the beauty of Berlin even ten years ago, that it was the most contemporary and the most avant-garde European city because it had these major vast areas of nothingness.
>
> (Koolhaas and Obrist 2007)

It is left to a journalist attending one of his talks to note wryly:

> At a press conference [about the Guggenhiem, Grozny], Rem Koolhaas only shrugs, 'It will be like the Berlin Wall, stronger in absence than in presence.' A reporter from the *Berliner Morgenpost* reminds the architect that the Wall did indeed make it difficult to get from the east side of Berlin to the west side, but Koolhaas merely shrugs again.
>
> (Lewinson 2005)

Epitaph

In 1991, the client of the Villa at Bordeaux died:

> 21 January 01/20.45
> Bordeaux 32 49 N 16 58 W
> Maison à Bordeaux
> After the death of the owner of the house, the empty vessel that he leaves becomes the receptacle for what the rigor of his regime – fatherhood, suffering, combativeness, love – had eliminated from the family's daily life: femininity, informality, hospitality, fun.
>
> (Koolhaas 2004: 374–5)

This, of course, is also a provocation. But here, the problematic contradictions in the work of Koolhaas and OMA are ultimately revealed, as the simultaneously poetic and functional devices of the Villa at Bordeaux suddenly have all their meanings emptied out, and the realities of lives, lived and lost, hit home. Here, too, is expressed a mainly conventional and commonsense usage of some stereotypical binaries around gender and the family. The disabled father (and his power, so celebrated in the building) is turned into a negative, the opposite of an assumed motherly, relaxed pleasure, whilst disability defaults to its normal location as 'suffering'. The creation of seductive design interventions, through linking and then juxtaposing particular social concepts with specific formal devices, turns out to show little adaptive or sustainable purchase on the much more complex, ambiguous and contradictory realities of everyday social and spatial practices, as experienced through dis/ability. And – for a moment – the awkward and problematic intersections between the routine practices of this household and the parallel universe of architecture's own internal discourses are revealed (as they are more generally in Lewinson's article about the Guggenheim Grozny) as something worth further unravelling. Thus, whilst the creative and inventive introduction of ambiguity and instability into architectural theory and practice has been a centrally important shift away from modernist preconceptions, these seem to end up being located in the *wrong place* – that is, in how abstract socio-spatial concepts are imagined and then interwoven, rather than in the ambiguities and instability of, on the one hand, actual lived social and spatial practices and, on the other, framings of architectural theory itself. This is something I will return to in the final chapter of this book.

5 On feeling and beauty

In the contemporary period phenomenological approaches to architecture have returned firmly to the centre of much architectural practice, particularly through the influence of architects such as Peter Zumthor, Juhani Pallasmaa, Alberto Pérez-Gómez and Steven Holl. This focuses on embodied experiences as a rich design tool, engaging with all the senses. This chapter aims to unravel some of the assumptions and tensions in phenomenology[1] as expressed architecturally by, as before, intersecting it with dis/ability, looking specifically at the writing and design work of Peter Zumthor. It suggests that, whilst these approaches bring a rich and vital articulation of all the senses into building design and have a central concern with occupancy, the assumption that there are archetypical spaces which we all share, a non-problematization of either the body or of perception, the obscuring of particular aesthetic preferences, and the lack of critical reflection around why spaces need to be experienced 'emotionally' in the first place, all produce difficulties for embedding dis/ability.

A phenomenological architecture

Phenomenology has been having a considerable impact on architectural thought for many years. Initially this was part of a critical response to the perceived mechanical functionalism of modernism, and its tendency towards the visual over other senses – that is, in focusing on what is seen rather than on what is felt. Phenomenology's concerns with experience, memory and, in particular, its articulation of spatial and aesthetic archetypes, have already led to many writings about, and built examples designed through detailed engagements with, the specificity of a site and place.[2] More recently, it has informed challenges to the emphasis on representation and meaning in post-modernism,

1 Phenomenology is the philosophical study of the structures of consciousness from a first-person perspective. In terms of architecture and design, phenomenology is the study and exploration of the physical experience of buildings, building materials and their sensory properties.

2 See, for example, Merleau-Ponty 1945, Rasmussen 1964, Bachelard 1994, Norberg-Schultz 1980, Hertzberger 2009, Shonfield 2000 and Holl 2000.

and the form-making of deconstructivist architecture. As Steven Holl, Juhani Pallasmaa and Alberto Pérez-Gómez write in the introduction to *Questions of Perception: Phenomenology of Architecture* (2006):

> The endless cultural limitations and contradictions inherent in artistic work, revealed with impeccable clarity and logic by the critics' deconstructive theory, are ultimately of limited use for the generation of architecture . . . Unlike the critic and the philosopher, the architect must embrace the contradictions between perception and logic, the slippage between architectural intention and realization, and the unpredictability of the future's judgement upon the acting present, and 'resolve' or confuse these aporias through his/her personal imagination.
>
> (Holl *et al.* 2006: 4)

A design method inflected with phenomenology enables what Zumthor calls the 'magic of the real' (1999) – the creation of places that have the ability to touch us deeply. A series of books and projects by this group of architects (Holl 2000, Zumthor 1999, 2010, Pallasmaa 2005) focus on the intimate experience of our corporeal engagements with artefacts and spaces. The aim is to generate an experiential intensity (that is, with poetic and spiritual resonances) in the physical and atmospheric quality of spaces, felt both through contemplative engagement and in experiential sequences. As Steve Rose writes about Zumthor:

> His approach is characterised by patient craftsmanship, deep understanding, and ascetic rigour. His buildings usually consist of very little, done very, very well. Zumthor is no minimalist, though; not for him ephemeral fashions in form and theory. He doesn't believe in architecture as a vehicle for communicating other forms of meaning, but rather as a language unto itself. The only thing Zumthor has labelled himself as is a phenomenologist, 'concerned with the way things look, feel, touch, smell, sound'.
>
> (Rose 2007)

Zumthor's book *Atmospheres* (2010) is a transcript of a talk to an architectural audience, describing this approach based on 'feeling' – on an 'emotional rather than a linear response', that is, intuitive and impressionistic rather than intellectualized. As in his other works, the writing is personal and conversational; offering itself as an honest and modest attempt to capture his particular method, framed around nine themes, supplemented with some personal preferences (that are merely listed rather than explained). These, in turn, frame how particular buildings are designed (Figure 5.1).

Most importantly, Zumthor aims to describe the means through which designed space can enhance the immediate sensations we get when we enter a space, and to show that this requires a considerable amount of work for the

Figure 5.1 Exterior of Thermal Baths at Vals, Switzerland, Peter Zumthor, 1996. Photography: p2cl. Downloaded from www.flickr.com/photos/p2cl/354225161 CC-BY-SA-2.0 (http://creativecommons.org/licenses/by-sa/2.0), via Wikimedia Commons.

designer – 'the task of creating architectural atmosphere [also] comes down to craft and graft'. His key points are that, first, architecture itself is like a material body *to* the body. In the section entitled 'The Body of Architecture' he writes that 'the material presence of things in a piece of architecture, its frame' is like an anatomy where different parts are brought together to make a whole, like our own bodies with skins covering, so that there are things we can't see:

> As a bodily mass, a membrane, a fabric, a kind of covering, cloth, velvet, silk, all around me. The body! Not the idea of the body – the body itself. A body that can touch me.
>
> (Zumthor 2010)

Thus types of materials and their constructional relationships are central. Material properties are also linked to the sound, temperature and lighting of a space. Interiors are described like large musical instruments based on their room shapes, surfaces, the way those surfaces have been applied and their temperature – used here as in 'tempering', that is as a kind of tuning system to achieve design harmonies. In addition are the effects of what Zumthor simply calls the 'light on things'.

Second, architecture needs to consider surrounding objects – that is, to engage with the deep relationships shown in how people bring objects together.

This care and love needs an architecture that 'creates these receptacles to house objects', not so as to capture a specific moment, but to imagine change because 'buildings also have to have their own future', nonetheless underpinned by a 'sense of home'. This is linked to the idea of personal preferences. He writes that buildings become part of a personal context and history (for example, a space can resonate with the memory of a first kiss) and that it is the ongoing use and experience of a space that matters much more than the architect's original intention. Third, architecture is about playing with spatial relationships, between, for example, intimacy and public-ness; or tensions between interior and exterior. This also makes it centrally about orchestrating feelings about movement in space – '"Architecture is a spatial art," as people always say. But architecture is also a temporal art. My experience of it is not limited to a single second.' This means both designing for the different spatial qualities of a variety of lived experiences, through a patterning of 'still' places, places with clear orientation, then places that are 'trying to coax you away'; and for expressing, through atmosphere, the meanings and functions of a specific building. As he writes, for example:

> and suddenly there is an exterior and an interior. One can be inside or outside. Brilliant! And that means – equally brilliant! – this: thresholds, crossings, the tiny loop-hole door, the almost imperceptible transition between the inside and the outside, an incredible sense of place, an unbelievable feeling of concentration when we suddenly become aware of being enclosed, of something enveloping us.
>
> (Zumthor 2010)

Here, the example connects the detailed embodied engagement of the action with the meaning of entrance (as an archetypically shared experience, as a personal memory and as an expression of the type of building being entered). It is these relationships, out of the experience and specificity of a situation, that generate form, which is thereby also beautiful. For Zumthor, then, there is no 'external' theory for this process. As he writes:

> Personally, I still believe in the self-sufficient, corporeal wholeness of an architectural object as the essential, if difficult, aim of work, if not as a natural or given fact . . . I am confronted here not only by the all-too-familiar awareness of the difficultly of eliminating artificiality in things created in an artificial act and of making them part of the world of ordinary and natural things, but also by the belief that truth lies in the things themselves.
>
> (Zumthor 1999: 30)

The reality of architecture is in the concrete body in which forms, volumes and spaces, come into being. There are no ideas except in things.

(Zumthor 1999: 34)

The power of atmosphere

The end result of this approach has been a number of built projects where infinite care has been taken over materials and their qualities; as well as over the orchestration of contemplative and sequential journeys through the building and its surroundings. This is predominantly interpreted as powerfully mysterious and spiritual:

> [Zumthor] has built dramatic hillside churches and hermit's chapels, but even his non-religious buildings tend to evoke a sort of spiritual awe, such as his refined glass box of an art gallery in Bregenz, Austria, or his thermal baths in Vals, a stone temple to water and bathing in the Alps. [At Kolumba] the sensation is of a sacred space: calm, powerful, unforgettable. Time seems to stand still; thousands of years of history are visible all at once.
>
> (Rose 2007)

Unlike OMA's buildings, which need to be described, initially at least, in terms of the conceptual and programmatic ideas that become translated into form, projects by Peter Zumthor tend to be most immediately outlined in terms of their actual embodied experience. Kolumba, for example, is an art museum in Germany, which shares its site with the ruins of a Gothic church and a 1950s chapel, and wraps a perforated facade of grey brick around both. Here is part of Steven Rose's description:

> This, the cavernous ground-floor room of Cologne's new Kolumba art museum, is a place of mystery and awe. You enter it from the museum's airy foyer, through thick leather curtains, and are instantly transported to another world. It is dimly lit, but fresh air and dappled sunlight spill in from honeycomb-like perforations high above. Embedded in the light brick walls are the blackened windows and arches of a ruined gothic church, onto which this new building has been grafted.
>
> (Rose 2007)

What is centrally important about Zumthor, then, is his ability to evoke, through designed elements, feelings of connectivity between people, spaces and objects; his attentiveness to detail attending to all the senses; and the quality of craftsmanship in his work. This approach of Zumthor, and of many others, has moved architecture on from both its modernist reliance on the universal user and a focus on the visual over other senses. It also avoids the difficulty of creative disruption covered in the previous chapter. This is because a phenomenological understanding of space directly concerns our experiences of this space; it is not caught up with, or even interested in, our distractedness or disrupted interactions with the material world as we go about our (other) business. Instead it is honed to a palette of human experience – linking back to feeling and memory, rather than function or activity – so simultaneously immediately sensual and almost transcendental in the emotional and poetic associations it triggers. This offers a radically different concept of 'fit'. What fits about these spaces is their assumed resonance with a shared human understanding of how space 'speaks' to us in its archetypical forms.

> **The world extends the form of some bodies and not others, and such bodies in turn feel at home in this world.**
>
> (Ahmed 2006: 129)

But, in intersecting dis/ability with this particular extension of phenomenological ideas into architecture, several basic questions have to be asked. First, to what extent *are* there underlying socio-spatial archetypes that, through their deep, almost intuitive embedding in personal memory, and what might be called a shared unconscious, can produce a similarity of sensual reverberations to diverse participants? Second, are there alternative forms of articulating our relationships to built space that such an attitude obscures or avoids? Here I want to suggest that, whilst designing space in intimate relationship with our bodies and senses should be a vital part of the architectural design process, the reliance on a general, but under-articulated (that is, not explicitly theorized or defined) phenomenology generates several difficulties when translated into architectural form. It builds a set of shared 'deep' meanings generated out of form, space and objects, that assume and delineate an archetypal ('normal') user. That this user remains the conventional mobile, autonomous and competent subject is obscured through the seemingly radical act of also attending to their emotions. In this process, we need to look harder at who is left out, either because they do not share the personal/unconscious experiences as designed; and/or because they also bring other forms of engagement beyond emotional contemplation of the building to their occupancy; and/or because they are framed not so much through archetypal emotional experiences but rather by the essentially *relational* encounters between people, spaces and objects, whose interactions are not necessarily obvious, poetic and shared, but more often complex and contradictory. As Melhuish writes:

> the deployment of senses and sensibility, and not only their content, is emphatically cultural – that is, the way that individuals use their senses and their particular responses to phenomena is highly determined by their specific cultural context and conditions, and not simply the result of universal human attributes.
>
> (Melhuish 2005: 207)

Further, we need to address more critically the tendency of phenomenological design to offer itself as non-theoretical (often in deliberate opposition to architectural design generated out of ideas), and thus as transparent, natural and 'obviously beautiful' in the quality of its resulting built form.

Whose house? What archetypes leave out

One of the enduring influences on architectural and interior design has been Gaston Bachelard's *Poetics of Space*, first published in 1958 (and translated into English in 1964). For Bachelard, the house is centrally important for study of our 'intimate' experiences of inside space because it is the archetype of our first essence, linking together in our shared psyches' associations between and across the primitive (or hermit's) hut, cradle and the maternal womb. Here, our earliest memories are built on positive feelings around shelter and protection. These kinds of spaces, then, are primordially shared by people, and as 'originating' spaces keep the *normal* consciousness 'well and happily housed' whilst the *abnormal* consciousness has been 'roughly or insidiously dislodged' (Bachelard 1994: 10). In architectural terms this means that – again normally:

> thanks to the house, a great many of our memories are housed, and if the house looks a bit elaborate, if it has a cellar and a garret, nooks and corridors, our memories have refuges that are all the more clearly delineated.
>
> (Bachelard 1994: 8)

But what constitutes the abnormal, outside of this oneiric (that is, related to dreams or dreaming) house with its spaces at the top and buried underneath, with its various patterns of light and dark, its different places of accessibility and exclusion, and its potential for poetic elaborations and extensions? Who does not have the possibility of this kind of dreaming? This is only dealt with by Bachelard in passing. First of all, there is the problem of inhabitation in the city – flats and houses that have spaces all on one level – so that 'the different rooms that compose living quarters jammed into one floor all lack one of the fundamental principles of distinguishing and classifying the values of intimacy' (Bachelard 1994: 27), which leads to oneiric incompleteness. In addition, because these places are not set in natural surroundings, the relationship between house and space becomes artificial, lacking a direct relationship, for example, to effects of wind and rain, or of winter cold. He also mentions people who have experienced trauma (illustrated by Jewish and Polish children's drawings of houses after experiencing German occupation (pp. 72–3)), who have also therefore had their range of poetic resonances stunted or depleted. But by blurring the potential gap between actual personal childhood memories (both his and those of other writers and poets) and universally shared archetypes and between individual perceptions of specific spaces and a generalized sharing by *everyone* of what feelings those spaces provoke, he makes 'abnormal readings' simultaneously negative – because stunted or depleted – and invisible, as we all partake of the same unconscious 'dreaming'. Since Bachelard's emotional archetypes originate in his own, both idealized and very specific, childhood memories of a large country house with servants and plenty of time alone, their generalization to the rest of the world needs at least critical reflection. This also means that *difference* is silenced; that by appearing to appeal to all the senses, the wider issues of *whose* senses are valued, and what other sense experiences are ignored, disappears:

> [What David Howes (1991) calls] the sensorium consists of the culturally specific ways our senses are hierarchically ordered: in the West, for example, vision is dominant. The notion of the sensorium is similar to the phenomenological insistence that '. . . there is no such thing as a simple act of perception since anything we are perceiving appears against a dense backdrop of past, present and future experiences' (Weiss 2003: 27) . . . Our way of sensing disability and making it sensible reflects the cultural education of the sensorium; it reflects the dense weave of historical experience that organizes perception and the relations among the senses.
>
> So, the sensorium has had an education. Wheelchair users (*for example*) either never show up or show up as a questionable presence; they are not necessarily perceivable in the course of daily life; thus, disability is not conceived as part of the ordinary sensibility of what it means to belong.
>
> (Titchkosky 2008: 50, italics added)

At the simplest level, this is about differential access to specific, supposedly shared and 'built-in' memories. Dis/ability complicates the appeal to our archetypical emotions, where 'the feel of the tiniest latch [that] remains in our hands' does not just bring back (even an imaginary) childhood:

> Trying to 'feel' the door 'click to open is a bit of a trial. Being told by a sign to *knock and wait* when . . . eh? What if there is no-one inside? Tap-wait-infinitum. Doors with small windows in them – very helpful. Going to the doctor nowadays is bliss, I walk in, tap onto a screen and wait for the announcement on the VDO. No more trying to communicate with a receptionist who may or may not be able to understand me. My right to converse is always caught in a fracas with the *need for ambience*.
>
> (Paul Redfern, *So What is Normal?* website comment, undated)

Spatial and aesthetic archetypes, then, may resonate in poems and dreams, but they have both differential meanings and enabling or disabling effects when translated into actual physical space. This is not to banally say that Zumthor fails because he does not always take accessibility into account. It is rather to suggest that there are inherent (but also creative) tensions in how built space is conceptualized, materialized and experienced, which need to be opened up to much more explicit engagement with dis/ability and difference. Gallery TOM, a museum for the blind and partially sighted in Tokyo, for example, has beautiful, large bronze door handles that incorporate Braille on their surfaces (Plate 16). The experience of using these handles is powerfully sensual, from the temperature to the smoothness to the feeling of the raised dimples. These handles, then, do not so much refer to memory as to the moment of entry to a specific building; embedding both feeling and information. Unlike, say, Zumthor's St Benedict Chapel, the entrance 'speaks' to a real and recognized audience, not to an archetype (Figure 5.2). Neither approach is more 'correct' than the other: the point at issue is how we open up alternatives to view, and to other kinds of intersections and relationships (Text Box 5.1).

Figure 5.2 Exterior view of entrance, St Benedict Chapel Sumvitg, Switzerland by Peter Zumthor (1988). Photography: unnamed author. Downloaded from http://commons.wikimedia.org/wiki/File:S._Benedetg.jpg via Wikipedia Commons (GNU Free Documentation Licence).

Text Box 5.1 Thea McMillan – Experiencing Zumthor (email exchange with the author, 11 September 2013)

The way that Zumthor's spaces are perceived: in Vals Therme, each space has been considered sensorially; the searing heat of the 40° bath reflected by burning red terracotta walls, which change from highly glazed to porous rough at the line where the water laps, contrasted by the cool turquoise water of the central pool and the sharp air rolling down from the surrounding mountains to lie on top of the outdoor pool. Guided by the continuity of the touch of the changing stone in each changing space; offering different sensory experiences, using contrast and heightened touch, hearing, and smell.

Perception: coming into the space from above, the sound is first, then the weight of the leather curtain pushed aside, followed by smell. For anyone disabled who has learnt to use their senses differently to complete pictures, this place offers many different clues. The spatial configuration of open plan and smaller contained spaces and the connections between them, gives a complex aural feedback for the visually impaired to construct the space in their minds.

Movement through the spaces, whilst not supportive of all wheelchair users, with its slow long flat steps, provides added layers of sensory experience for those who can climb them. As this almost offers the inclusive experience of moving through changing space, it seems a missed opportunity not to have a ramp.

This is about unravelling the underlying frameworks of both architectural discourse and design practice. And it is about (re-)centring design as a means to enhance people's lives, not just through the quality of their relationship to a particular building, but also in supporting what they *do* there. Sara Ahmed writes, in aiming at a 'queer' phenomenology:

> Phenomenology can offer a resource . . . insofar as it emphasizes the importance of lived experience, the intentionality of consciousness, the significance of nearness or what is ready-to-hand, and the role of repeated and habitual actions in shaping bodies and worlds.
>
> (Ahmed 2006: 2)

However, where its focus is only on the lived experience, and not also on the different *narrators* of that experience, then, she says, what is just as interesting is what gets relegated to the background. She re-explores Husserl's (1969) famous analysis of the experience of his work table (Ahmed 2006: 25–63), to show how there are people 'outside' of his detailed and poetic description who are *made invisible* by the concentration on the experience of the table itself, but are nevertheless an essential part of enabling the philosopher to undertake his work – his wife and children, the cleaner, the maker of the table, etc. To Ahmed, this suggests the additional concept of 'orientation':

> [O]rientations involve different ways of registering the proximity of objects and others. Orientations shape not only how we inhabit space, but how we apprehend this world of shared inhabitance, as well as 'who' or 'what' we direct our energy and attention toward.
>
> (Ahmed 2006: 3)

To properly analyse Zumthor's work it would be essential to unravel architects' assumed orientations of inhabitation in the design of the space, and to explore how this is interwoven with actual orientations, to see who is left out and where and whether it 'extends' some bodies rather than others (this is an issue

I will return to in the final chapter). How, for example, can we have a sophisticated debate about steps, often used by Zumthor, frequently to articulate moments of entrance, not just as the merely functional 'problem' of wheelchair users, but which also engages with their 'normal' location within architectural form-making:

> As [Bloomer and Moore] (1977) have noted, for instance, in modem architecture the multiple changes of level 'have often been used to delineate and enliven space' yet in ways which elevate the aesthetic above the pragmatics of use (p. 4). Thus, the interplay between levels, connected by steps, is integral to a design which seeks to display divisible, yet interconnected, functional, spaces.
>
> (Imrie 1998: 21)

Whilst Zumthor aims to supplant this kind of more formalist and visual manipulation, with the design of steps that are instead deeply imbued with feeling (of going up as to the attic or down as to the cellar, for example), neither approach makes explicit or challenges the assumed free-flowing characteristics of the user. Thus, stepped changes in level are sometimes used as an architectural device to deliberately interrupt *normal* bodies, so as to remind them where they are (of the qualities of architectural spaces themselves whether visually or emotionally); and – at the same time and without acknowledgement – confirm that certain bodies can *fail* to be extended. What does it mean for this design method if the creation of an effect of dappled sunlight, made by the honeycombed perforations in the facade at Kolumba, also creatively intersected with how such patterned light and shadow affects not only its sensual contemplation but also people's multiple and differential engagements with the exhibits on view, with navigating the space, or with conversing with each other? Why do these parallel interactions imply a stunting or depletion of the emotional experience (because they are 'merely' practical, pragmatic and ordinary), rather than the possibility of generating alternative but equally resonant details and atmosphere? What if architecture focused instead on how those who are 'disoriented' by the 'normal' orientations of architectural theory and practice are attended to with the same degree of passionate obsession that Zumthor shows in his works?

Whose truth and beauty?

> **Disability aesthetics refuses to recognize the representation of the healthy body – and its definition of harmony, integrity, and beauty – as the sole determination of the aesthetic.**
>
> (Siebers 2010a: 64)

Bachelard's poetic spaces and objects, whether attics, cellar, corners, wardrobes or boxes, are populated with feelings like solitude, cosiness, day-dreaming, secrets and fears. Crucially they are what he calls images of being, not metaphors for being; that is, they are immediate and intuitive with no need for a deliberate act of translation or association between a thing and its perceiver. Zumthor also aims to make direct, emotionally powerful relationships through space and matter, unmediated by more formalized thinking, interpretation or reflection on what is being experienced. But just as this attitude makes invisible the diversity of narrators (and their differential access to the power of making a particular, *implemented*, narrative) so it also hides processes of translation between design intention and resulting form. Instead, architectural form appears to grow straightforwardly and transparently:

> 'I think the chance of finding beauty is higher if you don't work on it directly,' Zumthor has said in describing his philosophy. 'Beauty in architecture is driven by practicality. This is what you learn from studying the old townscapes of the Swiss farmers. If you do what you should, then at the end there is something, which you can't explain maybe, but if you are lucky, it has to do with life.'
>
> (Kimmelman 2011)

Like many modernist architects, then, Zumthor insists that he has no 'style'. The very method he uses allows him to operate 'above and beyond all superficiality and arbitariness':

> not to stir up the emotions with buildings, I think to myself, but to allow emotions to emerge, to be. And to remain close to the thing itself, close to the essence of the thing I have to shape, confident that if the building is conceived accurately enough for its place and its functions, it will develop its own strength, with no need for artistic additions.
>
> (Zumthor 2010: 27)

And because the design process is truthful to itself, the end result will be beautiful. This is a deliberately non-theoretical stance, set in opposition to architects such as Koolhaas and his Swiss colleagues Herzog and de Meuron, who, he says, derive 'their theory of architecture as a form of thought'. And he goes on: 'personally I believe in the self-sufficient, corporeal wholeness of the architectural object as the essential, if difficult aim of my work, if not a natural given fact' (Zumthor 2010: 29–30). This makes Zumthor something of an architect's architect. His design choices become 'elemental'. Of course, he *does* have a recognizable – and fashionable – style to his works, a contemporary development of an alternative modernist tradition, both purist and a kind of expanded minimalism that is nonetheless 'explained away' through its persuasive and seductive justificatory narrative. Zumthor can also easily be made to conform to the stereotype of guru and aesthete, to be set against the cold commercialism of current 'Starchitects'. And by only undertaking a limited range of work, each a building type centred on contemplation (churches and chapels, baths, museums), the underlying limitations of such a phenomenological approach are not exposed, and the buildings appear to be the kind of work that most architects can only dream of creating.

But we also need to disconnect the particularities of the architectural quality of Zumthor's buildings from the phenomenological method that underpins them so as to open up a more critical engagement with what constitutes beauty in architecture. This is both because this kind of understated minimalism based on natural materials, crafted together and using the interplay of light and sound, is a *translation* by the architect that deserves to be critiqued, and also because it has particular *effects* – both good and bad – when intersected with dis/ability. This is not just about the avoidance of particular elements (the use of contrasting colour, for example), an issue to which I will return, but also about the assumed link between beauty and a specific version of architectural elegance. Tobin Siebers, exploring what a disability aesthetics might be, argues that such an assumption is locked into modernist beliefs linking health, cleanliness and nature with beauty:

> Beauty, order, and cleanliness in the built environment occupy a special position among the requirements of society because they apply to artificial bodies, such as buildings and landscapes, our preoccupation with our own body, including its health, integrity, and hygiene. Only an analysis of this powerful symbolic connection will explain why prejudices against the disabled body persist in the built environment, and only then will disability activists be able to shift emphasis from the individual human body to the imaginary bodies undergirding architectural theory, employment law, and conceptions of citizenship.
>
> (Siebers 2003)

If Zumthor's imaginary bodies are predicated more on their happy and healthy emotional states than their physical abilities, I would suggest that these earlier, modernist bodies still reverberate through designs. For Siebers, in fine art practice unlike architecture, disability has been central to the development of aesthetic representation; even whilst it has been neglected in theories, histories and criticism of the subject.

> Significantly, it could be argued that beauty always maintains an underlying sense of disability and that increasing this sense over time may actually renew works of art that risk to fall out of fashion because of changing standards of taste. It is often the presence of disability that allows the beauty of an art work to endure over time. Would the Venus de Milo still be considered one of the great examples of both aesthetic and human beauty if she still had both her arms? Perhaps it is an exaggeration to consider the Venus disabled, but René Magritte did not think so. He painted his version

> of the Venus, *Les Menottes de cuivre*, in flesh tones and colorful drapery but splashed blood-red pigment on her famous arm-stumps, giving the impression of a recent and painful amputation. The Venus is one of many works of art called beautiful by the tradition of aesthetic response that eschew the uniformity of perfect bodies and embrace the variety of disability.
>
> (Siebers 2010a: 65–6)

For Siebers, the idea of disability aesthetics opens up a very different corporeality to Zumthor's, one that is much more visceral, vulnerable, exposing, imperfect and messy (Figure 5.3), an imagery that will be returned to in the next chapter. Here, though, I am not just arguing for the substitution of one attitude to, or aesthetic for, the body over another. Rather, I want to show some of the underlying framings of contemporary architecture's knowledge base – and to remind us that its justificatory narratives are as much about fashionability and the seductive power of words, images and places as they are about 'truth'. Starting from dis/ability is one of the key means for critiquing the validity and relevance of architectural discourses, both conceptually as with Siebers, and in terms of the enabling and disabling effects of different architectural theories, methods and design languages.

Figure 5.3 Marc Quinn, 'breath', an 11-metre tall inflatable sculpture depicting a naked and pregnant Alison Lapper at the 2013 Venice Art Biennale. Photography: Jos Boys.

6 Bodies, buildings, devices and augmentation

In her seminal work 'A Cyborg Manifesto' Donna Haraway (1991, 1997) famously invoked the figure of the cyborg (see Glossary) as a means of re-thinking how bodies can be conceptualized. Intended as a tactic for going beyond the stereotypical and commonsense binaries of man/machine, human/non-human, woman/man and physical/digital technologies, the concept of the cyborg helped explore how our increasing ability to mix flesh and technology could also affect theories of, and actions in, the world. Whilst for Haraway this work was about challenging assumptions around the assumed separateness and difference of bodies from each other and from technologies, others have taken it up – through both theory and creative practice – to explore the impact of bodily enhancements; most particularly their powerful resonance and potential 'monstrosity' in making superhumans, or in encasing and taking over from vulnerable and fleshy bodies:

> The promise offered by human enhancement technology is at once exciting and unsettling, bringing into sharp focus both our hopes and fears about the future, while challenging our sense of identity as humans.
>
> (Sargent 2012: 4)

At the same time, many contemporary architects and designers are exploring emerging ideas, practices and potentials around robotics, body augmentation, bio-technologies, nano-technologies, and parametric and morphogenic (generative) design methods in order to develop new kinds of hybrid relationships between nature, bodies, machines and architectural form (Spiller 1998, Hensel *et al.* 2004, Leach *et al.* 2004). This has led to intense contemporary interest in architecture as an augmentation device, as a kind of prosthetic for humans; in the human body and nature more widely as an analogy for re-thinking the structure and skin of buildings; and in post-humanist[1] design approaches, that is, conceiving architecture

1 Post-humanism is a developing critical theory that has grown out of challenges to renaissance and modernist humanist thought, with its strict divides between minds and bodies, subjects and objects and humans and other species. Instead the post-human approach starts from trying to better understand the fluidity and ambiguity of inter-relationships, for example, between people, spaces, objects, animals and technologies. See Hayles (1999) and Wolfe (2009).

as not merely an amalgam of corporeal and technological components, but as a living, complex, integrative and responsive process. Where, then, do dis/ability in general, and disabled people in particular, 'fit' in these theoretical and creative dialogues? There are, after all, already many kinds of body augmentation devices, from hearing aids to canes to wheelchairs; but (as noted in Chapter 1) these tend to be perceived popularly as a limitation of, rather than an enhancement to, the human body – a sign of weakness and faultiness rather than superhuman power. This chapter will first critically examine some of the tensions of these contemporary framings of the body when intersected with dis/ability, and then go on to explore some recent architectural ideas around humans and contemporary technologies, so as to critically and creatively examine what the concept of augmentation might offer as an alternative way of thinking about dis/abled bodies.

A cyborg is a cybernetic organism, a hybrid of machine and organism, a creature of social reality as well as a creature of fiction. . . . This experience is a fiction and fact of the most crucial, political kind.

(Haraway 1991: 149)

A prosthetic impulse?

Many writers from across disability studies have critiqued how the concept of the cyborg has come to influence contemporary theory, yet leaves both disability as an idea and the realities of disabled people's lives completely out of the picture:

> The disabled body is a nightmare for the fashionable discourse of theory because that discourse has been limited by the very predilection of the dominant, ableist culture. The body is seen as a site of 'jouissance' that defies reason, that takes dominant culture and its rigid, power-laden vision of the body to task . . . The nightmare of the (disabled) body is one that is deformed, maimed . . . Rather than face this ragged image, the critic turns to the fluids of sexuality, the gloss of lubrication . . . But almost never to the body of the differently abled.
>
> (Davis 1995 quoted in Creal 2006: 3)

Thus, Davis argues, images of human/machine hybrids become an opportunity for celebrating a particular version of Otherness as a seductive, self-conscious *excessiveness* – an imagined monstrousness – as an exciting and pleasurable frisson that adds to, and even takes over 'ordinary life'. Being Other is no longer a threat or a problem but a *freely chosen* position by theorists who can then claim their radical 'transgression' (and ignore both their own privilege and abledness) by deliberately appearing to place themselves 'on the margins', outside of everyday conventions and stereotypes. In this framing, we can all be others, nomads, partial observers of the world. But this is a peculiar kind of Otherness, which values specific qualities – unproblematically imbued with autonomy, mobility and agency – whilst in fact obscuring the realities of diverse kinds of embodiment, and the persistent marginalization of specific groups. As Erevelles says, in this approach the writing of different bodies centres on the '(re)signification of such bodies to (re)possess emancipatory, transgressive, hybrid subjectivities that continually transgress borders and open up unlimited possibilities' (Erevelles, 1997: 1). These, then, are imaginary bodies, romanticized, often eroticized versions of transgression, but still fully autonomous and unhindered by bodily impairments. They are definitely not actual bodies, with diverse lived experiences, located within everyday social and spatial practices that restrict some whilst extending others. In the process disability disappears *twice*. This is, first, because in much contemporary cultural theory it is merely being added onto other 'identities' as a cursory inclusion, rather than explored for both its similarities and differences with other forms of Otherness (across feminism, post-colonial and cultural studies, etc.); and second, because the claiming of Otherness as a radical position in parts of that theory assumes abledness as the basis from which bodies can be 'played' with, as they (excitingly) intersect with machines. I will return to this issue in the final chapter. Here, I want to focus on how such an approach not only turns bodies into abstract concepts or figures, distanced from everyday life, but also encourages us to imagine prosthetic technologies themselves as independent, mobile entities which can even take on 'a life of their own'. Here, it is the machine that becomes monstrous, evoking a superhuman power, beyond and even without the human body. In critiquing these tendencies, Sobchack writes:

> Let me begin with the fact that I have a prosthetic leg – and thus a certain investment in and curiosity about the ways in which the 'prosthetic' has been embraced and recreated by contemporary scholars trying to make sense (and theory) out of our increasingly technologised lives. When I put my leg on in the morning, knowing that I am the one who will give it literal (if exhaustible) support, I don't find it nearly as seductive a matter – or generalised an idea – as do some of my academic colleagues . . .
>
> (Sobchack 2006: 17–18)

For her, there is a problem in much contemporary theorizing of the cyborg, when artificial enhancements become abstracted, mythologized and weighted with a figurative potential disassociated from real bodies. This is not because such a view does not align with the 'authentic' experience of wearing a prosthetic in everyday life (that is, as a simple opposition between the practicalities of existence and the realm of ideas) but because such approaches fail to explore the complex intersections *between* such metaphorical, imaginary extensions and a materially lived device:

> Perhaps . . . the prosthetic metaphor is most scandalous because it far too quickly mobilizes attention to (and fascination with) artificial and

> 'post-human' body parts in the service of a discourse always located elsewhere – displacing the prosthetic rather than living it first on its own quite extraordinary premises.
>
> (Sobchack 2004)

For Sobchack, then, coming from a phenomenological perspective, and concerned to integrate discursive, language-based interpretations with corporeal experiences, the aim is to ground current engagements with the 'prosthetic' across the arts and humanities as more than, and different to, simply a 'sexy new metaphor' (Sobchack 2006: 19). This means exploring how to interrogate the flourishing writing, artistic and design practices concerned with human–technological interfaces, that is, 'the joining of materials, naturalisations, excorporations and semiotic transfer that also go far beyond the medical definition of "replacement of a missing part"' (Jain 1999: 32), without leaving behind the literal functions as well as metaphorical ones; and thus failing to examine how bodies can and do take up various technologies:

> To be fair to all of us who use metaphor (and who doesn't?), we must acknowledge that metaphor is, by its tropological nature, a *displacement*: a nominative term is displaced from its mundane (hence literal, non-figurative) context and placed elsewhere to illuminate some other context through its *refiguration*. . . . Thus, primarily based on the relation of *ideas* rather than *objects* and on structural and functional resemblances rather than physical similarities, metaphorical usage does not owe any necessary allegiance to the literal object – such as a prosthesis – that generated it. Nonetheless, it does owe necessary allegiance to a 'common opinion' about the object and context that needs to acknowledge the resemblance sufficiently to 'get' the analogy.
>
> (Sobchack 2006: 21, italics in original)

Unlike Haraway's cyborg, which imagines a 'figure' in order to disrupt traditional notions of bodies as both whole and unproblematic (yet somehow male, white, abled, etc.), the concept of 'prosthesis' often comes to be celebrated as a deliberate visualization of difference, another version of playing with Otherness, that simultaneously makes it something more 'important' than the actual experience, and makes that actual experience invisible. The conceptualized or artistically produced prosthetic thus tends to express itself as resonant *presence*. As Sobchack notes, she does not experience her prosthetic leg in this way:

> Rather, in most situations, the prosthetic as lived in use is usually *transparent*; that is, it is 'absent' as in the rest of our body when we're focused outward to the world and successfully engaged in the various projects of our daily life. Ideally incorporated not 'into' or 'on' but 'as' the subject, the prosthetic becomes an object only when a mechanical or social problem pushes it obtrusively into the foreground of the user's consciousness

> – much in the manner in which a blister on the heel takes on an objective presence that is something other even though the body's own bodily fluid and stretched skin constitute it.
>
> (Sobchack 2006: 22–3, italics in original)

Prosthetic devices are, in fact, just an integral part of our more general lived experiences. What, then, are the implications in thinking and doing architecture in a period when these relationships between dis/ability, bodies, devices and built space are becoming increasingly intertwined?

Re-connecting discursive and lived engagements

Sobchack is proposing an alternative that goes beyond the perpetuation of commonsense relationships between the mundane and the conceptual that assumes disabled people are only concerned with 'banal' practicalities on the one hand, and designers or artists with the aesthetics of form on the other. This alternative encompasses intersecting processes where bodily practicalities and discursive understandings come in and out of focus (are more intense or more distracted) and are more or less enabling or disabling, dependent on the relational context. As already outlined in Chapter 4, this is the experience of everyone; a bodily complication or material obstacle or unexpected or unknown situation brings the inter-relationships between body, space, artefacts and others into jolting consciousness as the work involved in everyday life surfaces into attention. As I have also already said, this is bodily *work*, that will require more taking notice and time to support, for disabled people and will also be enabled or disabled by the shape of our material landscapes. I have also suggested that this leads to a particular prowess in reading space, not because of some special 'authenticity' carried by the disabled person, but because of the *effects* of living with the disabling conditions of the everyday world. Sobchack describes, for example, how this everyday work, with its enabling or disabling impacts can happen as both a sudden or gradual awareness of her leg as something that produces noticeable sensations, and therefore has to be paid special attention. Like the rest of her body, the experience of her prosthetic 'is not only *dynamic* and *situated*, but also *ambiguous* and *graded*' (2006: 26–7, italics in original). Such an understanding offers the potential for exploring dis/ability, not as a simple binary opposition, but through its complex, nuanced and simultaneous intersections of material conditions, lived enactments and discursive experiences.

In the previous chapters in this section on Rem Koolhaas/OMA and Peter Zumthor, I have suggested that architects can tend to translate human activities and bodily characteristics *into* building form (that is as a means to generate particular types of formal, spatial and aesthetic manipulations) rather than designing *for* occupancies, through the kind of dynamic and multiple registers across our emotional, social, conceptual and practical experiences of inhabitation that Sobchack describes. Like her, I have suggested that much discourse produces the problem of orienting agency *to* artefacts and spaces and *away* from participants, just as the prosthetic can come to be substituted for the human who uses it. In looking next at how contemporary architecture is engaging with the many new and developing inter-relationships between bodies and machines, I will again propose that this kind of slippage occurs, that is, from actual bodies (however enhanced) to the metaphorical body of the building; and that whilst this work is richly informed by, and engaged with, new technologies for and of the body, the complex and dynamic registers of occupancies by diverse bodies disappear just as resolutely.

Architecture as prosthetic?

> What is liquid architecture? A liquid architecture is an architecture whose form is contingent on the interests of the beholder; it is an architecture that opens to welcome you and closes to defend you; it is an architecture without doors and hallways, where the next room is always where it needs to be and what it needs to be. It is an architecture that dances or pulsates, becomes tranquil or agitated.
>
> (Novak 1991)

There has long been an interest in architectural theory and practice in destabilizing the (unfortunate) solidity and gravity-restricted qualities of building. With the increasing impact of digital design technologies and of developments in nano- and bio-technologies, this potential for creating fluid, non-static forms seems to finally have a realizable potential. Architects such as Marcos Novak (1991), Asymptote (Rashid and Couture 1995) and Greg Lynn (2011) are exploring this new, mainly computer-generated form-making.[2] This is leading some architects to re-imagine the very nature of the subject. Here, for example, is Marcos Cruz, Director of the Bartlett School of Architecture in London, whose research, teaching and practice:

> is dedicated to a future vision of the body in architecture. It questions our 'human flesh' and its altered relationship with a new contemporary 'architectural flesh'. Different body conceptions are analyzed in historic and aesthetic terms, helping to recognize the emergence of a present condition known as Cyborgian Body – a widely accepted new existential condition that still needs to be redefined. The underlying argument of this investigation

2 There is no precise definition of computer-generated parametric design (also called morphogenesis, and neo-plasmatic design) and there are other related terms and synonyms. The key issue is that its uses algorithms to creatively repeat and adapt operations so as to be generative of forms, rather than merely reproducing them. Whilst Greg Lynn has explicitly examined generative 'Blob' and 'Fold' architecture, Ben van Berkel and Caroline Bos of UN Studio have been interested in using computational tools to design large urban infrastructures by inputting a range of parametric criteria set to time and motion with animation software. There are increasing numbers of built examples, including Foreign Office Architects' (FOA) Yokohama International Port Terminal of 2002 (Plate 15).

> is that today's architecture has failed the body with its long heritage of physical detachment, purity of form, and aesthetics of cleanliness. But a resurgence of interest in flesh, especially in art, has led to politics of abjection, changing completely traditional aesthetics, and is now giving light to an alternative discussion about the body in architecture.
>
> (Cruz 2014)

For Cruz, this is less a matter of representing that abjection (or its inter-relationships with ordinary social and spatial practices) in built form, and more about re-conceptualizing the building as a type of body:

> Through the comparative analysis of a variety of 20th century and also contemporary projects, along with the design of new building typologies, 'flesh' is proposed as a concept that extends the meaning of skin, one of architecture's most fundamental metaphors. Hence, in a time when a pervasive discourse about the impact of digital technologies risks turning the architectural skin ever more disembodied, the aim is to put forward a 'thick embodied flesh' by creating architectural interfaces that are truly inhabitable.
>
> (Cruz 2014)

However, whilst in this process Cruz is concerned that 'a variety of social, cultural and political factors are taken into account', such as the influence of local traditions and the development of socio-economic conditions, he is most interested in what shapes the architectural form itself, which is:

> above all, the decisive role of digital design in the spatial/formal re-qualification of contemporary cities . . . complemented by a coherent employment of innovative technologies in the field of renewable energies and materials. In this context, a range of digital techniques, such as intense 3D modeling in addition to CNC, CAD/CAM and rapid prototyping are implemented. This research focuses on new experimental design solutions that are not only based on the usual planimetric/diagrammatic and predictive thinking, but rather on a high level of formal, material and spatial three-dimensional complexity. The city and its endless interfaces are materialized from inside-out as a dynamic convolution of multiple three-dimensional cartographies, constructs and operations; as an urban manifold, or, in other words, understood as an ever-mutating Urban Flesh.
>
> (Cruz 2014)

> **Rarely is a broader perspective on the creation of technology taken, acknowledging how it is shaped by the role of professional groupings and specialized knowledges, or the politics of technological systems.**
>
> (Goggin and Newell 2003: 9, quoted in Anderberg 2006b: 48)

Designed space, then, comes out of the interplay between the conceptualization of the building as 'thickly fleshed' and the potentials offered by the new technologies for architectural design; that is, what kinds of visualizations, three-dimensional form-making and generative processes these enable, beyond the more traditional techniques of sketching, orthographic drawing and hand-crafted model-making. This, part of a much wider interest in parametric design is often called Blob architecture. Part of this exploration of making building flesh has been through exploring 'wall-conditions that prompt new forms of architectural embodiment' (Cruz and Colletti 2005: 6). This envisions walls as inhabitable interfaces – 'as a new means of human interaction: interfaces with which we can engage and eventually merge'. In his project 'Cyborgian Interfaces' (2008), Cruz proposes a domestic environment with wall-embedded devices, which include Communication Suits (wall-incorporated synthetic neoplasms that integrate new haptic technologies and promote, in a physical and virtual manner, a tactile engagement of the body in architecture), Relaxing Cocoons with embedded synthetic neoplasms, Storage Capillaries and Gestural Tentacles (Figure 6.1). As Cruz explains:

> In the last 20 years, a lot has been said about our existential condition of being cyborgs, but very little has been designed that suggests how

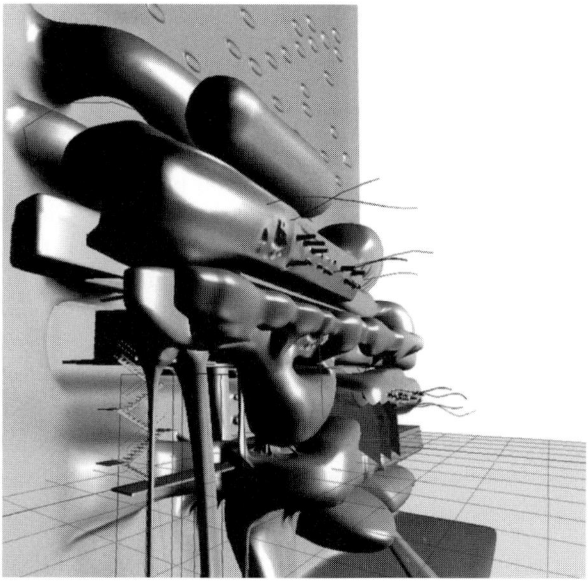

Figure 6.1 Marcos Cruz, *Hyperdermis/Cyborgian Interfaces*, 2004–7. Overall view with communication suits, in-wall sitting, relaxing cocoons, storage capillaries and gestural tentacles.

> this cyborgianism is affecting our built environment. William Mitchell's famous argument that our human inhabitation is gaining a different meaning – 'one that has less to do with parking your bones in architecturally defined space and more with connecting your nervous system to nearby electronic organs. Your room and your home will become part of you, and you will become part of them' – is still left unanswered in terms of design. In this sense, Cyborgian Interfaces are a response to Mitchell's challenge, and feature a home for cyborgs that goes beyond the traditional notions of dwelling. It is a place of hyperconnectivity in which inhabitants step into their surrounding walls in order to spend most of the time in (virtual) communication with others . . . In these wall interfaces, essential domestic functions such as sitting, sleeping or communicating are transferred from the traditional room space into the walls.
>
> (Cruz 2008: 56)

This is more than just the image of, or metaphor for, a responsive environment. Rather the house details a series of different kinds of *practical* enactments with the wall. Each of the service devices is articulated as a series of variable layers 'defined respectively as an outside protective layer, an in-between structural layer, and an inside sensitive layer' and each relating to different programmatic requirements. So, for example, with the Communication Suit, the inside layer increases and decreases levels of viscosity along the human body. In cases such as this, the stiffening that occurs makes the substance behave less like a liquid or gel and more like a sticky solid. As Cruz goes on to explain:

> The service devices of Cyborgian Interfaces are equipped with different types of haptic technologies embedded in the walls: basic force feedback devices that work in two dimensions between user and screen, and exoskeletal devices that exert tactile pressure on the skin, allowing for a three-dimensional engagement of body in virtual space. For Storage Capillaries and In-Wall Seats, computer-manufactured textiles such as micro-fibres are employed; that is, extremely fine and soft woven fabrics with crease-resistance and sheer appearance. Digital definition makes it possible to weave the micro-fibres densely enough to make them windproof, water resistant and breathable all at the same time. They are able to maintain a constant temperature in oscillations of hot and cold conditions. For the design of Relaxing Cocoons and Communication Suits, a different technology is required. As long-term inhabitable environments, these surfaces function as skin-sensitive and micro-textured surfaces, as well as enabling high degrees of hygienic care. Artificial skin is inserted in their interiors, a procedure that requires high levels of control and maintenance, and is monitored and kept alive via numerous small bioreactors that supply the skin with nutrients and regulate its environmental conditions. For Gestural

> Tentacles, 'shape memory polymers' are reinforced by an embedded prosthetic armature that is movable by artificial muscle fibres, enabling these extremities to move freely in space.
>
> (Cruz 2008: 56–7)

The detailed application of specifically articulated technologies offers a sophisticated development of the prosthetic into fully developed bodily augmentations, which are to be fully customized to, and by, diverse bodies. But the current framing of such a sustaining architecture – whilst it considers actual body–technology relationships in valuable detail and depth – remains abstracted from dis/ability and occupancies more generally, both in its hopes and in its avoidances. First, it relies on the implicit and conventional architectural trope of an inherent flexibility, wishfully believing that these devices will offer their suitability for *everyone*, that dreams of a world untouched by the effects of normative everyday social and spatial practices, or the realities of economic and socially inequitable contexts. Second, it does not problematize who users are, what technologies 'mean' or the situated and difficult entanglements between bodies, technologies and spaces. Third, it often employs a particular language of 'excessive' metaphorical bodies, deeply influenced by not only the celebration of the cyborg with which this chapter began, but also with architecture's own internal discourses around new kinds of digitally inflected buildings, already outlined. Again, we have another version of the commonsense 'anyone' to 'not anyone' slippage that makes dis/ability vanish down the gaps (as discussed in Chapter 2). Cyborgian architecture is thus a powerfully seductive design approach – currently having a huge impact across architecture – but one that seems to be failing to include any kind of critical engagement of the type that Haraway has pioneered. It does not seem to use ideas of form-making as a means to question what might constitute either existing norms or their enhanced variations. It does not, following Sobchack, often work with and across the different *registers* through which bodies, devices and spaces simultaneously interact conceptually, emotionally and practically. In the process, the problematic shape of architectural design knowledge around occupancies in general and dis/ability in particular continues to be avoided. Compare this to Anderberg who, when exploring assistive technologies for a range of disabled people, critically and creatively differentiated between relationships with technology that imitate normal bodies and social practices, those that mimic conventional experience but through alternative mechanisms and those that can generate the feelings of an experience, when its actuality is not possible to achieve (Text Box 6.1). This is not to say that architects should work more like rehabilitation engineers, only that explicitly thinking about the complex relationships between bodies, prosthetics and buildings can, in fact, generate some other kinds of creative ideas and spaces. Or take the work of Revital Cohen, who explores the intersections between humans, machines and animals in a rich and deeply thought provoking way (Figure 6.2, Plate 7).

Figure 6.2 Revital Cohen (2008), 'Respiratory Dog' drawings as part of *Life Support* project. www.cohenvanbalen.com/work/life-support

Text Box 6.1 'Parrot, Chameleon and Poodle Methods', excerpt from Anderberg (2006b), *FACE Disabled People, Technology and the Internet*, Doctoral Thesis for CERTEC Division of Rehabilitation Engineering Research, Department of Design Sciences, University of Lund, pp. 24–5. Download available from: www.arkiv.certec.lth.se/doc/face/face_final_version_5.pdf.

> It may be appropriate to question, at the very outset, whether the solution should imitate fully the solution for a non-disabled person (the parrot method), have the same purpose but a different form (the chameleon method), or be completely different and only retain its fundamental characteristics, its very core (the poodle method).
>
> (Jönsson and Anderberg 1999)

The parrot method

If it is possible to imitate, like a parrot, the way a non-disabled person would handle a certain situation, this may be the best solution (at least from a social perspective). This means that the system, consisting of the person with a disability and her technology, is capable of doing exactly what she would otherwise have been able to do without her technology: She chooses exactly the same approach to problems that other people can handle without the aid of technology. Examples are: glasses, prostheses, corrective medication . . .

The chameleon method

The aim might be to perform the same task as the non-disabled person is able to do, even if it is not meaningful to imitate the way in which it is carried out. Instead, like a chameleon, one tries to change the 'color' of the solution by changing technologies to achieve the same result.

Examples of chameleon solutions for people with visual impairments would be using Braille, speech synthesis or audio books instead of ordinary text (the purpose is the same as it is for sighted people: being able to take in something that has been documented). Using wheelchairs and guide dogs are other examples (the purpose is the same as for sighted people: being able to move about independently).

The poodle method

Like Goethe's metaphor in *Faust*, this is about getting to the heart of the matter; about finding the innermost part of the dream, the wish, or the need. Even with technology, it may not always be possible to do what you want to do. And even though it may be possible, it might not be worth it to make the original dream come true at any cost. Perhaps the specific activity is not the most important – another activity that yields the same feeling might serve the same purpose.

An example: a young man used to enjoy sailing very much, but after a neuromuscular disease his muscles were too weak for sailing. He liked the challenge of the sea, feeling his body working and strong, feeling his powers. So to him an automatically operated sailboat controlled simply by pushing two or three buttons was meaningless. That was not what he experienced in sailing; it had nothing to do with his need and wishes. What was the driving force for the sailing activity? Was it the physical or the intellectual challenge? Is it possible to find an activity that can be physically experienced just as much or even more so? An activity that will make the body buzz with exhaustion and joy? Perhaps there is an altogether different activity that would provide the same intellectual challenge.

The dreams of discourse and the multiple registers of experience

The fact that it can seem unfair to critically intersect the ideas and design experiments of such innovative architects with 'reality' is itself an aspect of architectural discourses' own justificatory and self-perpetuating framings. If, though, we do investigate the multiple registers through which such propositions might be viewed – starting from dis/ability – we need to also explore how technologies are currently intersected with disabled people. As already suggested, new technologies have in many cases enormously improved the lives of disabled people. At the same time, though, it is important to investigate why and how such technologies are often badly designed and poorly implemented, reinforcing disability as marginalized and unimportant. Customization to individuals is all too often a make-do-and-mend resorting to tape and hand-made inserts. In addition, many 'assistive' technologies continue to be predominantly articulated through a functionalist interpretation of dis/ability, lacking any idea of the seductive or excessive. Simultaneously, we should be learning from disability studies (and, as I will suggest later, from science and technology studies) which are opening up this area to critical view; by theorizing how the inter-relationships between bodies, devices and spaces might be better articulated; by exploring the multiple registers through which diverse disabled people engage with different augmenting devices, and by challenging the commonsense assumptions that such technologies should be about making disability more 'normal'.

To challenge these everyday assumptions, Anderberg starts from the inseparability of people and their augmenting devices. Rather than imagining particular (seductive) devices taking on a life of their own, or being found awkward by the abled (wheelchairs, white canes), or just 'ordinary' and 'nothing much' (cars, computers, spectacles), his focus is on how *relations* between people, things and spaces come together in different ways:

> Where does the person end and the technology begin? It is difficult, often meaningless to try to figure out where the person ends and the technology starts. You touch the ground and feel the pavement with your wheelchair and when you turn around, your wheelchair turns with you. You are part of a functional system consisting of your body, your wheelchair and the ground beneath you. The boundaries you have for experiencing the world go beyond the physical limitations of your skin and are determined by the system for experiencing the world in which you exist.
>
> (Anderberg 2006b: 40)

There are now a considerable number of studies that have understood dis/ability in this way (Moser and Law 2003, Winance 2006, Roets and Braidotti 2012), which both explore the complex inter-relationships between humans, machines and environment and bring to light some of the dynamic patterns of differential access and inequality, both enabling and disabling:

> Technology can be seen as a manifestation of economic, political, social and cultural concepts as well as individual wishes and ideas, and the question of power is embedded. The possibility of empowerment or risk of disempowerment is strongly dependent on the power relations in the system in which the technology is introduced. The perspectives of the users or the task of changing power structures 'is not at the heart of technical research unless social science perspectives are integrated' (Östlund, 2005). Optimization from technological factors alone is seldom fruitful when it comes to assistive technology. Technology that is used to empower people can also be used for the construction of the image of the 'disabled person'.
>
> (Anderberg 2006b: 48)

The increasing number of studies that explore these issues has a potential value for the development of 'liquid' architectures, if only by exposing the gaps in an architectural design method that tends to start from individual – both figurative and real – bodies, and then slips sideways into a fluid and elegant form-making, increasing abstracted from real bodies and everyday social and spatial practices, whether current or imagined for the future (Figure 6.3).

Figure 6.3 Examples of student work from Unit 20, *Porosity: A Material Shift Towards an Architecture of Permeability* (MArch Architecture), Bartlett School of Architecture, University College London, End-of-Year Exhibition 2013. Unit tutors: Marcos Cruz, Marjan Colletti and Richard Beckett.

An excessive aesthetic?

In 'CyberBaroque and other DigiTales' (2008) Cruz's architectural partner, Marjan Colletti, explores what kinds of imagery are appropriate for these transformative inter-relationships between bodies and technologies and suggests that:

> after the initial period of definition and discovery of disembodied virtual realities, data-scapes and cyber-realities, the endeavour now is to establish a debate in which experimentation, technology and progress do not exclude the actuality of emotions, traditions and identity.
>
> (Colletti 2008)

For him, this is best expressed through a contemporary version of the baroque:

> The CyberBaroque is at hand because once again it convolutes (i.e. synthesises, overlaps and blurs) the dichotomy of rational and empirical thinking, as well as the morphing of classical-digital architectural semantics into playful theatrical tectonics and typologies. In fact, the most contemporary manifestation of digital architecture achieves the synthesis of poetic expression and intuitive knowledge, of culture and tradition as well as industry and progress. In its virtuosity, the digital CyberBaroque avant-garde reconciles the actual with the virtual/digital, the technological with the poetic/intuitive, the mathematical with the artistic/blissful, the gestural with the figural/figurative, the intermediary with the medium/mediated, and the symbolic with the social/reflexive.
>
> (Colletti 2008)

As with the cultural theorists, already critiqued above, here technology is expressed conceptually and in representation as excessive, alien – both seductively pleasurable and potentially monstrous (Figure 6.4). As Colletti says, 'both in text and image, the vocabulary of architectural design is broadened beyond common standards, flirting with the extravagance and richness of the CyberBaroque: lavish, sexy, sophisticated and most of all, avant-garde.' These forms are generated through what he calls DigiTales: 'digital narratives about the strange, other and alien as well as the familiar, intimate and contextualised – that discern (actually reveal) a whole series of events and haecceities [the properties that uniquely identify a thing from other things] within digitality beyond the usual aspects of techniques, technologies and technics' (see Colletti 1999). These are experiments with dynamic pattern making, either in physical form or digital space, a kind of performance or staging, through generative form-making, which explicitly aims to mimic the baroque.

As Colletti concludes: 'does not the convoluted nature of the subject matter go beyond the functions of complexity and intricacy? Does it not invoke something ranking above beauty, elegance and smartness? Does it not evoke the sublime, the blissful and the mysterious. . .?'

Figure 6.4 Emily Yan, *Inhabitable Thresholds, Undulating Apartments, Hong Kong*. From Unit 20 (MArch Architecture), Bartlett School of Architecture, University College London, End-of-Year Exhibition 2013. Unit tutors: Marcos Cruz, Marjan Colletti and Richard Beckett.

Whilst such vocabularies of form are powerful, and in many ways overlap, for example, with the kinds of arguments Sieber makes for a much more visceral disability aesthetic, and can also be used to deliberately transgress the often banal and clinical imagery linked to disability (Text Box 6.2), their very seductiveness can act to blur the complexities with which such forms are dealing. To return to Sobchack:

> The theoretical use of the prosthetic metaphor tends to transfer agency . . . from human actors to human artifacts. Paradoxically this transfer of agency indicates a certain technofetishism on the part of the theorist . . . As an effect of the prosthetic's amputation and displacement from its mundane context, the animate and volitional human beings who use prosthetic technologies disappear into the background – passive if not now completely invisible – and the prosthetic is seen to have a will and life of its own.
>
> (Sobchack 2006: 23)

Here, as I have said before, it is only the exotic (erotic) technologies that take on a theoretical power, for, as Sobchack also notes, nobody is interested in her crutches or canes. There is, in the architectural language preferred, just this kind of separation out of body and prosthetic, with its privileging of the latter, and its disavowal of real bodies, of dis/ability and of occupancies in all their 'complex and dynamic ambiguity' (Sobchack 2006: 27). As before, the aim of this chapter is not to criticize these architects for not considering disability. Rather it is to open up architectural ways of thinking to other kinds of investigation. The interesting question becomes: what happens to both a form-making method and its dominant aesthetic when intersected creatively and constructively with dis/ability? For the new kinds of computer-generated and bio-cultural architecture, I would argue that this concerns, first, how to incorporate corporeal diversity and difference into initial analyses of the inter-relationships between bodies, nature and technologies; and second, how to develop designing techniques which can interrogate the multiple registers of bodily engagements with material space and devices.

Text Box 6.2 Robert Adams on the Asclepius Machine: www.designboom.com/project/the-asclepius-machine-genetic-diversity-and-extreme-urban-euphoria-resubmit-with-video

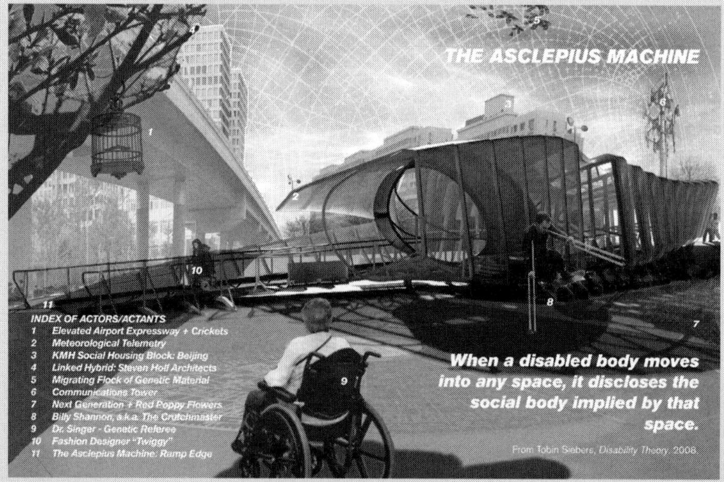

The Asclepius Machine, Beijing – sited between Steven Holl's Linked Hybrid and the social housing block, Qing Shui Yuan (2011)

The Asclepius Machine is an exuberantly designed wheelchair accessible ramp and computationally pervasive architecture. The Asclepius Machine is to the 21st century what the arcade was to the 19th century

– an animated passage – a civic infrastructure and space capable of producing extreme urban euphoria. In contrast to the passive labor of 20th century infrastructure designed with a singular understanding of fitness and beauty through frictionless auto-mobile bodies avoiding the more extreme capacities of the human experience, the Asclepius Machine is a complex and interactive environment thriving among human technological and mechanical diversity. Located between the scale of furniture and a pedestrian bridge, the Asclepius Machine animates and extends the operative range of our bodies. If assistive devices such as motorized wheelchairs or white canes for the seeing impaired are mechanical extensions of a sensing body, the Asclepius Machine is a biomechanical hybrid between mechanized bodies and extreme urban environments. Unlike most wheelchair ramps and other accessible forms of infrastructure that perform simply in service to those with so-called special needs, the Asclepius Machine is a performance vehicle that exceeds necessity, and motivates a more robust understanding of how our collective genetic diversity contributes to the vitality of everyday life.

The fear of pain, loss of gender identity, and the unease of the grotesque body have incapacitated the agency of architecture to produce spatial models that broaden the expectations of the social body further isolating the disabled body. The primary drive of this work is to co-produce urban machines that rethink and network civic infrastructure, genetic diversity and disability constraints to improve the quality of our lives in the ephemera of architecture as an ancient form of locative media. The design seeks to extend the range of architecture's capacity to enroll a more intricate understanding of the public sphere to the extreme limits of perception regardless of bodily ability. The objective of this work is to reconfigure cultural codes through producing devices, formal structures and pervasive environments that advocate for a more actionable and responsive architecture that does not simply ameliorate or re-engineer the perceived challenges of disability, but that produces a wider range of civic paradigm empowering design for all.

Robert Adams
Associate Professor – Architecture
Taubman College: University of Michigan

See also: Adams, R., 'Making a Scene: A Vivid Genealogy of The Asclepius Machine', in *Scapegoat Journal: Architecture, Landscape, Political Economy: 0.4 Currency*, CreateSpace 054/02/2013. Available for download from: www.scapegoatjournal.org/docs/04/04_Adams_MakingAScene.pdf (accessed 6 February 2014).

And 'Asclepius Machine' video: www.youtube.com/watch?v=rajgw8O2OuA (accessed 6 February 2014).

Why the sidestepping?

Then there is also a question that has to be asked of architectural theory and practice more generally. Just why does this kind of sidestepping go on, with its avoidances of engagement with the multiple experiences of others, and of the difficulties of conceptualizing such processes – actual social and spatial practices – within its theoretical discourses? If disabled people underline the untenability of conventional and modernist notions of the user, they also expose the unwillingness of much contemporary architectural theory and practice to risk its theories and approaches beyond the academy; to open up its assumptions and beliefs to wider debate and criticism; to listen to outsiders rather than just 'play' at being Others. These newer trends responding to changing relationships between bodies and machines have powerfully enabled a re-energized design process, with some resonant and thought-provoking propositions, but still fail to create spaces for articulating dis/ability as a concept worthy of integration into contemporary architectural discourse; or of formulating design methods that constructively and creatively engage with both the differential effects of everyday social and spatial practices and the multiple registers through which both disabled and abled people intersect with material space. In these dominant practices – however radical the architects consider themselves – disabled people continue to be non-existent or wrongly located, and framed in ways that they do not recognize. They can be over-visible within the limitations of the accessibility debate as 'abnormal' users defined only by their disability; or mainly invisible in mainstream architectural thought (and cultural theory more generally); or they can find themselves subsumed into some poorly fitting notion of 'hybrid', 'nomad' or 'cyborg', that obscures and displaces dis/ability just as it seems to be celebrating it.

In many ways it is not surprising that those in the avant-garde of architectural theory and practice (with its preferred location both 'outside' of mainstream commercial practice and as challengers to architectural discourses historically) slip away so often from the complex and messy realities of everyday practices and encounters into evocative abstractions about bodies and occupancy. For how does one encompass the full variety of personal preferences, individual needs and desires in the design process? What can one do in the multi-faceted and many-variabled procurement, development, design and delivery of buildings to make space useful, enjoyable and appropriate for everyone? Throughout this book I have noted that this is a complex, even impossible, position for architects, who can only do the best they can, and are never likely to satisfy everyone. But I have also been arguing that architectural theory, practice and education needs to embed a better understanding of occupancies into what it does; not as separate to, or more important than, spatial and compositional modelling, but as a creative and relevant mode of thinking and doing. I have also proposed that starting from dis/ability offers a way into this alternative mode of operating.

The next section, then, begins to explore some alternative techniques for thinking and doing dis/ability differently. This starts from a critical attentiveness to disabled peoples' narratives and strategies so as to take better notice of the kinds of work involved in our everyday survival in, and making sense of, the world. It offers some methods for interrogating the differential enabling and disabling effects of ordinary social and spatial practices. And it explicitly engages with dis/ability and occupancy across its multiple registers in theory and practice. This requires both constructively and creatively intersecting architectural discourse with disability studies and extending current architectural design methods, crucially explored as 'translation' techniques that open up the gaps between space and its everyday, diverse occupancies.

Plate 1 Leigh Bowery, video still from Katherine Araniello and Aaron Williamson, *The Disabled Avant-Garde Today!* Originally shown at Gasworks Exhibition, 7 September–22 October 2006. www.youtube.com/watch?v=fLAA5mUIQ2M

Plate 2 Noëmi Lakmaier, *We are for you because we are against them.* 9 June 2009 The LAB, Dublin. Curated by Liz Burns. Photography: Hugh McElveen. www.noemilakmaier.co.uk

Plate 3 Sue Austin, *Creating the Spectacle*, Unlimited commission as part of the 2012 Cultural Olympiad, co-curated with Trish Wheatley. Copyright: www.wearefreewheeling.org.uk. Photography: Norman Lomax.

Plate 4 Jon Adam and Mellisa Myston, Installation at InQbate, University of Sussex as part of Architecture-InsideOut (AIO) workshop, *A space where 2 people meet*, 10–11 April 2008. Photography: Jos Boys. www.architecture-insideout.co.uk

Plate 5 Liz Crow, *Bedding Out*, 48-hour durational performance at Salisbury Arts Centre April 2013. Photography: Mathew Fessey/ Roaring Girl Productions. www.roaring-girl.com

Plate 6 Architects Ash Sakula with disabled artists Tony Heaton and Chris Ankin: 'How many ways can U get from A2B?' from Architecture-InsideOut (AIO) event *Opening Up!* Turbine Hall, Tate Modern, 10 May 2008. Photography: Jos Boys. www.architecture-insideout.co.uk

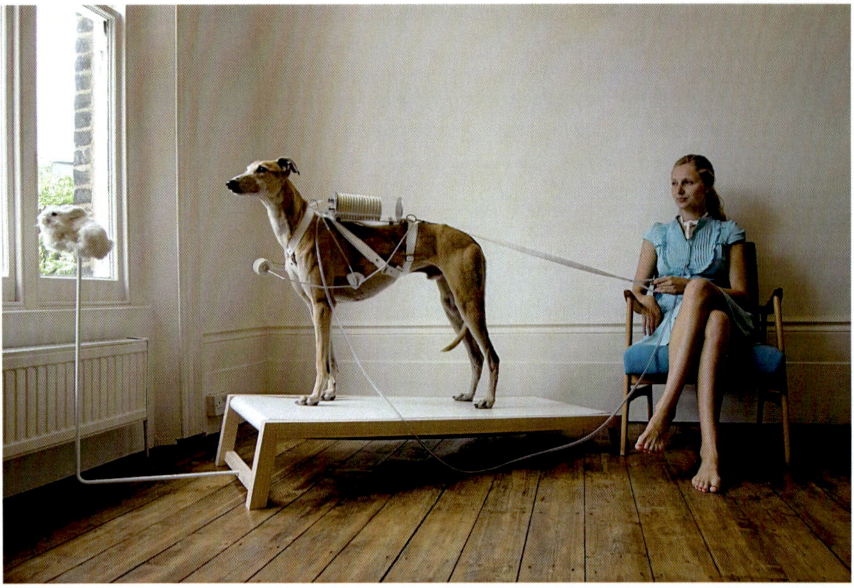

Plate 7 Revital Cohen (2008), 'Respiratory Dog' as part of *Life Support* project. C-type print on aluminium. www.cohenvanbalen.com/work/life-support

Plate 8 Henry Franks, *Confused Coathangers*. http://henryfranks.net

Plate 9 Louella Forrest and Edmond Brooks-Beckham, Cover illustration from Fox *et al.* (2008) *Overalls: A Blank Canvas.* Project and publication from Access to Art artists, University of Brighton/CUPP, showing overalls used as memory and methods note-taking device. Photography: Andrew Kingham.

Plate 10 Matthew Lloyd Architects, with Architecture-InsideOut (AIO) and the Royal Engineers, *Prototype Water Lift*, Duke of York steps, as part of London Festival of Architecture June 2010. Photography: Jos Boys. www.matthewlloyd.co.uk/#/project_39

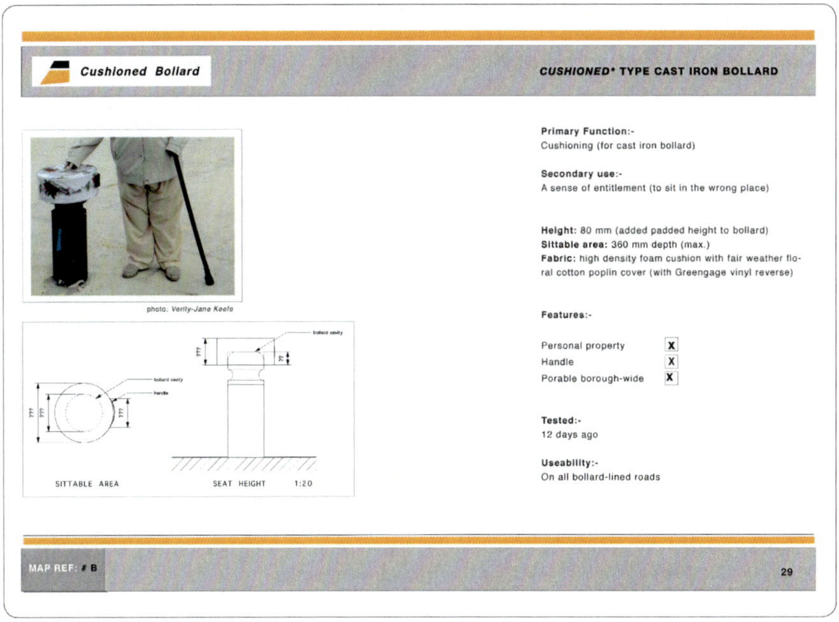

Plate 11 Ageing Facilities: Diagram from *Alternative Seating Guide*, www.ageing-facilities.net

Plate 12 Interior view, Chambers McMillan Architects, *Ramp House*, Portobello, Edinburgh 2011. Photography: David Barbour. www.cmcmarchitects.com/the-ramp-house

Plate 13 Architype, *The Willows*. Interactive mounted wall poem, facilitated and designed by artist Ruth Sparke, combining letters and Makaton symbols. Photography: Leigh Simpson. www.architype.co.uk/page3

Plate 14 Graeae's *The Limbless Knight – A Tale of Rights Reignited* at National Paralympic Day featuring the Mayor's Liberty Festival for Disability Arts. Queen Elizabeth Olympic Park, 7 September 2013. Photography: Kois Miah.

Plate 15 Foreign Office Architects, Yokohama Ferry Terminal. Photography: Jos Boys.

Plate 16 Door handles, Hiroshi Naito and Associates Gallery TOM (Touch Our Museum) Shibuya, Tokyo 1985. Photography: Jos Boys.

Plate 17 David Gissen (renderings by Victor Hadjikyriacou), *Proposed Reconstruction of the Acropolis Ramp* 2013. http://davidgissen.org/Project-Disability-and-History-Reconstruct-the-Acropolis-Ramp

Section III

Doing architecture and dis/ability differently

7 Alternative mappings

The previous section of this book engaged with some key exponents of contemporary architectural theory and practice, to open up gaps and opportunities for doing dis/ability and architecture differently. This final section explores what kinds of ideas, attitudes, methods, activities and practices can help in this process by combining existing examples with imagined possibilities. This chapter looks particularly at alternative forms of mapping that can provide a more attentive engagement with dis/ability and can offer a variety of methods for creative investigations, commentaries and analyses. Examples included here suggest how students, tutors and practitioners can open up dis/ability as an integral aspect of what they think about, centred on the *architectural* interest it offers. As I have said before, this is about how disability opens up our understandings of the work involved in everyday life; disrupts conventional categories and oppositions between the unnoticed abled and disabled 'others'; and helps to unravel and expose what is involved in performing ordinary social and spatial practices as well as their implications for architectural design.

> **The movement from being disabled to becoming dis/abled leaves it empirically, methodologically and conceptually open as to when, where, how, and how extensively people become enabled or disabled.**
>
> (Schillmeier 2010: 116)

Welcome to the dis/ordinary

As has been said many times here, the diverse ways in which disabled people live their lives can reveal the kinds of everyday work involved, and expose the enabling or disabling effects of different encounters, artefacts, spaces and contexts. In her book, *Waist-High in the World: A Life among the Nondisabled* (1996), Nancy Mairs aims to make 'storyable' a life lived with an increasingly impairing disability, that refuses the distancing tactics 'often practiced by those in whom disability triggers unbearable anxiety' so that 'a cripple, in order to earn a shot at social discourse with "normal" must never publically lament her state, must preferably never mention it' (Mairs 1996: 7). As with some of the narratives outlined in Chapter 1, she challenges these stereotypes by showing how much disability is just about the business of getting on with living – 'the ways in which life is indistinguishable from any other sort: fueled by the same appetites, fraught with the same anxieties, replete with the same delights . . .' But, as she goes on to say:

> In scrutinizing some of these elements common to the human condition – among them adjustment to change, body image and sexuality, the need for both independence and nurturance, the ceaseless search for equality and justice and pure pleasure – through the lens of my own experiences and those of the people I know well, I can bring to life their particular significance in terms of disability.
>
> (Mairs 1996: 11–12)

In her writing, then, Nancy Mairs interweaves the complexities, ambiguities, joys and struggles of being ordinary, interacting with the world and having an impairment as a loss, but not a *lack*:

> The spatial and temporal exigencies of a life shaped by severe physical disability – a life bound by permissions (I have to weigh every act in terms of whether I can or cannot perform it) and obligations (I must overcome inertia to do the least thing) . . . I am literally diminished by my disability, reduced to a height of about 4' 8", consigned to gazing at navels (generally shrouded) other than my own. But diminution is not the whole of it. 'Waist-high' also resonates with 'knee-deep'. This is no piteous deprived state I'm in down here but a rich, complicated, and utterly absorbing process of immersion in whatever the world has to offer.
>
> (Mairs 1996)

The everyday work required (weighing every act, overcoming inertia) shifts and changes, inevitably getting worse, but also demands inventive management:

> The bare rehearsal of my progressive disability conceals an increasingly intricate set of exercises in problem-solving that have kept me on my toes (even though off my feet) for nearly a quarter of a century. What to do when sacks of groceries become too heavy to carry? Ask the clerk to pack more of them with fewer items. What to do when I got too weak to carry them at all? Buy a little four-wheeled wire cart. What to do when I could no longer push the cart? Request that someone else carry them to the car . . .
>
> Virtually every activity, no matter how automatically most people would carry it out, has necessitated for me this sort of attention, resourcefulness and adaptability.
>
> (Mairs 1996)

Mapping stories like these resonantly reveals what 'normally' goes by unnoticed as the abled are 'racing from the kitchen to office to supermarket to fitness centre to political meetings'. And it opens up a potential *design* space, in the potential for creative translation *between* our everyday actions and the devices and material landscapes through which these are performed.

> **I'm now divorced from the nondisabled, bounding around heedlessly and hailing one another through the empty air above my head.**
>
> (Mairs 1996: 15)

Disabled people are not only more likely to actively read material environments for their potential supports to everyday life (how to enter a building, finding the toilets, finding somewhere to sit down) but are also aware that disabling effects operate at the intersections between functional, emotional, societal and contextual relations:

> Sometimes it is the physical dimensions of a building that is focussed bearing in mind accessibility for wheelchairs and rightly so. However, often overlooked is how we engage with space and the built environment on a psychological level. So what is the space from the door to the front of house like, is it easy to step into, comfortable, is it too large, psychologically inaccessible – anxiety creating? What is the language of the space – often very overlooked by architects – is it public, private, public-private shared – a cafe, a gallery, etc – all have their own languages. Is a wall a wall or is it really a giant door or window – moveable – that influences how people feel – negotiate and engage with the space they are in. People don't just have physical disabilities. The hidden or not so obvious must be attended to as well.
>
> (Aidan Moesby, Disability Arts Online (DAO))

In Chapter 6 I outlined Sobchack's argument for engaging with dis/ability across multiple registers, which recognizes the situated complexity of enabling and disabling effects. Here, what is particularly important to map, through taking notice of diverse disabled narratives, is the role of both devices and spaces in affecting these layered perceptions and experiences. Sobchack visualizes it as a kind of dynamic 're-scaling' of material space, as a coming in and out of focus, of – not attentiveness to the architecture – but of the feelings, interpretations and practicalities through which everyday life is performed:

> My consciousness has been altered at times by a heightened awareness of such things as the availability of handicapped access and parking and also of the way in which city streets, although still the same objective size, have

> subjectively expanded in space and contracted in time so that crossing the street before the traffic light changes now creates a heightened sense of peril and anxiety that I never felt before my amputation.
>
> (Sobchack 2006: 32)

What, it is worth asking, would an architecture based on this kind of mapping comprise? Such effects are felt of course personally and differently, but also reinforce how disability is viewed more generally, as separate and unimportant relative to 'normal' everyday life:

> Getting re-routed is a common part of the disabled experience. Being asked to do something differently in order to do it in the first place, is problematic. It is these little journeys 'up the goods lift' or 'round the back' that can be so devoid of comfort, creativity and humour.
>
> (Sarah Pickthall, *So What is Normal?* website comment)

As before, this is not an oppositional relationship between abled and disabled needs; it is a patterning and re-patterning of everyday social and spatial practices, with differential effects in different situations. For designers, then, it is not about 'doing what disabled people want' (or not) but about recognizing – even enjoying – the creative tensions in the difficult relations *between* dis/ability, artefacts and space. Anderberg details the kind of interesting ambiguities produced, using his mobility scooter as an example:

> If I drive my three-wheeled powered wheelchair scooter to work, is it an assistive technology device or is it a vehicle with which I go to work? When my personal assistant drives it home, because I have to go somewhere else with a car, is it still an assistive technology device? When my sons borrow the scooter to drive around the park outside the house because it is fun, does it cease to be an assistive device and become a toy?
>
> I cannot get off it and walk if I wanted to, but my personal assistants and my sons can. I, my scooter and the surrounding environment make up a functional system that is necessary for me to get to work. That is what makes it an assistive technology device for me. But if I try to go down to the beach, in the fine-grained sand, or go up two stairs, it ceases to assist me and to be assistive technology, because it does not provide any function in those settings. But does the actual wheelchair cease to be an assistive device at that moment?
>
> Some of my assistants refuse to sit on my powered scooter when they need to take it home or anywhere else. Sitting in a wheelchair makes them feel uncomfortable, although not in a physical sense. Some of them would rather take on the complicated and risky task of walking next to it, trying to manoeuvre it from the side. One assistant who was driving it home said that he felt that everyone was staring at him, and he felt so uncomfortable that he had to stop and get off the scooter and walk around for a while so

> that everyone would see that he did not have an impairment. He felt that people's attitudes towards him changed considerably when he was driving the scooter. The actual device signals the disability. That is not inherent in the technology per se, however, but an aspect of the attitudes towards disabled people is transferred to the technology associated with them.
>
> (Anderberg 2006b: 46)

Similarly, he gives the example of spaces for wheelchair users in theatres, which not only 'locate' disabled people in a particular place, but also offer cues to everyone else about the *value* of having a disability. This, then, becomes not just about disabled people and their 'special needs', but about exposing the specific social and spatial practices of doing 'being ordinary' and the detailed particularities of differential entitlements and markings that are involved:

> Instead the analysis concentrates on ontological peculiarities, on how disability is simultaneously experienced through bodily functions, constructed in social and cultural norms, anticipated and manufactured in policy-making and technology development, and created in architecture.
>
> (Galis 2011: 835)

This also has implications for what kinds of *spaces* come to the fore; that is, the mapping of dis/ordinary spaces. John Walker is undertaking a project with deaf people that investigates their memories of school, mainly at a time when deaf children were required to learn to lip-read and speak rather than sign. For these interviewees the important spaces were those where they could go together to sign; often secret, non-noticed parts of the school and its grounds. For exponents of Deaf culture, this offers an alternative kind of architectural mapping – of Deaf spaces of resistance (Text Box 7.1).

Text Box 7.1 Deaf Spaces of Resistance by John Walker, Senior Research Fellow, Community University Partnership Programme (CUPP), University of Brighton, UK

Deaf people have always interacted with non-deaf people. In the 18th and 19th centuries, the Parisian Banquets were spaces where Deaf people met and discussed current affairs in French Sign Language. Non-deaf Parisians, noblemen and aristocrats respected them and often visited their gatherings; they posed questions to the Deaf fellows and pondered over their answers. This period has been described as a 'golden era' of Deaf life, where its cultural norms were revered.

In 1880, it was proposed that signed languages should be banned from education and it gradually fell out of favour, in preference for an imposed oralist approach. In the UK, the 1889 Royal Commission on the Deaf and Dumb led to a resistance organisation, the British Deaf and Dumb Association, founded in 1890. This resulted in 130 years of resistance in various forms.

In residential specialist education, signed languages persisted when Deaf children, unknowingly, shared their signs and stories in hidden parts of the schools. Walls with glass doors and locations in the grounds provided respite from the regime; these spaces allowed them to 'break the rules' while still keeping a lookout, through reflections and shadows, for a teacher. But the schools had spaces that restricted their movements, positioned at the front of the classroom under the eye of the teacher. However, the teachers were never really in control.

It is not possible for Deaf people to return to the Golden era, the pre-colonial state, when Deaf spaces were places of respect. Presently, Deaf people are experiencing a post-colonial period of resistance and resurgence. The design of spaces will influence whether Deaf people will visit, temporarily stay, cohabit the space or endorse it as a new Deaf place.

See also: Sussex Deaf History: Celebrating Deaf people's histories in Sussex: www.sussexdeafhistory.org.uk.

Mapping spaces from the experiences of diverse disabled people thus suggests other ways of thinking and doing that remain considerably under-researched. This is not just about asking people what they like, or don't like; it is about starting from disability to offer alternative kinds of interpretations of material space beyond those within architectural discourse (Text Box 7.2). Importantly, this is also about enabling dis/ability to connect with well-known, contemporary architectural examples, rather than with the clinical and functional languages with which it is usually associated. As Zoe Partington-Sollinger writes, for example, whilst on a CABE-funded scholarship (see Plate 15):

> During my visit I also went to Yokohama to see the immigration port designed by Foreign Office Architects. I have to say stepping on to the surface and traversing across the space filled me with a sense of joy and the idea that urban space can be sexy, vibrant and uplifting in a grey, wet environment overwhelming. It was a (wood) surface but level access, no steps incredible undulating curves mirroring the landscape rolling countryside or sand dunes. It was not perfect by any means but it had potential and was of enormous significance in my view as it was a beautiful engineered and designed urban space. You could use other features to make it more inclusive and still retain the style, elegance and space to be a place that is uplifting and enjoyable.
>
> (Partington-Sollinger 2008b: 17–18)

As I have already said, these voices are worth listening to not because they are 'authentic', but because they can open up different kinds of engagement with material space, as alternative kinds of precedents for architects (a point I will return to in the next chapter). They also again raise the question, often returned to in this book, about why architectural discourse has such a difficulty in connecting with 'ordinary' people's descriptions of their experiences of material space.

Text Box 7.2 Spaces that work for sensory impaired people by Dr Nicholas Vogelpoel, Head of Arts and Wellbeing, Sense (www.sense.org.uk)

My work is with deafblind people (some who are artists), or people with single sensory impairments and associated disabilities around the UK. I was up at a Museum in the North of England a while back, and they have this new extension on the building that is basically a big, open plan, high-ceiling, white learning space. It is impressive and has great views of the sea. It's physically accessible – you can get into the building without going through a back entrance. Navigating the space is almost impossible though. The aesthetics of the building are contemporary and cool. There is low or no contrast, small print, no contrasting light, vacuumed acoustics and immovable objects. It struck me as odd, since we were meeting to discuss inclusive museums and galleries.

Likewise, I often get into long conversations with architects who call for consultation about accessible buildings. Like most, they operate on the premise that once the building is built, and the programmes are set, some audio looping, Braille on toilets, and an introductory BSL video on the website should do the trick. But, I caution them, what is the experience for people with alternative communication methods? They seem to have their answer cloaked in do-gooderism, and inclusivity remains an afterthought.

But then, this morning I encountered a revelation. The Wolverhampton Art Gallery has a spectacular sensory exhibition space. It is inclusive, tactile, accessible, interpreted, and so well designed. The curatorial team deserve serious celebration for taking such an intuitive move to make art and culture accessible. They didn't design a new building, they didn't build a new building, they just worked intelligently. The result is a fine and genuinely inviting sculptural exhibition, full of tactile experiences and multi-communicative options.

Mapping the ambiguities of the disabled–abled divide

Another key theme has been to challenge the commonsense stories that get told about (rather than by) disabled people, which all too often frame their lives as tragic or heroic – less than human or superhuman: they can be either passive victims or extraordinary people, but definitely not 'normal' in their desires and attitudes. I have suggested that we need to challenge these simplistic stereotypes, by recognizing that dis/ability is both ambiguous and relational:

> I ask my students to design a 'normal' human, to construct their own categories and taxonomies and come to some conclusions about what's normal and what's not. We have fun with this exercise, obviously. Students often joke that, for example, men should be about six feet tall and women should weigh about 120 pounds, until I remind them that such 'norms' conceal as well as reveal culturally desired attributes . . .
>
> So they designate broad categories that seem promising: physical, mental, emotional, psychological, sometimes behavioral. Most students feel competent to itemize the physical norm, so I ask something such as, what if a person has one eyebrow higher than another or an extra metatarsal bone in one foot? . . . If anything, our attempts at classifications become more hotly disputed – and absurd – as we move on to the mental, emotional, and psychological categories. Well before we get to the behavioral category, someone in class will usually (and mercifully) bemoan the fact that by our standards some, if not all, of the members of his or her family are abnormal. Exactly!
>
> (Wilson 2000: 150)

J. C. Wilson's aim here (working with medical students) was to enable the students themselves to see how 'unmanageable' artificial divisions between disabled and able-bodied are, when they are critically explored. Is someone with cancer disabled, or someone who is fatter, or larger or smaller than the norm?

In another project from the early 2000s, listed on the Universal Design Education Online website, students' commonsense about what makes a 'normal' building was challenged. The *Seven Deadly Sins* project was for students enrolled in the third year of an architectural technology programme by a professor called Bob Topping at Sheridan College – a community college near Toronto, Ontario. As part of a design elective course, 'Universal Design', where students had studied the principles of universal design, they were here asked to design an entrance that *excluded* as many people as possible. Designs included buildings where you can only get in via a rope ladder, opening up to exploration of the idea that pushing the boundaries of what constitutes disabled to include everyone except the super-fit reveals the ambiguity of assumptions about what is a normal way of entering a building and what is special for a 'non-normal' contingent.

A final example from Universal Design Education Online:

> In the fall semester of 2002 a seminar was offered to architecture students at the University of Arkansas. This seminar, entitled Post-Modern Critiques and the 'Unhealthy', examined a cross-section through post-1965 architectural theory and synthesized inquiries concerning the production

of architectural ideology. The course surveyed several interdisciplinary readings and films, facilitating a discussion of diverse (and perverse) social, psychological, and spatial desires of (un)healthiness. This was a questioning of architectural and non-architectural conditions that have been termed 'unhealthy'; the course examined the implications of this act of classification on the production of tectonic space.

Throughout the semester, the following questions were posed: Generically, how does cultural dogma affect the production of architecture? What limits, what discriminations, are placed on architecture by status quo convictions? What conditions have been segregated or denied from tectonic manifestation? What is architecture's role – historically, currently, and prospectively – in accommodating (or refuting) the 'unhealthy', of allowing/disallowing the pursuit of perverse desires?

These inquiries allowed students to recognize their own desires, preconceptions, and perversions – and analyze (and potentially alter) their attitudes toward various states of (un)healthiness.

(Smith 2002)

Here Korydon H. Smith, Assistant Professor of the School of Architecture at the University of Arkansas, asks students to challenge both their own and commonsense societal concepts of what constitutes 'health' and to critically and creatively map how these are embedded into everyday attitudes and practices.

Expanding the senses

Unfortunately many design projects introducing disability into architectural schools can perpetuate abled assumptions that disability is a 'tragic' lack, by framing its experience both through what is 'missing' and how this can be 'mended'. When students are asked to imagine themselves as disabled (perhaps by being blindfolded or going around in a wheelchair for a day), they are likely to notice mainly the unnerving feelings of not being able to see or walk. The problem for most disabled people about this approach is that it does not accurately express the realities of living with an impairment *ordinarily*, that is as the creative management of everyday living. A student blindfolded, for example, will compare themselves to how they 'normally' see. Compare this to Sally French's description of normal blindness:

> We cannot always engage in the same activities as sighted people, we cannot do things as fast, we need more time to see, and we need the time to use our other senses to the full. When we are together, getting lost and having problems, we are engaging with the world far more than we ever could from a car or at someone else's pace. We might not do as much, but what we do, we do on our own terms and at our pace without any need to explain ourselves.
>
> (French 1999: 27)

It also means that sense experiences *from* disability are not even noticed. In the same piece, French offers an example:

> As a small child I had a dislike of going out on windy days. My mother, no doubt exasperated, asked me why this was so, to which I replied 'the wind gets in my way'. I do not remember this incident but it is recalled, as an amusing family story, to show what a quaint and peculiar child I was. As a visually impaired adult I know exactly what I meant. The wind makes noises which obscure the small auditory cues which, though rarely appreciated until they are absent, are so helpful when walking about . . . I was right, the wind does indeed get in my way.
>
> (French 1999: 21)

A research project aiming to open up the senses beyond the visual appreciation of much architectural practice and criticism, called *Buildings Revis(it)ed*, needs to be treated with care because of this issue, but does open up to awareness alternative ways of mapping buildings (Froyen *et al.* 2008). As part of their work, the team invited architecture critics to return to a well-known public building while being blindfolded and guided by persons who were visually impaired.

> Afterwards, they were asked to report on this visit in an article for an architectural magazine. The initiative aimed at drawing the attention of the critics – and, by extension, the readers of their articles – to the need for accessibility, usability and comfort for the real diversity of users, but also to architecture's potential multisensory richness.
>
> In the short term, *Buildings Revis(it)ed* offers architecture critics an opportunity to catch a 'glimpse' of how persons with different capacities and limitations experience the built environment. In the long term, it aims at triggering a change in mentality; at sensitizing architecture critics – and the readers of their articles – to pay more attention to these persons' multisensory and spatial experience and, more in general, to accessibility, usability and comfort for all, when designing, describing and assessing architecture.
>
> (Heylighen *et al.* 2009: 1–2)

They note how one of the critics, Caroline Goossens, was both struck by the 'realization that the rigid frames which structure life so routinely are actually extremely thin', but also 'pleasantly surprised to discover how changes in temperature, light, smell and sound reveal architecture's invisible borders, and how materials and details offer body and mind something to hold on to' (Heylighen *et al.* 2009: 3).

Another, Koen Van Synghel, used his resulting magazine article to suggest that

> architecture is a medium that should provide comfort – not in the sense of luxury or lazy relaxation, but in the sense of consolation, of solace. That is

exactly what a handrail offers when you are climbing a stair with a blindfold, handed over completely to what you feel with your white stick or, even more elementary, with your hands.

(Heylighen *et al.* 2009: 4)

His conclusion was that architects should become more involved in ordinary details, such as handrails, with guiding lines in footpaths and floor tiles, and with contrasting materials. Whilst these comments raise interesting issues, they perpetuate a view from sightlessness, that is, by asking the abled to experience – only momentarily – a 'loss' of sight, and then valuing and reproducing these interpretations rather than those, for example, of their visually impaired 'companions'.

In a 2007 Art Council South East funded project, bringing together Vocal Eyes – a professional audio-describer's organization – with students from the University of Brighton, we attempted to create instead a dialogue between blind and partially sighted people and interior architecture students. The 'Sense of Place' (Figure 7.1) project aimed to bring together disabled experiences of space with students' verbal descriptions of those spaces, through the process of developing audio-descriptions for blind and partially sighted architectural tours. Students worked with blind participants, to both find out more about how they understood space, and to learn themselves to describe spaces both accurately and poetically. Thus, we attempted to combine students' learning towards an

Figure 7.1 University of Brighton Interior Architecture student developing an audio-described architectural tour with blind and partially sighted participants, Brighton 2007. Photography: Jos Boys.

increased understanding of blind experiences of space, and to develop the range and accuracy of their language in 'explaining' architectural form. However, whilst this project did raise awareness of disability and extend students' engagement with all the senses, what it did not do was make explicit or critically challenge the dominant commonsense assumptions of the abled *about* disability. How, then, continuing with the example of blindness and visual impairment, can we map the world alternatively by instead starting *from* disability?

Starting from disability

Tanya Titchkosky offers another – more radical – form of mapping, one that investigates the gaps *between* abled assumptions and disabled perspectives:

> I (first) met Rod as a blind man, but one who could see. He could see . . . but not quite; what I could understand, count on or see as seeing was never all that clear when I was with Rod. It was a confusing state of affairs that threw into question for me what seeing and blindness are supposed to mean . . .
>
> This confusion flowed from my conception of blindness and sightedness as radically opposite. Either Rod was sighted or he was blind. Fixed oppositions according to Scott (1998: 33) 'conceal the extent to which things presented as oppositional are, in fact, interdependent'. Not only did my conception of blindness as opposite to sightedness conceal their interdependence in Rod, it also concealed from me the need to think about this interdependence.
>
> (Titchkosky 2002: 102)

As she goes on to say, the most common cultural map of blindness is as 'not seeing' – 'defining blindness as a kind of negation of sight is regularly expressed in everyday life' (Titchkosky 2002: 103). As Rod (Michalko) himself writes, if blindness is seen as strange and opposite to sight as the familiar, then the experiences of blind people themselves are negated. He observes the interaction between Jenny, an eight-year-old girl blind from birth, and her Orientation and Mobility instructor, Cheryl, who is teaching her to use a white cane. Following a long conversation about what the qualities of objects she encountered were, and Jenny's own interpretations of these, Michalko goes on to note:

> Jenny depicted knowledges (of the sky and carrots) to Cheryl and to me and did so from the location (standpoint) of blindness. Cheryl saw a problem with this depiction . . . it was knowledge gleaned from the location of blindness and thus defective. Cheryl learnt nothing of the sky or of carrots from Jenny. Cheryl learned only what she already knew – that Jenny had a lot of work to do on concept development.
>
> Jenny was learning how to use a white cane as a mobility device and she was learning about carrots. But there was a hidden curriculum and Jenny

> was learning something else – she was learning that she had local knowledge, knowledge that came to her through her blindness . . . Jenny is learning that her knowledge is located only in the space of her blindness and that this knowledge does not count and is even defective in the imagined geography of sightedness. Jenny is learning that the space of blindness is a private space and that it is a detriment to her movement and understanding of the public space of sightedness.
>
> (Michalko 2002: 178–9)

Here, the understandings of the world from a blind person's perspective are being constantly downgraded in relation to the experiences of sightedness as the 'obviously correct' interpretation.

This framing of blindness *through* sight also has an effect on how accessibility and inclusive design are imagined and implemented. Stephen Hetherington provides a good detailed example in relationship to how, for example, museums can frame blindness in particular ways rather than others, as much structured by wanting to be *seen* to do something, as in the actual value of the doing.

> The museum's overarching concern is with *accountability*. The Parthenon marbles are a controversial set of objects and the British Museum has for some time now been on the defensive about its custody of them . . . The idea of visitors being given greater access through the facilities in the introductory galleries is one way of the museum trying to continue to justify its possession of these artefacts . . .
>
> Access is not just something that museums can become; it is also something that they can do. To do access is to be accountable in a visible and distal way. . . . So such facilities, as elements of a policy of social inclusion, can mobilize the figure of the visually impaired visitor within the discourse of access precisely because such facilities are in place.
>
> These practices constitute the visually impaired person and their embodiment through these processes of monitorable practice and their signifying properties. The visually impaired person is now written into the space of the British Museum and is thereby disposed of as a gap. Their embodiment is constituted through the book, the moulded cast section and the audio guide that has been designed for them. Not only *what* but *how* they touch is already defined by the materials that have been provided.
>
> (Hetherington 2003: 113)

The built-in assumption is that all information needs to about aiding touch, rather than noticing that touch 'can simply be for itself – a proximal form of understanding'. In the process Hethrington suggests that several things happen. First, the museum can be seen – at least at the level of appearances – as being accessible; that is, it has taken account of disabled people and of regulatory requirements. At the same time, touch is here re-producing the 'normal' visual interaction with a museum, as a process of identification and interpretation of objects.

> Touch is treated as a distal form of knowledge, its proximal sensitivities, not necessarily interested in identification, visualization and representation are ignored and remain unknowable. The tactile aids are used as optical prostheses, there to supplement an impaired and unfinished body and, by implication, aiding an 'impaired' subjectivity. As such, they constitute disability negatively through the idea of non-sight rather than more positively through an understanding of skilled, sensitive touch.
>
> (Hethrington 2003: 115)

Refusing to construct blindness *via* sightedness (that is, as both in opposition and inferior to 'seeing') can bring us to a different 'place' for both disability and ability:

> Insofar as seeing is cultural, sight is a social accomplishment and blindness is a kind of forced consciousness of the work necessary to achieve it. This is a key lesson that accompanies my shift away from attempts to reduce disability to a concrete reality and to mapping disability as a complex set of social interactions.
>
> (Titchkosky 2002: 107–8)

For as Schillmeier writes:

> Spaces of sightedness and blindness become present differently, and still they are not opposite or separated in social praxis. They criss-cross, connect and separate, and become present and absent for each other.
>
> (Schillmeier, 2010: 127)

In his book, *Rethinking Disability: Bodies, Senses, and Things*, he offers many examples, such as his explorations of blind and partially sighted people's interactions with ATMs:

> Cash machines are effective and efficient because they are self-restricted and lack flexibility . . . They are what cybernetics calls 'trivial' machines, as they know and accept only standardized procedures: they do what one wants perfectly well, in a secure and trustworthy manner, but only under their conditions; and these conditions are highly visually designed and configured. . . . One is made blind, as a consequence of not being able to read and follow the instructions of an ATM. To put it differently, ATMs cannot put up with the complexities of different sensory practices, such as those of blind people. As a consequence, ATMs enact the normality of visually dominated practices *and* visualize blindness.
>
> (Schillmeier 2010: 137–8, italics in original)

As he goes on to note, this produces a problem because it is also associated with the valuing of autonomy and competence:

> Spaces where money circulates enable 'effectiveness' but only as long as the people performing 'money practices' comply with certain standards. But

> if such money practices are disrupted then money space shows its fragility and vulnerability: money spaces stop being effective and people who cannot conform to their practices are excluded . . . Blind peoples' practices visualize quite vividly the power of money and of money technologies . . . which normalize and configure the 'normativity' of their users.
>
> (Schillmeier 2010: 137–8)

This leads him to a conclusion that will be explored in much more detail in relation to disability and architecture in this book's final chapter:

> [B]lindness and sightedness are not inherent properties, but effects constituted out of heterogeneous relations involving different materialities and technologies, different people, and different (sensory) skills, which make up the practices of social space and the social spaces of practices. Put differently, the differences between blindness and sightedness is stablised not by a fixed state or condition of blindness or sightedness itself, but as the *mediation* of heterogeneous materialities and practices.
>
> (Schillmeier, 2010: 138, italics in original)

Alternative descriptions

Another route to mapping disability differently is through engaging with disabled people's own creative interpretations of the world, precisely operating at, playing with and subverting this 'mediation of heterogeneous materialities and practices' (Schillmeier, 2010: 138). The work of internationally famous artists such as Yinka Shonibare, Tacita Dean and Ryan Gander may intersect with – but is not constrained to, or only about – their disabilities. Exploring these commentaries is in some way always about how we each place ourselves, and are placed in the world. It opens up to creative and poetic expression relationships between, for example, bodies, space, stereotyping, vulnerability, boundary-making, imperfection, exclusion and power. Ryan Gander's work, for example, though deliberately difficult to pin down, offers tangled narratives, through which he 'frequently elaborates, exaggerates and lies which, in turn, makes it difficult for him to remember where things began and differentiate between fact and fiction' (Chaillou undated). Like Araniello and Williamson – the two disabled artists with whom this book began – he plays at the interface between the absurd and the 'normal', offering up dis/ordinary situations that disorient their audiences' assumptions. But whilst Araniello and Williamson revel in reclaiming the spectacular freakery through which disability used to be partially constituted (Garland Thomson 1997b), Gander is a much more contemporary trickster:

> Gander's Artangel project is called *Locked Room Scenario*, but it's more the Case of the Missing Exhibition. I patrol the warren of shabby rooms and immaculate corridors leading into deathly gloom; riffle through piles of uncollected mail heaped in corners, and hear complaining voices on the

> other side of the loo wall. Above the churning cistern, I heard the names Martin Creed and Mike Nelson, so try to eavesdrop some more.
>
> Gander's project is full of in-jokes, arch clues and misdirections. It has so many levels of contrivance and accident I haven't a clue what matters. There seems to be an exhibition – but is it going up or coming down? The whole thing is as shadowy and enigmatic as the figure whose silhouette I spy, rippling on the other side of a locked, frosted glass door.
>
> (Searle 2011)

Locked Room Scenario makes a series of spaces where material landscape, objects and occupancy cannot be separated. One does not merely reflect or reinforce the other in a resonant and associative cycle, but instead opens up the gaps and confusions between them. Within these spaces, we, the participants, are made lost both actually and conceptually, as the 'normal' clues of everyday social and spatial practices are removed, or shifted.

This deliberate loss of the inherent control and power of the ordinary have also been important concerns in Noëmi Lakmaier's work. If Gander mainly acts as a choreographer of his audience's social and spatial experiences, she has increasingly performed the complexities of 'amending' her own body:

> Noëmi Lakmaier's work explores notions of the 'Other' ranging from the physical to the philosophical, the personal to the political. The individual's relationship to its surroundings, identity, and perception of self and other in contemporary society are core interests in her predominantly site-responsive, live and installation-based practice.
>
> Lakmaier's work aims to emphasize and exaggerate the relationship between object, individual and space . . . she constructs temporary living installations – alternative physical realities – exploring the psychological implications of power, control and insecurity, the drive to belong and succeed as well as feelings of self-doubt and otherness.
>
> She is interested in the presence of the viewer as voyeur and how this presence can act as the catalyst that galvanizes an event and creates a tension and a divide between 'Them' – the passive observer – and the 'Other' – the objects of their gaze.
>
> (www.noemilakmaier.co.uk)

Experiment in Happiness, for example, is a giant ball covered in hundreds of shoes, to which, at a live event, she attached herself (already illustrated in the introduction to this book). Spectators were then invited to push the ball, taking control away from her. By using her own body in the artwork, she intensifies the relationship between viewer and object, challenges her fears of relinquishing control, whilst also positioning the viewers in an uncomfortable relationship to her. Other pieces deliberately re-shape her body, and that of others (Plate 2). For example, she squeezes herself into a 'weeble', crawls along the pavement, or appears as an 'ordinary' office worker who is, in fact, drenched in water (Text Box 7.3).

Text Box 7.3 Interview with artist Noëemi Lakmaier

Jos: There is a whole history of artistic work around performing the body. How do you think your work is informed by/relates to this?

Noëmi: It developed without me really realizing it, in the difference between performance and live art. There are artists who perform a part, playing a role not a person. In my work it is always me or an objectified version of me. The scenario is planned but the rest is real. So the work is created through making an absurd situation, rather than a 'different' persona, and then putting me in it.

The body becomes just another material, like plaster or paint. It is like trying to become part of an art object, even though that is impossible.

Jos: When I look at your work, I know that it is informed by much more than the fact that you use a wheelchair. But I do feel that you often come to the body from a different angle to many non-disabled artists who make performative work. Does that make sense to you, or am I just reading into something that is not there?

Noëmi: Because my body is visibly disabled that body will always be read into my work, so it is probably worth considering from the start rather than ignoring it.

But my work is really about taking the risk of being out of control. This comes from being brought up in an environment with someone with obsessive compulsive disorder, who had to be in control of everything to be 'normal'. So I wanted to take it to an extreme, as in *Exercise in Losing Control* (2007) where you no longer have control over yourself. And putting the audience in charge, to see how far they will take it.

In *Working Moments* (a collaboration with Sabine Gruhn and Mark Erickson) we explored the 'imposter syndrome'. So there is this aspect of office psychology – that has a name as a condition; and I was interested in when feeling uncomfortable and exposed at work is just part of being human.

Working Moments (Photographers' Gallery), 2010, photograph by Sabine Gruhn

Jos: Your work seems to have increasingly entangled body and a kind of dynamic relationship to space. How important is site to you, and can you talk about how you respond to physical space?

Noëmi: Space comes before the body in my work. Everything is about where the work takes place. In *One Morning in May*, where I crawled from Tower Hamlets in London to the City, I wanted to show the social and political distance between poorest and wealthiest. It is something we don't notice, because these places are so geographically close, so easy to walk to. This was about mapping at a much slower pace and in a more arduous way the real social and economic distance. Doing the journey on my hands and knees was to create this slowing down.

Then, in the various versions of *We are for you because we are against them* (Plate 2) organizing a dinner party – an event full of social conventions about behaviour – but with people wearing weeble suits, set up the absurd situation; nobody could eat elegantly. When we did it in Dublin, the group became quite relaxed and no longer minded not being in control; they started to find out what they could do in the suit. But when we did it in Belfast with politicians from different parties, everyone was extremely self-conscious and very stiff.

The specific space is completely part of the situation, it shows up how people react when they are put in an unexpected position.

Exercise in Losing Control, 2007, photograph by Joy Stanley
www.noemilakmaier.co.uk

If each of these artists makes work that operates, I suggest, across the complicated and unstable interface between the ordinary and the dis/ordinary, others have explored how disability might be expressed affirmatively, recognized in its own right as a life to be valued. As part of the UK Cultural Olympiad and its Unlimited commissions, Sue Austin, performed a piece called *Creating the Spectacle* (Plate 3) exploring how to 'open up a *thinking space* around the materiality of the wheelchair . . . used as a *metaphor* to raise questions about the value of diversity to society through raising the profile of "difference"' (www.susanaustin.co.uk). As she writes, this is not about merely being didactic, but about creating

> *portals* or multiple entrances into the resulting artwork (e.g. through live art, associated online and multi-platform presentation, etc.,) so that it can find a way to ask questions but at the same time leave space for the audience to generate their own meanings.
>
> (www.susanaustin.co.uk)

By going diving in her wheelchair, Austin intersects a strong visual and affirmative visualization with a set of ongoing theoretical interests in the effects of representational forms:

- The socio-cultural implications of the presences and absences (Derrida) created by the 'traces' left by the wheelchair;
- The surreal, unexpected juxtapositions arising from the image of the Underwater Wheelchair which act to reshape cultural preconceptions about disability (Narrative theory);
- The appropriation of the semiotics of display (e.g. those used in car commercials) to attach concepts of drama and glamour to the objecthood of the wheelchair;
- The power of repositioning 'extensions to the body' through associating the glamour and adventure of scuba equipment with the extensions to 'being' provided by the wheelchair;
- Creating associations that act to make the NHS wheelchair, visible, iconic and valuable.

(www.trishwheatley.co.uk/suetheory.html)

Creating this spectacle, then, acts to shift perceptions of what wheelchairs can or can't do, and what the people who use them are capable of.

In addition, some disabled artists have engaged directly with the material world, using site, installation and spatial relationships to reveal the complexities in the relationship between disability and its landscapes, and to examine the critical and creative tensions that are produced. I have already described in Chapter 1 Liz Crow's *Bedding Out, Bedding In* project that deliberately juxtaposes spaces normally kept apart – the 'private' zone of coping with illness or impairment and the public world where ableness is assumed, and where sometimes it is just easier for disabled people to 'pass' (Plate 5). By making her bed in the public space of the gallery, Crow reminds us how material space acts to separate out and make invisible some aspects of everyday living.

Joseph Young is a sound artist, who is also partially deaf, and is therefore interested in the inherent tensions in the 'noise' of space:

> It's amazing what the brain can do to adapt to functional impairments, I realised that for years I had been filling in the auditory gaps and had already started to develop unconscious strategies of listening with my left ear forward to better catch the flow of conversation in crowded pubs and busy public spaces. It's not that I can't hear at all what a person is saying to me; I am often able to make out, say, 1 word in 3 and have learnt to interpolate the rest. But because the human voice and background noise both occupy the same part of the frequency spectrum, that's what it all sounds like to me – NOISE, and one noise can be virtually indistinguishable from another.
>
> Not that I find the noise unpleasant you understand, on the contrary, I have made an entire artistic practice out of listening to urban noise and finding creative ways to transform it. And that is the point – I realised the diagnosis had led me pursue the search for meaning in the constant stream of indistinguishable sounds (the wealth of information hidden inside the urban drone) and this was forcing me to listen harder and more carefully, ultimately driving forward my artistic practice.
>
> (Joseph Young, discussion piece for Architecture-InsideOut (AIO), undated)

Young uses binaural microphones that capture sound from around the body, recording it in its three-dimensional ambience. For him, playing with these recordings in his own work picks up 'the beauty and complexity of the urban soundscape' – an attentiveness to all its subtleties:

> The way that sound literally surrounds us as we walk through the city – sounds of people, chatter, shouting, crying; vehicle noise of all different pitch, vibration and tone; recorded music, mobile phones all playing off each other in a random, yet surprisingly coherent way when listened to carefully.
>
> (ibid.)

At the same time, he recognizes his own and others' preference for a clear soundscape, so that, for example, conversations are audible – coming to the conclusion that:

> How we experience public space is as much to do with how we hear a space as to how we see it, an equivalence that is rarely expressed in the building design. Sharp edges and hard materials all serve to amplify the reflections that create background noise and attenuate certain frequencies over others. Whilst I am a massive fan of the brutalist architecture movement that celebrates concrete and glass, I also understand that these very materials impair hearing access in the buildings that utilise them. Not being

> an acoustician or architect, I do not have answers as to whether these sorts of buildings can be adapted to absorb rather than reflect sound or whether they should carry a health warning that says 'This building constitutes a hazard for the hearing impaired'. Either way, this article is a small call to arms for artists and others to engage creatively with those responsible for public planning to suggest creative responses to the problem of buildings that unintentionally amplify background noise.
>
> (ibid.)

An early project by Architecture-InsideOut (AIO), an ongoing series of collaborations between disabled and Deaf artists and architects, funded by Arts Council South East and based at the University of Brighton, also examined sound as a relation between disability and space. A number of disabled artists were given the brief of 'a space where two people meet', both to explore working together and to respond specifically to a 'spatial' issue (Figure 7.2). Melissa Mostyn and Jon Adams found their point of contact in imagining themselves meeting in a crowded room. For Adams, his Asperger's meant that incoherent and dense noise became intimidating and disorienting. For Mostyn, the space and light for easy conversational signing were prevented by such a setting. They therefore expressed the discomforts of such a space of meeting (Colour Figure 4).

Figure 7.2 Architecture-InsideOut (AIO) event, InQbate Creativity Zone, University of Sussex, UK, 10–11 April 2008. Photography: Jos Boys. www.architecture-insideout.co.uk/?location_id=31

Critical devices

A recurrent theme of *Doing Disability Differently* has been the way 'devices' come to be articulated in relation to both disability and ability. In Chapter 1 I showed how enhancements for disabled people are often 'marked' problematically compared to 'normal' objects. And in Chapter 6 I looked at some contemporary explorations of relationships between the body and technologies, particularly in its (sometimes problematic) resonances with the concepts of cyborg and prosthetic. These debates have also informed critical design. Work by Anthony Dunne and Fiona Raby, directors of the Design Interactions programme at Royal College of Art (RCA), for example, articulates objects as a deliberate social commentary, rather than just 'normal' products (Dunne 2008, Dunne and Raby 2013). Revital Cohen, when a second year MA student at the RCA, won the CABE 'Designing for our Future Selves' environment award for her conceptual project 'Life Support', which has already been illustrated in a previous chapter (Figure 6.2). She was interested in re-imagining support equipment for people who were on dialysis or oxygen, not as machines but as assistance animals (www.cohen-vanbalen.com/work/life-support). This work is deliberately difficult, provoking post-humanist questions about the intersections between health, life, bodies and animals. Here, as already noted, rather than the seductive resonance of the superhuman enhanced by a machine, we are faced with the reality of clinical technologies. The 'normal' dialysis machine performs only a function, failing to offer anything more to the person who is connected to it. By replacing it with the blood – and company – of a domestic pet, she offers simultaneously the potential of a more 'humane' relationship, and an unnerving extension of the intimacy and interconnection that that implies (Plate 7).

Other product designers have looked to start from disability, as a form of material commentary and a means to improve function. Henry Franks, a product design graduate from Northumbria University, has re-imagined a collection of everyday objects as a way of expressing his dyslexia through form 'to create products which have dyslexia and function better as a result':

> One of Franks' products is a coat hanger with two hooks, so it can be hung either way round. 'The Confused Coat Hanger wasn't paying attention when being told which way round it was supposed to be,' Franks explains. 'As a result, it has a double-hooked head and can hang either way round when hanging your clothes up.
>
> Coaster Plinth, an oversized cork drinks coaster, ended up as an elevated platform rather than a flat disc because it 'misread the dimensions it was supposed to be and hasn't understood the question,' says Franks. Despite the apparent precariousness of a cup placed on top of the plinth, it makes the cup more noticeable so it's less likely to be spilled.
>
> (Dezeen 2013)

Here a developing range of 'dyslexic objects', designed in response to Franks' own dyslexic condition, aims to encourage the user to re-engage with ordinary objects and subject people to products with a higher emotional function (Figure 7.3, Plate 8).

The *Overalls* project grew out of an Access to Art programme for adults with learning disabilities (Fox *et al.* 2008). These students learnt in collaboration with students from art and design courses at the University of Brighton; everyone wore white overalls, which became a place to record or collect images (Plate 9). The course tutors then explored how this impromptu activity could be developed into a useful reflective tool for everyone. By noting down their ideas, or things to remember, an individual artist's overalls become a map for, and about, their own art practice:

> Overalls offers a new and creative look at ways of engaging in reflective practice and proposes a shift in how students gather, reflect upon and reveal their thoughts around learning. Here we have an innovative, transferable model for inclusive learning across subjects, which is of use to mainstream and learning disabled students alike.
>
> (University of Brighton 2008)

Again, starting from disability suggested a creative technique for remembering artistic procedures and preferences, that was useful and engaging for everyone involved, not just the disabled students, and could easily be extended to other situations.

Figure 7.3 Henry Franks, *Muglexia* – mugs designed to illustrate how dyslexics often deal with inversion, here resulting in cups that are more stable and more balanced in the hand because of the handle position being upside down and lower down than normal. http://henryfranks.net

Criticality through participation

I have already outlined some of the potential difficulties with participatory design projects, both in how relationships between 'users' and 'designers' can fail to be critically reframed, and because – in focusing only on case-by-case examples – disability becomes a special (and difficult) category that only needs to be dealt with *sometimes*. In architectural education, such projects tend to be about a building *for* disabled people, and, as outlined in Chapter 3, fail to challenge the much stronger demands on students to conceptualize their work primarily through architectural concerns with formal, spatial and aesthetic manipulations. In the *Making Discursive Spaces* project at the University of Brighton (Boys 2007, 2008) we attempted to sidestep these problems by offering a more general design project (artists' studios) and by employing a number of disabled artists as tutors (Figure 7.4).[1] As we wrote at the time:

> Bringing together Deaf and disabled artists with interior architecture students in a collaborative space both enables richer descriptions of material space and disability than traditionally discussed and opens up interpretations of the built environment from different 'positions' to creative and constructive review. We hoped this would produce more creative

Figure 7.4 Interior Architecture student tutorials, *Making Discursive Spaces* project, University of Brighton, UK, 2007. http://www.discursivespaces.co.uk

1 This interior architecture studio, taught with Theresa Hoskyns, worked with disabled artists Rachel Gadsden, Noëmi Lakmaier, Caroline Cardus, Miles Thomas, Rubbena Aurangzeb-Tariq, Sarah Pickthall and Damian Toal. Student participants were Kerry Alford, Charlotte Brisley, Matt Everest, Laia Martin Marqueda, Lettie McCall, Alex Paduano, Rohini Pophale, Dominie Shelley, Vasiliki Stylianou, Ellie Taplin, and Rebecca Whythe.

> complexity, and therefore deeper levels of understanding so as to enrich design quality, not just for Deaf and disabled people but for everyone.
>
> (Boys 2007)

But, as with the research already discussed, the project was only partially successful, lacking critical purchase on the already existing complex relationships between architectural education as a practice, and the contradictory 'location' of accessibility and inclusive design within it. Whilst the collaboration increased design students' awareness of their own bodies, and of differences between bodies, it did not challenge their already existing assumptions about what makes 'good' design and how to go about it (that is, by starting from a concept and then moving into increasing detail). Within this framework, disability continued to be disconnected from the parallel universe of 'proper' architecture. There was therefore what one participant called 'a problem in translation'; that many second-year undergraduate students struggled with finding ways of translating their awareness and feelings about the qualities of space – and about these new ways of thinking disability – into design. They could recognize the artists' different insights but had very few tools to take these forward into a design method or realization. In addition, students were all too aware that this element of the project was not officially assessed; and therefore felt insecure or split about whether to engage completely with the artists, or to rely more on what they conventionally understood as a design project. A small minority of other tutors were also not supportive of incorporating disability issues into the design studio, which made students confused about how they should respond. This added extra layers of complexity – not just about disability and design but also about educational experiences and levels, about design education frameworks and about what risks students felt they could take during their studies. But if this was our own evaluation from the project, an external critic was much more scathing:

> Ah, but at the end of the day . . . you're still in control as the one with the design expertise . . . so what are you really risking? Are you prepared to risk the explosion of the hegemony of standards and aesthetics in the design industries if that's what it takes to fully liberate disabled people from their imposed silence? Wouldn't it be interesting to stretch this to examining whether the interior design and architectural fields' inherent structures are even capable of apprehending the shattering impact of a completely Other set of knowledges . . .?
>
> (Anonymous external reviewer comment 2008)

Another approach was Squarinthecircle?, a public arts programme initiated by the Disability Arts development agency Dada-South with Diablo Arts, in partnership with the University of Portsmouth, St George's Beneficial School, the Portsea community and disabled artists. The project involved architecture students, other local young people, the Portsmouth Disability Forum, local disabled artists and the University estates team. It included workshops by Signdance Collective with architectural students and with schoolchildren; and the commissioning of a sculpture from disabled artist Tony Heaton (Figure 7.5). The aim of the project was to develop a dialogue with local groups who can often feel excluded from plans about their own built environment. The project allowed them to contribute to new developments being proposed by the University.

The University of Portsmouth also employs Jon Adams, an artist with dyslexia and Asperger's syndrome, as a Research Fellow, to work with students on projects, including architecture students. Again, raising awareness of disability, and opening up students to a different way of looking, has been a central intention (www.disabilityartsonline.org.uk/Jon-Adams).

Minding the gaps

The examples of alternative mapping introduced here have, to varying degrees, started from disability as a means of making explicit the kinds of work involved in both everyday living, and in order to help us better understand how 'normal' social and spatial practices come to be unconsciously perpetuated, and can be critically and creatively exposed. But I have also argued that in order to do disability differently, we need to critically map where and how architecture as a profession, practice and product continues to both re-produce 'normal'

Figure 7.5 Tony Heaton, Squarinthecircle? Sculpture, commissioned by the Arts Council and sited at the University of Portsmouth. Photography: Chris Smart. www.tonyheaton.co.uk/squareinthecircle.htm

everyday social and spatial practices; and to intersect these with what I have termed the parallel universe of architectural discourse.

As well as beginning such a project in Section II, I have also already outlined Titchkosky's valuable work here on the (non-)implementation of accessible toilets at her university and her analysis of the justificatory narratives that perform an assumed willingness to exclude disabled people, whilst agreeing that this is unacceptable. I also have outlined some work examining how disability is implemented or not within architectural education. Disability studies offer many other illustrations of these processes. Lellis (2011) argues, for example, that universities should take on a social leadership role in relation to disability rights but – by examining how one (North American) university responded to the American Disabilities Act in the 1990s – shows that this has not been historically the case. In fact, rather than offering a '"stomping ground" for advocacy, equality, and activism' (Lellis 2011: 809) universities became just one of the many public and private institutions that have struggled to implement accessibility, and where it was precisely the perceived 'difficulty' of access that shaped how disability was discussed, rather than any wider concerns with discrimination or inequality.

As already outlined in relation to the response of the architectural profession to disabled people, accessibility becomes the *problem*, not the solution, which in turn enables it to be downgraded or ignored. This suggests that we also urgently need more alternative forms of analysing architecture *itself* as a particular form of professional organization, with a specific repertoire of practices and discourses. Besides some basic data on the number of disabled people within the UK profession (Manley *et al.* 2011) this area remains seriously under-researched. There is thus much more mapping still to do.

8 Strategies and tactics

This chapter explores different ways of working for architects and others involved in the shaping of our material landscapes, beyond relying on conforming to regulatory requirements and accessibility guidance. It looks at some innovative ways of engaging with disability in architectural education and practice that neither limits it to the 'special needs' category nor avoids it, by blurring it within a more generalized rubric about designing for 'everyone'. It offers some examples of educational and architectural projects that have done dis/ability differently; for example, by examining how buildings and spaces mark out difference, and by working with disabled people in innovative and creative ways. Finally, it looks at how to re-connect dis/ability with other central architectural issues, particularly sustainability, by bringing human occupancy and social inequality 'back' into the heart of the subject. As with the previous chapter, the examples offered here are neither exhaustive nor comprehensive. The intention is to suggest different kinds of architectural thinking by starting from dis/ability as a means of generating constructive and creative opportunities and debate, not to provide a solution to a 'problem'.

> **The space of a tactic is the space of the other.**
>
> (de Certeau 2011 : 37)

It should also be noted that both strategies and tactics are seen as potential opportunities to act on dis/ability. Michel de Certeau, in *The Practice of Everyday Life* (2011), locates strategies at the level of governmental, corporational and institutional power and tactics as moments of creative resistance by ordinary people, by the subjugated. This book does not divide the world so securely into binary oppositions between oppressors and oppressed. Just as disability and ability are ambiguously fluid, so too are our ongoing, variable positionings in relation to everyday social and spatial practices; we are not just abled or disabled as fixed identities, but enabled or disabled, perpetuating or challenging inequalities, dependent on situation and context. What de Certeau reminds us, though, is that both strategies *and* tactics cannot operate either 'from new' or from 'outside' existing everyday social and spatial practices, but will always be in *relation* to those practices as moments of continuation, adaption, challenge and transformation. Change thus occurs through the accumulation of many such 'moments', both defensive and opportunistic, as we act to intervene in the spaces between the 'normal' rules and products that already exist in culture, which shape us, but do not determine us.

Building on the best inclusive design

Whilst this book focuses on how to go beyond the framing of disability and architecture through the narratives of accessibility, it remains essential to recognize, and learn from, the huge amount of good design practice in inclusive design. As David Bonnett, Principal of David Bonnett Associates (DBA), notes, the historical shifts forced by disability activism in the UK since the 1970s have resulted in a commitment in many places to well-designed and accessible buildings. He gives the Athletes' Village (now East Village) and the Queen Elizabeth Olympic Park in London as an illustration, part of the original bid to make the 2012 Olympic and Paralympic games 'the most accessible Games ever' (Text Box 8.1, Plate 14). Without exception, the 2,500-plus flats in the development were all designed to Lifetime Home standards, which allow flexibility for change, and around 10 per cent of the units are designed to meet the needs of wheelchair users. The sheer scale of this project, the commitment to accessibility throughout the process (including legacy planning) and the comprehensive approach from transport links through to internal design standards make it an important example. The 2013 National Paralympic Day and Liberty Festival enabled disabled artists to both celebrate and interact with the newly re-opened Park (Figure 8.1).

Text Box 8.1 David Bonnett on the impact of the 2012 London Olympics on accessible design

The UK has a reputation for innovation in the design of new towns and more recently the design of accessible buildings and public spaces.

The breakthrough for accessible buildings was legislation passed in the 1970s and 80s that led to the requirement for accessible public buildings (Regulations). This innovation, exclusive to just a few countries in the world, allowed further UK legislation in the mid-1990s (the Disability Discrimination Act or DDA) to call for even greater accessibility than before.

This applied over time to all public buildings (without exception) and even to public transport. However, it did not apply to our public spaces, streets and roads, parks and squares. These have been slow to follow, but the Olympic Village and Park, built in East London for the 2012 Olympics moved things on. It is the first large-scale development to comprehensively deliver on access, with inclusive design a key consideration from the outset.

Every single flat and house is designed and built to be accessible; all the roads and pavements including street parking too. So also the local school, theatre and health centre, the local shopping centre, railway station – in fact, everything. Furthermore a proportion of the homes are designed for wheelchair users, available on all levels (not just on the ground floor), all sizes and (cleverly) indistinguishable from their neighbouring dwellings.

Anyone, more or less regardless of disability, can live a fulfilling life here, go to the local school, shop or catch a train to London, or onward even to Paris and Brussels. The challenge now is for disabled Londoners and their families to know what's on offer and check it all out!

Olympic Village, London 2012 (now East Village). Photography: David Holt London www.flickr.com/photos/zongo/7683085900) (CC-BY-SA-2.0 (http://creativecommons.org/licenses/by-sa/2.0), via Wikimedia Commons.

Other architects, particularly those working within heritage, museums and galleries where public accessibility is increasingly well embedded, have also been developing an elegant and well-mannered repertoire of interventions over many years.

For example, the Royal Festival Hall's 2007 refurbishment by Allies and Morrison involved the comprehensive restoration and reconfiguration of the auditorium and foyers, and a new public face to the River Thames (Figure 8.2). As Stephen Bayley has written:

> the majority of their work is a highly ambitious but very subtle rehabilitation of the 1951 original. It is unusual in a normally egomaniacal architectural profession for a leading firm to dedicate itself to such patient revision of someone else's work. I asked Graham Morrison what visitors will

Figure 8.1 Marc Brew and Rachel Gadsden, *Cube of Curiosity*. Performance at Liberty Festival, Queen Elizabeth Olympic Park, September 2013. Photography: Hamish Roberts.

> notice: 'First impression will be of a restored clarity,' he said. 'The recovered transparency of the main foyer will remind everyone of the concept of the egg of the auditorium raised up in a box. The new works are not radical: they simply help reveal the original design.'
>
> (Bayley 2007)

As David Bonnett also notes:

> The process of achieving improved access and inclusive design during the refurbishment works involved close collaboration with the Access Group over many years. The result and improvements include new shops and restaurants outside the building and less clutter internally, making the internal circulation and wayfinding easier for everyone. There are new step-free entrances into the building, with power-assisted doors, a new internal glass lift and step-free access to almost all internal areas both for the public and at back-of-house.
>
> Within the Auditorium, the acoustics have been greatly improved, the seating has been reorganised to provide more legroom and the accessibility of the seats has been increased significantly. There is now a choice of spaces for more than 32 wheelchair users and 345 'easy-access' seats reached by only 1–2 steps from the Foyer.
>
> (www.davidbonnett.co.uk)

Figure 8.2 Exterior detail, Royal Festival Hall London refurbishment, Allies and Morrison with DBA 2007. Photography: Fæ (CC-BY-SA-3.0 (http://creativecommons.org/licenses/by-sa/3.0)), via Wikimedia Commons.

(Precedent) studies allow us to look at architecture holistically and within a specific context, and take away lessons that can inform our future design thinking.

(Studio H 2010)

It is worth asking here why such projects do not feature as useful architectural precedents offering a wealth of both strategic 'overviews' and detailed tactics; in a similar way to which other buildings and built elements often inform new design projects. Other architects' practices have designed projects using participatory methods with disabled clients and users. A project by Architype for Wolverhampton City Council (2011) has brought together a special school for 4-to-19-year-olds with a mainstream primary school. The aim was to transform 'the school's determination to create a happy, safe place for these children into a welcoming, light-filled, easily navigable building. A simple coherent plan allows easy circulation around the building, with shared facilities located in a central linear zone' (www.architype.co.uk/page3). Overall, though, the aim is to use the same form for both schools, so as to give equivalence rather than separation between them (Text Box 8.2, Plate 13).

Text Box 8.2 Mark Lumley, Associate Director, Architype Architects on the Willows School, Wolverhampton, UK

The Willows became an exceptional project for a number of reasons; a major one being the enhancement to the design process that was brought about by a well-funded Arts Programme that ran concurrently with the consultation and the evolution of the schematic design. We were very lucky to find Zoe Partington-Sollinger to work with us as an Arts Coordinator, who brought a wealth of contacts from the arts world. Importantly for a project that co-joined a specialist school – accommodating a wide range of disabilities – with a single form primary school, she drew on a group of artists that had experience of inclusive practice; enabling all the children to participate in a diverse range of workshops. This included work with filmmakers, performance artists, sculptures, historians, visual artists, and we plugged ourselves in as architects.

The aim right from the beginning with this programme was to engage the school communities in the process of change and transformation that would be manifest in their new building. Through early consultation we understood that this move could be particularly traumatic for some of the children who need stability and constancy in their physical environment. We also wanted to use the arts funding to enrich and extend the children and staff's experiences that would influence the finished building and what went in it. For example, the mounted wall poem is situated at a central point in the new school, the results of the work of the artist Ruth Sparke. The loose letters and Makaton symbols are set on a magnetic strip, allowing the children to write their own words. Ruth was one of the artists who played a pivotal role in bringing the two school communities together, through the running of joint workshops with the children and teachers.

In this process, architects have learnt about alternative ways of thinking about and doing dis/ability. When Ash Sakula worked directly with Graeae Theatre, the client, Jenny Sealey, said:

> together we found possibly the most inaccessible buildings – an old disused boiler house in the midst of London Metropolitan University. Their designs made me realise that access is always possible and it can be beautiful, theatrical and dignified. The whole process was extraordinary but unfortunately the University pulled out. The learning we gained in terms of access as a concept, a necessity and a starting point will stay with us all.
> (http://ashsak.com/?page_id=2165)

Whilst Cany Ash, a partner in architectural practice Ash Sakula, has commented:

> It was fun working with a group who were looking at how different people approach space rather than one size fits all. We made friends with tiny people who were brilliant actors and deaf people with a fantastical sense of humour. You say, well of course, but working alongside an extreme variety of people gives you that first hand personal experience and it allows you to escape the PC attitudes and see the real relativity and complexity of all human ability, the challenges and talents that might be less obvious outside the theatre context but are still there. We talked about the ambience of spaces which is not talked about nearly enough for spaces that are not expensive restaurants. How would that make you feel? That was a common question when looking at the various corners of the design.
>
> (Cany Ash, email exchange, August 2013)

There are also fine examples of architecture *starting from* disability, where disabled people have been integral to the development of the programme. Gallaudet University, in Washington DC, was the first school for the advanced higher education of Deaf and hard-of-hearing people in the world and is still the only higher education institution in which all programmes and services are centred on Deaf and hard-of-hearing students. It is bilingual, using both American Sign Language and English in all classes. A group of Gallaudet students, with Hansel Bauman of HBHM architects, developed the concept of DeafSpace, initially as part of a taught course at the university that guided the design of a new building on the campus, the James Lee Sorenson Language and Communication Center (SLCC). This enabled students to act as designers, articulating 'the fundamentals of space as it relates to their unique sensibilities' (www.gallaudet.edu/campus_design/deafspace.html). This led not just to the design and development of the SLCC, but also a set of DeafSpace Design Guidelines (www.hbhmarchitecture.com/index.php?/ongoing/deaf-space-design-guide) for application across other projects:

> It has since propelled the renovation plans for a residence hall, steered a proposed 'innovation lab' beside the Gallaudet campus, and inspired collaborations with other students of function-focused design concepts. Bauman said that Gallaudet has embarked on a 'radically inclusive process' that brings the University community into the planning process at every step.
>
> (Gallaudet University 2009)

As Robert Sirvage, a graduate of the Department of American Sign Language and Deaf Studies' master's programme at Gallaudet, who was a member of the original DeafSpace class, puts it:

> We wanted to get away from learned behavior and see how our physical sensibility shapes our cultural experience as we make connections with

> space and navigate through it. That it is where DeafSpace principles come into picture as a guide for design with the intention of producing forms that will encompass and enrich it.
>
> (ibid.)

The designers of the SLCC, SmithGroup, then created five basic aesthetic principles to complement DeafSpace principles around space, light, form, composition and materiality, aiming to create a place that would 'celebrate the natural condition of deafness and incorporate the community'. The interior provides full visual access to each part of the building and the outdoors, and ease of navigation, using glass walls, open spaces and curves. The length and placement of the building also helps to link together other parts of the campus.

A yellow ball bounces down the steps . . ., out the door, and rolls across Hanson Plaza. Gaining momentum, it careens down the . . . sidewalk and takes a turn at the Hall Memorial Building, cutting a trail across campus. The ball symbolizes a Gallaudet student, but it is more accurate to say that it represents any deaf person, whose language and culture are best suited to an environment that, like the ball, is spherical and free flowing.

(Bryd 2007)

The students also argued for circular and open rather than rectilinear and enclosed forms, which they juxtaposed as 'maluma' rather than 'takete' type spaces:

> Space that comprises free flowing, circular movements is associated with the anthropological term 'maluma', which conjures up images of a soft, flowing aesthetic – the essence of deaf language and culture. The opposite of maluma is 'takete', a rigid, sharp, angular aesthetic. When designing homes for a hearing person, for example, the architect is conscious of the desire to create walls that enclose space – takete – which translates into a feeling of security. But in performing the same task for a deaf person, for example, the architect needs to be cognizant of the desire for visual access, which means less walls, and in their place 'implied enclosures' – maluma. This can be accomplished through designing partial walls that are less than floor-to-ceiling height, or using building materials such as clouded glass as an alternative to brick, concrete, or drywall to create rooms that afford privacy yet preserve a sense of openness.
>
> (Byrd 2007)

An alternative diagramming?

The fact that critical engagement with examples such as these – either strategically or at the level of detail – is not part of the 'normal' architectural practice of learning from precedents illustrates just how deeply embedded is the 'inclusion by exclusion' of dis/ability in architectural design education and practice. Similarly, and as I have already noted in Chapter 2, the 'location' of accessibility in the bundle of activities most usually at the end of the design process – technical specifications, detailing, regulatory compliance, costing adjustments – and the continuing tendency for practicalities and detail to be less valued than conceptual frameworks (except in specific cases, as discussed in Chapter 5) also continues to associate disability with the more 'inferior' end of architectural design practices.

Next, then, I want to briefly explore what might happen to many of the conventional practicalities of inclusive design if they were to be better embedded within the design process, rather than tacked on the end. I noted in Chapter 4 how architectural designing often differentiates between (and deals differently with) situated programmatic concerns on the one hand, and the generation of an underlying approach and method on the other. With more recent interest in 'diagramming' (Eisenman 1999, Vidler 2000, Garcia 2010) these divisions are being re-thought and re-arranged. Diagrams are used in design practice as a means to extract ideas from the multiple properties and tendencies of all aspects of architecture – its materials, spatial arrangements and/or structural combinations. This is both analytic and a modelling technique. Building design becomes the practice of various processes of selection and combination, aiming at realizing a set of conditions and/or potentialities:

> The diagram is an invisible matrix, a set of instructions, that underlies – and most importantly organizes – the expression of features in any material construct. The diagram is the reservoir of potential that lies at once active and stored within an object or environment (or in any aggregate or section of these). It determines which features (or affects) are expressed and which are saved.
>
> (Reiser and Umemoto 2006: 12–13)

However, whilst there is general agreement that diagramming as a method needs to move beyond the representational and metaphorical to instead investigate underlying processes[1] *what* is analysed can vary hugely – as Vidler writes:

> this tendency is exhibited on every level of meaning associated with the term diagrammatic, and runs the gamut of a wide range of approaches and

1 Reiser and Umemoto (2006) suggest an example of this. They see a shift from Le Corbusier's aesthetic analogy between object and function through the image of the streamlined car, to its processes and their creative and energy potentials; that is, through ideas instead about the internal combustion engine.

styles that at first glance seem entirely disparate – from diagrammatic caricature to theoretical discourse, modernist revival to digital experiment.

(Vidler 2000: 2)

I suggest that the new diagramming tends to concentrate on compositional form-making, whether through digital modes of generation – as with the architects discussed in Chapter 6 – or through more traditional typological descriptions, the kind of exposing of 'traces' as famously theorized by Eisenman in his *Diagram Diaries* (1999).

Operating between form and word, space and language, the diagram is both constitutive and projective; it is performative rather than representational.

(Vidler 2000: 6)

What then could be the effects of intersecting dis/ability and diagramming as a way of modelling space, especially when digital technologies open up to analysis the dynamic (and generative) relationships between people, movement, behaviours, time and space? Here, I can only make a few suggestions of what kinds of relationships might be modelled, by aiming to capture some key entanglements between bodies, material landscapes and everyday social and spatial practices, that also – crucially – include interrogation of architecture's own assumptions and fashions. I start with what might be called 'levelling up and widening out' that is, finding ways of mapping and analysing material space starting from a disability perspective, to reveal its assumptions of ordinary mobility.

The fact of the matter is that disability access is usually an afterthought. Even for a lot of disabled people. Well, for me anyway. Despite having the balance and grace of a toddler and using a walking stick around 50% of the time, access issues never enter my pretty little head until I come across somewhere inaccessible. Even then it sometimes takes landing on my ass to remind me.

(Dave Watson, *So What is Normal* website comment)

Alternative diagramming is not be about designing 'solutions'. Instead it is a means to open up to proper notice and consideration the complexities, ambiguities and unevenness produced through the interactions between architecturally designed space and everyday social and spatial practices. For example, a project by artist Tony Heaton (1989) installed a timber bar measuring 28" × 2" × 1" with the words 'Wheelchair Entrance' on it with two hanging ropes. His intention was to literally map into space the different 'shapes' of movement; and to make a commentary on the assumptions built into the

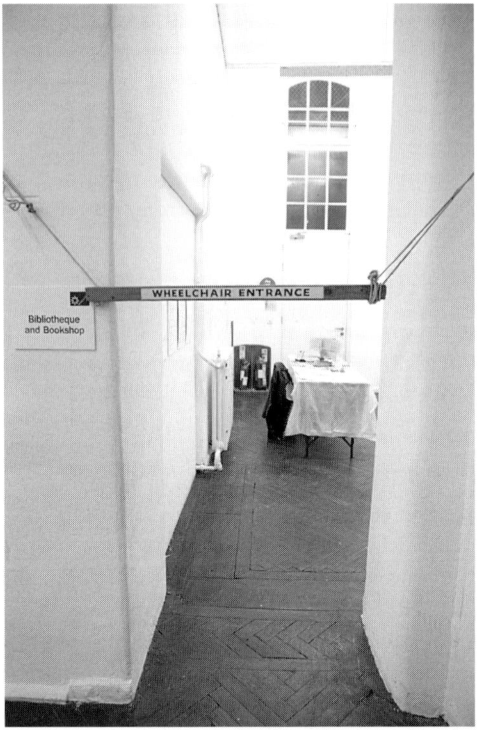

Figure 8.3 Tony Heaton, *Wheelchair Entrance sculpture/Intervention* (1989). www.tonyheaton.co.uk/wheelchair_entrance.htm

everyday sizes and shapes of material space The piece was designed to hang in a doorway at a height that will impede ambulant people but give clear access underneath it to wheelchair users (Figure 8.3).

Another analytical possibility lies in what could be called 'public care'. Where are the moments that act to support diverse bodies as we go about our ordinary lives – from door handles, to handrails, to places to sit, to public facilities? What kind of diagramming might investigate sequences of such moments within public buildings and spaces? There is already a considerable amount of work exploring the social and spatial practices of bathrooms and toilets, for example (Cavanagh and Ware 1990, Shove 2003a, Knight and Bichard 2011, Penner 2013), to show how changing ideas about hygiene, privacy and cleanliness have affected the provision and design of such facilities. How, then, could contemporary assumptions 'built into' public toilet design, that indicate their relative unimportance, and functional and clinical framing, be unravelled diagrammatically? What is the 'fashion' that demands vacant/engaged locks to be so discreet and invisible, rather than large, exuberant and graphically strong? Why is the paraphernalia required in each cubicle always treated as an

Figure 8.4 Signage in public toilet illustrating the ambiguousness of equipment categorized by different user groups. Photography: Jos Boys.

afterthought? How can we open up the social and spatial assumptions around what 'normal' or 'accessible' toilets should be like, and which currently insists these are different and separate spaces, despite the much more blurry relationships of diverse bodies to this activity (Figure 8.4)?

Another project refuses to accept the 'normal' categorization of older people, as relatively incapable. Ageing Facilities is initiated and managed by Sophie Handler, with support and funding from the RIBA/ICE McAslan Bursary and the Arts and Humanities Research Council UK. It describes itself as 'an alternative urban research initiative that actively explores different ways of "making space" for older age'. One of its current projects is called *Resistant Sitting* and looks at different ways of sitting in public places:

> Based on 6 months' worth of repeat visits to a pensioner's lunch club in Canning Town [London] the project locates those spaces (low walls, commercial seating, borough-wide bollards) that are regularly appropriated by the elderly as informal, ad hoc seats where standard street furniture is not available.
>
> A series of conversations in the lunch club identify the location and use of these spaces (past and present) revealing, in turn, an articulate knowledge

> of public space as it meets up with the changing physical and psychological needs of older age. The otherwise invisible 'use' of these alternative sitting spots is mapped out and made visible as a useable borough-wide resource (uploaded onto a dedicated Ageing Facilities website and recorded in an ongoing video project animating these sitting spots).
>
> Here, the smallest of everyday, ordinary acts (sitting down) reveals a resourcefulness and adaptive capacity of the changing-ageing body that challenges stereotypes of elderly need and passivity (that is dependent on provision), and reveals instead a quiet form of generational defiance and active resistance to public provision for the elderly.
>
> (Handler 2010)

By perceiving older people not as passive and frail but as creative – even potentially subversive – transformers of existing material landscapes, the work of Ageing Facilities playfully shows up gaps and opportunities in ways of thinking and doing architecture, built on what has also been emphasized here – a design engagement with the everyday work involved in surviving in, and making sense of, the world (Plate 11, Figure 8.5).

Other areas for exploration could be around buildings as communication devices, that is, in the array of visual and aural patternings across space (light, shadow, colour, decoration, sound, informational encounters). This would need to critically intersect, for example, ideas around DeafSpace with the designerly

Figure 8.5 Ageing Facilities *Resistant Seating* Project: 'Portable Cushion'. Photography: Verity-Jane Keefe.

tensions between 'clarity' and 'intensity', and between and across various architectural enthusiasms and fashions (for example, in the modernist restraints of monochrome and more recent tendencies towards using colour on surfaces). It would also need to more deeply investigate not only the ambiguities between diverse bodily perceptions and experiences (as a way of illuminating design decision-making rather than generating over-simplified design guidance) but also contradictions and overlaps in what kinds of spaces suit what kinds of bodies. At Gallaudet University, for example, ramped walkways turned out to also work for Deaf people:

> A ramp for wheelchair users leads to a second-floor entrance, lending barrier-free access to deaf people walking while engrossed in conversation. The ramp is symbolic of the 'third person' in deaf culture – typically, when three deaf people walk together, two converse while the third acts as a guide, looking out for obstacles and charting the course.
>
> (Byrd 2007)

Finally, I suggest that in mapping morphological and typological patternings of architectural space interwoven with both dis/ability and everyday social and spatial practices, we need to investigate *generosities* – that is the differential provision of location, amount and types of spaces for different activities, the ways in which certain ways of being and acting are privileged over others; and thus, the particular moments and places where creative interventions could make a big change for the least noticed in society. As before this is not a simple matter of oppression, but a complex unravelling of how socio-spatial inter-relationships are or could be played out. J. Kent Fitzsimons in his review of both Koolhaas's villa at Bordeaux and Peter Eisenman's *Memorial to the Murdered Jews of Europe* in Berlin (2012) offers an example of how diagramming might be used as a questioning mechanism – as an opening-up to creative tensions – rather than just a development tool, when architectural discourses and dis/ability are intersected. As he notes, the Eisenman project, made up of over 2,700 stelae or concrete slabs of different heights, organized on an orthogonal grid, was targeted by disability activists as 'discrimination against people with disabilities for purely formal reasons'. As Fitzsimons adds, 'Disability rights organizations judged particularly distasteful that a memorial dedicated to some of Nazi Germany's victims be inaccessible to those who share the physical traits of other victims' (2012: 250). Eisenman's diagramming method for the Memorial (2006) builds from the relations between the repetitive elements, the formal grid and the idea of time. He argues that rather than a monument that is 'looked at', as a static representation, the Memorial aims to become just of itself:

> In this monument there is no goal, no end, no working one's way in or out. The duration of an individual's experience of it grants no further understanding, since understanding is impossible. The time of the

> monument, its duration from top surface to ground, is disjoined from the time of experience.
>
> (Eisenman in Cassara 2006: 154, quoted in Fitzsimons 2012: 252)

But as Fitzsimons shows, not only does this also make invisible what has not been thought through diagramming, but it also fails to address assumed divisions between disability as access, and the 'experiencing' body within the work. When it came to the Tribunal, these unresolved complications resulted in the odd decision that 'at least 13 of the 130 paths traversing the site would have to meet the accessibility code'. As Fitzsimons goes on:

> Why not more, or all? The Tribunal argued that too much modification would harm the work's 'artistic concept'. The court apparently noted that the paths are not simply functional elements that provide access to the memorial. [But] if the paths do not function as access to the memorial, they do not fall under the provisions of the law. But it is precisely because of their narrow and undulating nature that they *are* the work, rather than merely its access route. In other words, it is by not meeting accessibility norms that the paths are excused from their application.
>
> This strange bit of reasoning, whereby a path is not a path, betrays some interesting design principles. In particular, it creates a distinction between a path as access and path as substance. Eisenman's memorial is an extreme case where there seems to be full coincidence between circulation and sense, between movement and meaning. But the Court's statement implies precisely that, normally, there is a distinction. It opposes two sets of terms: on one hand, access-circulation-functionality, and on the other hand, experience-substance-meaning . . .
>
> We might ask if any one path best produces this divergence between perception and concept or if, on the contrary, any path makes it manifest as well as any other. More radically, we might wonder if one must pass by each of the two thousand stelae, on all four sides, from every possible arriving itinerary, to every possible departing itinerary, in order to realize the work's meaning, its potential, to experience it in an appropriate way for it to be the memorial that it is. Since it is practically impossible for any one person to exhaust the possibilities, the meanders, the turning in circles, the disorientation, is the Berlin Memorial really fully accessible to anyone?
>
> (Fitzsimons 2012: 252)

Both the Tribunal ruling and Eisenman's original design thus open up important critical and creative questions around what is being thought and modelled through architectural space when it comes to dis/ability. This suggests a potential shift in what we *ask* of our diagrams:

> Bringing disability into architecture usually raises the question: Can everyone, including those with mobility or sensory impairments, experience

> this building? The Berlin Memorial helps formulate a different question: To what modes of experience does this architecture lend itself? Or, to paraphrase Kristeva: What ways of being does it anticipate and realize?
>
> (Fitzsimons 2012: 254)

(Re)freshing tactics: starting from dis/ability

Starting from disability means not imposing assumptions about what disabled people are like, or want, but, as already said, taking notice of the diversity of narratives and strategies. At the same time, we need new ways of working that engage with disabled people in co-designing spaces; not only on a case-by-case basis, but also through projects which enable creative and constructive involvement with how dis/ability and architecture can be better interwoven. The group Architecture-InsideOut (AIO), mentioned in Chapter 7, is an Arts Council South East funded project bringing together architects with disabled artists to explore innovative new ways of designing buildings and spaces which improve the built environment for everyone. Its mission is 'to promote activity that develops and captures models of new practice for the built environment, led by the creativity and experiences of disabled and Deaf artists' (Figure 8.6). The group aims to do this by:

- enabling creative and constructive collaborations between disabled artists, architects, educators and related agencies;

Figure 8.6 Caroline Cardus explores the Turbine Hall, at part of an AIO event, Tate Modern, 10 May 2008. Photography: Jos Boys.

- capturing, publicizing and debating the best work so as to continually inform current and future practices;
- developing the capacities of disabled artists, so as to make an impact on the built environment by improving the accessibility and quality of public spaces.

(www.architecture-insideout.co.uk/?location_id=28)

Architecture-InsideOut has run a number of events, for example a one-day intensive design charrette in the Turbine Hall at Tate Modern London, involving groups of architects and disabled artists working together, called *Opening Up 1*. The eight teams[2] responded to a brief that asked them to make an intervention based on the motto 'enter this place that is a joy to us'. Groups responded in a variety of ways. One performed a 'security detail' that used mobile barriers to block or channel incoming visitors in unexpected or confusing ways. Another made a critique of the gallery's Changing Places facilities that although a recent and very valuable addition to the other accessible toilets nonetheless has a clinical 'non-designed' interior, the only space in the whole of Tate Modern to be treated in that way. The group deliberately and excessively decorated it. Another, entitled 'How many ways can U get from A2B?', used the main entrance slope to celebrate the variety of forms of mobility (Plate 6). There were also experimentations in playfulness, turning the space momentarily into a giant playground (Figure 8.7). This was a means of expressing and enjoying childishness, so as to both creatively reverse its often patronising use in labelling disabled people, and to see both space and disabled people as active and energetic. The event wanted to experiment with alternative ways of architects and disabled people coming together, as a means of capturing and generating different design modes beyond 'accessibility' (Figure 8.8).

One spin-off from these events was the creation of a prototyping project for the London Festival of Architecture (LFA) in July 2010. Matthew Lloyd Architects, together with Tony Heaton, disabled artist and SHAPE Director, the Royal Engineers and RIBA London developed a temporary proposal for making an important set of public steps accessible. Not being able to use the historic site of the Duke of York Steps (running between The Mall and Waterloo Place near Lower Regent Street in London) makes for much longer journeys for everyone. The test rig, which was built and used during the festival, was a solar

2 Participants at AIO Tate Modern were artists Jon Adams, Chris Ankin, Rubbena Aurangzeb, Sue Austin, Caroline Cardus, Lynn Cox, David Dixon, Stephanie Fuller, Sabine Gruhn, Tony Heaton, Joolz Cave Berry, Noëmi Lakmaier, Barbara Lisicki, Melissa Mostyn, Zoe Partington-Sollinger, Sarah Pickthall and Aaron Williamson. Architects were from Architype, Anne Thorne Architects, Ash Sakula Architects, AOC, Fluid, Architectureplb, Sarah Wigglesworth Architects, Matthew Lloyd Architects, Avanti Architects, HLM Architects and Robert Barnes Architects. The Tate was represented by Marcus Dickey Horley. Chris Higgins and Martin Gent from Map Consortium acted as facilitators, Gwen Webber and Mandy Legg provided additional support, and Rachel Gadsden, Abigail Norris and Joseph Young undertook process capture.

Figure 8.7 *Balls!* One of a series of performances exploring disability through playfulness, Turbine Hall, Tate Modern, London by Architects Architype and disabled artists Caroline Cardus and Joolz Cave Berry, as part of Arts Council South East funded Architecture-InsideOut event (AIO), 10 May 2008. Photography: Jos Boys.

Figure 8.8 Rachel Gadsden capturing the process during the AIO Tate Modern event, 10 May 2008. Photography: Jos Boys.

and water-powered lift, making it both sustainable and not reliant on a fallible power supply. Its main aim was to celebrate (rather than hide) improved access by designing a device that is enjoyable for everyone to use, deliberately slowing the 'rush' of everyday Londoners whilst making things much easier for those with limited mobility (or with pushchairs or bicycles), and giving everyone an opportunity to take time to enjoy their surroundings.

Matthew Lloyd Architects worked with disabled artist Tony Heaton and the Royal Engineers to develop a lift proposal that uses water tanks to counterbalance body-weight. As people enter the lift additional water is added, so as to make them 'heavy enough' to go down. Renewable energy from solar panels is then used to pump water back to refill the system. The lift allows people to enjoy the view, whilst hearing and seeing water flowing and gurgling around them.

Unlike many access projects, this proposal aimed to take centre stage on its historic site, organized centrally and on an axis with the column and statue at the top of the steps, rather than hidden as a side entrance or some other more discreet location. At the same time, it is sensitive to the location because it does not require extra fittings, and therefore does not damage the existing fabric. The towers act as a beacon to highlight a major route and to celebrate the importance of universal access, whilst the mechanical elements of the lift are on display so that people will be able to decipher how it works (Figure 8.9, Plate 10).

Figure 8.9 Tony Heaton, Matthew Lloyd and Will Alsop use the prototype Water Lift, London Festival of Architecture 2010. Photography: Jos Boys.

David Gissen is an architectural historian, theorist and critic who also intervenes in this critical and creative space, to open up assumptions within architectural practice and discourse about dis/ability. As part of his history, theory and criticism (HTC) experiments series at California College of the Arts, Gissen has made a design proposition that challenges architecture's own knowledge base about itself and about its history. He re-inserts disability differently, into a reconstruction project for the Acropolis in Athens. He shows both the nineteenth-century path to the top and the current access route, as being set in their own time – one aiming to capture a deeply romantic and nationalist notion of the journey as deliberately difficult, and the other to meet the needs of disabled people. He argues instead that a sixth-century BC path should be re-instated, one that provides a ceremonial ramp from the base to the top of the Acropolis (Plate 17, Text Box 8.3). He thus re-maps both our assumptions about 'inclusive design' and the history of architectural interpretations of this site:

> Virtually every project or text on disability and architecture is envisioned in either a medical context or brings a medical sensibility to existing spaces. This has two important effects: This makes disability into something that is seen as a clinical condition versus a category of thought – a way of seeing and being seen in the world. This also has the curious effect of eliminating the presence of disability from a deep and longer engagement with history, particularly the history of architecture. Disability, while a modern term, is not a contemporary category absent from pre-modern life.
>
> (Gissen 2013)

Text Box 8.3 Excerpt from 'Reconstructing the Acropolis Ramp' by David Gissen (2013)

The path to the summit of the Acropolis might be one of the most famous in the history of architecture. The arduous climb up a winding walkway has been written about by architects from Le Roy to Le Corbusier.

In the 19th century, various poets, artists and philosophers praised the difficult walk up as an act of personal and historical discovery. The acropolis ascent achieved its significance at this time because it embodied the aesthetics of Romanticism, which simultaneously celebrated the discovery of ruins and sensations of physical duress. The pressures of historical time and the lived time of a perceiving subject became conjoined.

In the 1950s the path was remade into a marble-stone lined walk by the Greek architect Dimitris Pikionis – a construction that related to the revived nationalistic ambitions of the post-war Greek state, rooted in a return to Hellenism.

Other, more minor paths have spun out of Pikionis'. Of these, the most recent is a special route for the disabled. Responding to repeated criticism of the inaccessibility of the site, the organization that oversees the Acropolis built a wheelchair accessible path to the north that terminates in a modified construction elevator. The elevator accommodates one person and scales the side of the Acropolis, going up to the summit.

We would like to enter into this three-hundred-year consideration of the Acropolis ascent by proposing another route to the top – a reconstruction of the original path to the top that existed here from the 6th century BC to the middle-ages. In the 6th century the government of Athens funded the construction of a massive ramp that connected the outlying areas of the Athenian Agora to the northwest to the top of the Acropolis . . . The now-destroyed ramp is a significant aspect of the history of the Acropolis but unknown to virtually all who come to the site today.

If Pikionis' route positioned a nationalist figure within this robust ascent, a possible remade Acropolis ramp represents the reconstruction of a different, but no less historically constituted public. In contrast to nationalism or romantic athleticism, we see the ramp as a reconstruction of different subjects, of a commons yet to be fully configured – one evocative of the origins of Western concepts of urban citizenry, city space, architecture and its history, but which simultaneously refers to more recent concerns of self-hood.

Revis(it)ing histories

In addition, the history of designs for buildings specifically relating to disability demonstrates extraordinary shifts in typology and form.[3] By looking at these designs we see how society defines the normal citizen and how it chooses to accommodate the individuals that do not fit these criteria. We see that in some periods of history architecture has been instrumental – even central – in constructing visions of society, in incarcerating, segregating and categorizing people because of their differences. The built environment is not simply something that needs to be made accessible or modified for its many different users. It has had (and still has) an active role in shaping that environment, in realizing social policy and legislative change, and in constructing our ideas of who and what is normal.

While it is tempting to imagine that we have moved on from some of the more disturbing designs produced by architects of the past we might also use this historical material to reflect on the current forces, beliefs and legislation which shape our own architectural principles. And by looking at buildings

3 This section was researched and written by Katie Lloyd-Thomas, as part of the CETLD-funded *So What is Normal* Project (SWIN). Many thanks to the staff at the British Architectural Library (BAL) collection at the RIBA for their support in this work.

designed 'for' the disabled, we can also tell a lot about society as a whole, about what constitutes ability as well as disability: about what is viewed as an ideal community; about the place of work; and about what makes for a 'fit' citizen. Looking at the history of disability and architecture thus enables us to look critically at changing concepts, categories and building types.

For example, one of the photographs at the British Architectural Library (BAL) shows what now appears to be a grim classroom in a hostel – 'the first of its kind' – that gave adults with cerebral palsy a chance to study. It was built in the UK in 1965 before the Disability Discrimination Act, before Part M of the Building Regulations and before there were any manuals or standards about design for disability. Then the building was commended for its lack of sentimentality, for its impeccable modernism and use of colour and for the way the built-in furniture was perfectly scaled to suit spaces which were 'a bit bigger than normal' to accommodate the wheelchairs and involuntary 'sometimes quite violent' movements of its residents. We might not agree but, whatever we think of the building, the architect Dennis Pugh and his innovative clients couldn't reach for a manual to find the 'right' solution but had to debate and take their own decisions on questions about the normal body and difference, about inclusion and exclusion, about community and how architecture can define the experiences of its users.

Disability activism, building regulations and anti-discrimination laws have led to shifts that mean many fewer people are incarcerated in institutions, and many different kinds of people and bodies have improved rights to access the built environment. But behind the certainty of the dimensions and diagrams of inclusive design principles and design guidance lie big questions. In another photograph in the BAL collection two men are writing a response to the question chalked on the blackboard – 'What obligation has the state to the social outcast?' Reviewing architecture's own history of buildings for disabled people opens up changing attitudes in a relevant and important way. It's disappointing to note that histories, surveys and appraisals of contemporary buildings, theoretical discussions concerning disability and the built environment are yet to be compiled. But researching 'hidden' parts of architectural history not only opens up issues around disability but also lets us see some glimpses past the usual histories of famous architects and landmark buildings.

The English Heritage-funded *Disability in Time and Place* has made an important start to this process, showing how disabled peoples' lives are integral to the heritage all around us (Figure 8.10). As they say: 'from leper chapels built in the 1100s to protests about accessibility in the 1980s, the built environment is inextricably linked to the stories of disabled people, hidden and well-known'. At the same time, there are 'alternative' histories being compiled that aim to capture the experiences of disabled people themselves. John Walker, a researcher at the Universities of Sussex and Brighton, has worked as part of *Hidden Histories: Intercultural Dialogue (2011–2012)* to capture oral history narratives on Deaf Education in the 1970s. This is part of a larger project funded by the European Union Grundtvig programme

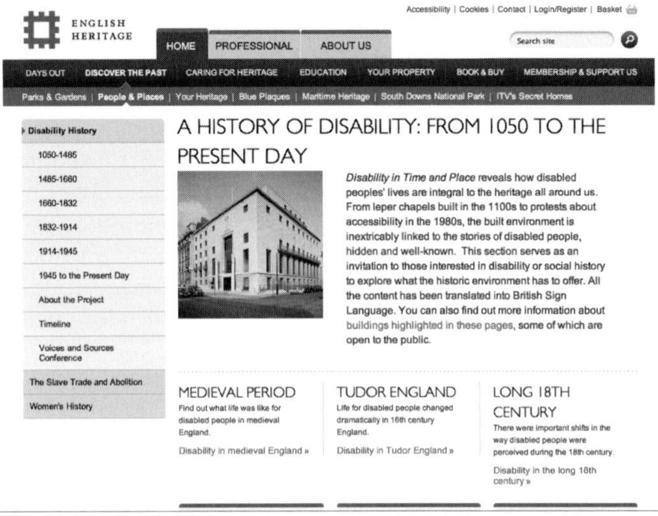

Figure 8.10 Illustration from English Heritage's *Disability in Time and Place* website, www.english-heritage.org.uk/discover/people-and-places/disability-history

that is exploring hidden histories in England, Ireland, Finland and Austria by recording community experiences in rural, nomadic, and Deaf communities (http://hiddenhistories.euproject.org). And artist Liz Crow has been investigating disability history as a way of contextualizing the current experiences of disabled people in Britain (Text Box 8.4).

Text Box 8.4 Excerpt from Liz Crow, '"Strivers not Shirkers": echoes through the century', 4 July 2013, www.roaring-girl.com/blog/strivers-not-shirkers.

I've been at the Bristol Records Office recently, trawling through the archives of The Guild of the Brave Poor Things. One of a network of membership groups for disabled people, the Bristol Guild was founded in 1896 and became the first to have its own purpose built headquarters. Bringing together disabled people in a social space, the Guild lay on entertainment, companionship, training, sales of works and apprenticeships.

Membership was pretty exacting: you needed the right impairment (physical or sensory, visible), and enough of it but not too much. It helped a lot to be male. Most of all though, you needed the right moral character, exhibiting the 'Guild spirit' and signing up to its ideals. Above all, the Guild set out to prevent disabled people from being a burden on society.

As I read the reams of closely written copperplate from almost 120 years ago, the sort of disabled person you needed to be and the drive towards work for independence, wellbeing and morality, feels so very contemporary. I can hear the Coalition [current UK government] mantra echoing through the century: 'Strivers not Shirkers'. Now, as then, the aim is that disabled people should overcome and inspire all the way to economic self-sufficiency. Then, as now, employers were not always keen to be a part of the solution.

And yet there's one critical difference. Then – for all the charitable and tragic overtones – there is a feeling of liberation unfurling. Against a backdrop of poverty, inaccessibility and social exclusion, and long before the welfare state was formed, lives were being transformed. The Guild of the Brave Poor Things was not a self-help group, but certainly it was a place where group identity had a chance to form.

The Bristol Guild (eventually renamed The Guild of the Handicapped) continued right up to 1987 when the building was sold and it re-registered as a charitable trust. The same year, oblivious that the Guild had ever existed, a small group of disabled people held our inaugural meeting for what would become Avon Coalition of Disabled People. We gathered through the generosity of Community Service Volunteers, in the middle of their busy lobby, since Bristol then had not a single public building that was accessible. CSV is just 200 yards up the road from the Guild.

Redefining the normal

Ultimately, these kinds of alternative strategies and tactics are aimed at, first, designing with an integrated understanding of affective and practical experiences for diverse dis/abilities; of challenging the commonsense of ordinary, everyday social and spatial practices; and of resisting and challenging normative attempts to make disabled people invisible or marginal, to treat them as a problematic special case, or just to make them more 'normal'. This is not to forget the essential role of design in enabling our material landscapes to be accessible to disabled people, and the importance of making these improvements. Rather it is about critically and creatively reviewing what are considered everyday social and spatial 'arrangements' in architecture. Ultimately, of course, the aim is re-define what constitutes the normal. In designing the Ramp House in Portobello, Edinburgh, architects Thea Chambers and Ian McMillan designed a house for their own family (Figure 8.11, Plate 12):

> The principle of the ramp house was to design and build a family home for a little girl who is a wheelchair user, where the whole house enables her to lead a barrier-free included life. We are often confronted with the physical barriers that the built environment presents; in our own home we were able to design a fully inclusive place which, by using a ramp to access all levels, provides an equality of space to us all. We have designed spaces along the ramp so that the experience of the house changes as it unfolds.
>
> The difference that the ramp makes is in how the spaces are experienced; this is both linear and sectional, and allows opportunities to look back or forward into other spaces. The ramp contributes both width and height to each of the different pausing places along the way. As we inhabit the house, we can see how this provides variation, complexity and flexibility in the

Figure 8.11 Exterior view of Ramp House, Edinburgh, UK. Chambers McMillan Architects. Photography: David Barbour.

everyday use of the house, how many spaces can be used concurrently and how it reaches its potential when it is inhabited: movement around it, by foot or on wheels brings the experience to life. For a child who cannot move around independently the connectivity of the spaces becomes all the more important; if Greta is in the living room, there are six different spaces that we can be in and move between, and she is still able to see and hear us, and communicate with us.

(www.cmcmarchitects.com/the-ramp-house/our-experience)

Here movement through the space is not separated out as 'accessible circulation' but formally interwoven with both how family life is lived, and with the multiple registers through which we engage with the material world simultaneously. Greta is neither a special case nor an unconsidered 'anyone': she is just one of the members of the family; as she says herself, 'I'm just a very busy eight-year-old and like everyone else, I just need a place which allows me to get on with things.'[4]

Alternative architectural manifestos: Slow Space

Doing Disability Differently has proposed that whilst concepts of accessibility and inclusive design have been very important to improving design of the built environment, they have also obscured as much as they have revealed. Instead (or as well as) we need to find strategies and tactics that can help us do disability and architecture as a (potentially avant-garde) practice that is *deeply embedded* within architecture's own knowledge of, and assumptions about, itself as a creative, professional and socially responsible discipline. Finally in this chapter, I want to outline an alternative manifesto – as a potentially real campaign, as a provocation, and/or simply as an example of a different kind of practice – that is intended to be positive, thought-provoking, useful and resonant to architectural students, tutors and practitioners. Again, the aim is to start from dis/ability but also to open up connections with other important things architects are currently thinking about and responding to.[5] The idea grew out of work with Architecture-InsideOut artists and in the dialogues which supported the *So What is Normal?* (SWIN project). We have called this approach Slow Space. It explores overlaps between and across dis/ability, equality and sustainability (Text Box 8.5). Slow Space is also offered as something of a challenge to that aspect of sustainability in architecture that tends to see nature as an unambiguous category and as a technological fix (see for example Gissen 2000).

4 Greta does not communicate through spoken words (although she understands them); rather her mother Thea tries to communicate with others how she thinks Greta is perceiving things.

5 Conversations between the co-producers of SWIN and artists involved in AIO also began to generate notions about connecting dis/ability with ideas of an 'imperfect' architecture and what might be called Augmentative architecture. However, these ideas have not yet been explored very far; they just indicate possibilities.

Text Box 8.5 David Watson on Slow Space (written as part of the So What is Normal? project)

We live in frenetic times

We work harder and longer than our parents did, spend more time at the office, less time with our loved ones. When we do eventually go home we're checking emails on our laptops, our Blackberries, our iPhones, texting our colleagues while microwaving a pizza. We're never out of touch, always in the loop. We've got Wi-Fi on the trains and cellular phone masts up mountains. Conspicuous consumption, rampant consumerism, runaway recession, information superhighways, instant messaging, fast food, speed reading . . . We're obsessed with speed, bodies in constant motion, racing through life like it's a competition. We're a roadrunner culture and like sharks we have to keep moving.

When exactly did haste become a virtue?

Sometimes you just have to slow down and smell the flowers

Beginning with a protest outside a McDonald's in Rome in the mid-'80s the Slow Movement represents a seismic cultural shift away from consumerism in favour of slowing down life's pace. We've now got Slow Food, Slow Travel, Slow Design, Slow Fashion, Slow Cities (a few of which, ironically, can be found in Norfolk) and Slow Sex. There's even a Slow Email movement which advocates checking your emails just twice a day. The common factor that binds these movements together is their emphasis on time and its reclamation; it's time to slow down, adjust the pace of our lives and savour the day-to-day experience.

Slow Space and disability

For many disabled people though we've no choice but to take life at a slower pace. A mobility or cognitive impairment can mean it takes longer to accomplish tasks than a non-disabled person. I'm 35. I became disabled when I was 21 after a series of strokes. Suddenly I had to rethink my life and radically change pace. Tasks that were second nature suddenly required thought, planning, practice. Mobility and balance impairments meant I had to slow down. It's hard to rush with a walking stick and the natural grace of a toddler. For me, slowing down meant taking more time, taking more care. I learned to appreciate experience, any experience. I was going slow before I even knew there was a movement.

Love the experience

Perhaps one of the most relevant aspects of the Slow Movement for disabled people is the concept of Slow Design. Slow Design focuses more on the individual experience. A longer design process gives the designer more time to research the individual and unique needs of the user, allowing them to test and fine tune. Slow Design tends to make use of local materials and technologies, supporting local industry and craftsmen and it designs for human behaviour, usability and sustainability. Slow Design is patient, innovative, constantly evolving. It's not about speed; it's about thought and deliberation. If something's worth doing, it's worth doing right. And that takes love. The Slow Movement isn't a manifesto for laziness. It's a clarion call to love the experience.

Starting from the notion of Slow contains a deliberate element of 'reclaiming' for disabled people. Slow can too often have negative connotations: that someone is a bit stupid, their movements restricted, laborious and therefore time-consuming, or needing 'support'. In a world which highly values mobility, speed, independence and personal autonomy, slowness is a problem; the response to taking time 'unnecessarily', to needing 'help', is often one of irritation or awkwardness (Chapter 3). This is not to suggest that disabled people are 'slow' or even want to 'go slow'; it is to open up to view the interconnectedness of unthinking abled mobility, instant gratification, the reduction of everyday life to superficial consumed experiences, and the speed at which we are using up planetary resources. The Slow City movement (Cittaslow) grew out of Slow Food festivals in Italy. It was founded in Orvieto in 1999 and has now extended to towns and cities in several European countries, including the UK:

> The Cittaslow Charter has 7 principles and 55 'requirements for excellence'. One central principle is: The goal is to foster the development of places that enjoy a robust vitality based on good food, healthy environments, sustainable economies and the seasonality and traditional rhythms of community life.
>
> (Knox 2005: 1)

Slow Space also extends concerns with sustainability, to make difference – and engaging with difference – central. Like the Hannover Principles (McDonough and Partners 1992), Slow Space has an explicit commitment to diversity, health and well-being, and inter-dependencies. The sustainability agenda must be as much about human resources as natural resources, social inclusion as well as material processes. But this is not just about disability, or only 'for' disabled people. Architecture based on Slow Space would explore what happens both when we enjoy taking time in our lives; and when 'slowing things down' helps us closely, critically and creatively interrogate the particularities of our different social and spatial relationships. Rather than living our lives in a state of (harassed) distraction, where we take the 'normal' for granted and fail to notice other perspectives on the world, living in slow space offers opportunities for new kinds of close looking.

Masa Kajita's 2007 MA project at the Royal College of Art in London was for a proposed health education facility focusing on nutrition to improve the health and lifestyle of residents in Hackney, London (Figure 8.12). Here, then, is an example of 'Slow' action – the design concept emerged in dialogue with the older people and children, and was about allowing time for changing clothes, meals and other activities. The design aims to avoid distinctions between static space and movement space. It is long and thin in form, absorbing level changes through gently sloping floors and generously accommodating differences in experience through programmatic proximities set in layers.

Thinking slowness, then, is simultaneously an attention to detail, sensory clarity and richness, careful thoughtfulness and increased enjoyment in the immediacy and particularities of each moment. It allows time and a heightened awareness, to see the translation work in, and develop a critique of everyday social and spatial practices.

This is also another way of making the ordinary extraordinary – not by making the strange 'familiar' as a means to intensify our relations with the building itself, but to enhance occupancy. It suggests that design can be generated from a deep attention to, and celebration of, our differences – the rich diversity in the ways that our bodies work and the many and various relationships we have to things, spaces and each other. This is architectural design as a kind of craftwork, not just of materials and how they go together and the archetypal (or other) meanings attached. It is about taking time and giving notice to the task of designing for a diverse and sustainable occupancy:

> [Craft] advocates a kind of patient attentiveness, a kind of waiting that is so often derided as a waste of time in an age obsessed with purpose, targets and goals. . . . why is this kind of enduring enthusiasm regarded as 'weird' or 'sad' . . . Have our interests become so undemanding, easily dropped and often put towards another purpose (career, profit)?
>
> (Bunting 2007: 25)

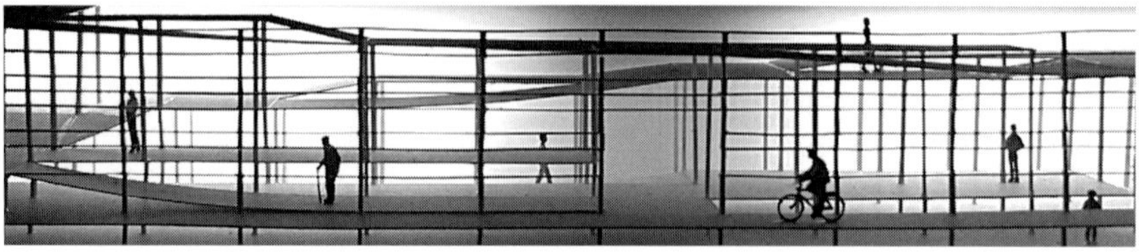

Figure 8.12 Masa Kajita's MA project at the Royal College of Art, 'Action-Rooms'.

Figure 8.13 David Dixon, *Signs of Life* (2008). A site-responsive piece, set in a derelict house, using the long accumulated dust as its material. Part of the Liverpool 2008 Biennale *Three Weeks in November*.

Here, we are proposing that 'crafting' has the potential to be at once highly conceptual and practical – that ideas can be generated from close attentiveness to the detailed quality of inter-relationships and everyday spatial practices (rather than starting from abstract ideas, which are then detailed 'up'). This crafting joins the sensual with the social (Figure 8.13).

It is only at slower speeds that events can be both more carefully observed and more fully lived; that patterns of encounters can be explored and analysed to see if and where some are disadvantaged compared to others. This means not taking everyday small-scale seen but unnoticed practices and encounters 'for granted', as transparent and obvious to 'anyone'. And this kind of attentiveness starts to help develop a critical awareness of difference and its potential for generating creative action. We want architects and other designers to be idealistic and passionate about positively transforming the world, but to remain happily embedded in the messy compromises of everyday life. We want design processes to include the taking of time over creative processes of transformation, via noticing, meeting, sharing, making and interpreting.

Part of this more careful and critical noticing/thinking means being attentive to the gaps, flaws and unintended consequences in our assumptions about what is 'normal'. As I have said before, language connects 'slow' to making mistakes, and to being faulty or inferior – the opposite of 'getting things right'.

Figure 8.14 Ben Cove, *Practical Mechanics*, solo show at Cell Projects, 2006.

But working with inexactness and the beauty of imperfection can offer alternative and interesting ways of thinking about the design of the built environment. Ben Cove, who initially studied architecture and now works as an artist, has used an over-sized version of a pantograph (a simple mechanical tool for enlarging or reducing drawings using a pivot while tracing over the original) to make inherently unstable and inaccurate copies of the plans of famous buildings. The work expresses exactly the impossibility of getting it completely right, and even the pleasures in the human qualities that his more wobbly lines add to the drawings (Figure 8.14).

This kind of slowness is not backward-looking or conservative or lazy. It demands innovative thinking and practice, energy and social engagement. We think that imagining what Slow Space might be like can challenge the thoughtless unevenness that the built environment offers to different people in terms of both functional access and emotional pleasures. It demands that we refuse to continue building barriers to equal participation in society and develop a more equitable and sustainable distribution of resources. Enabling everyone to take time to enjoy and enrich the diversity and difference of experience is a positive and creative aim. Material space costs money and time. It is a limited resource, which benefits some people more than others. We want to be more generous, especially to the people who currently get the least, in terms of our buildings and cities. Slow Space is thus not just about making better spaces for disabled people – although it is also centrally concerned with this – but also about being part of a larger progressive movement.

9 Re-thinking the normal

> Critical disability studies starts with disability but never end(s) with it; disability is *the* space from which to think through a host of political, theoretical and political issues which are relevant to all . . . with a shared opposition to the conditions of disablism and ableism that continue to marginalize disabled people from the everyday realities of social life.
>
> Disability is therefore not a stigmatizing embodiment of an individual but a social portal that leads to an investigation of exclusionary practices in society at large.
>
> (Goodley *et al.* 2012: 4)

Architecture is what is known as a weakly bounded discipline (Cousins 1998); that is, it tends to appropriate its theories from other, 'external' subjects, and then translate them into new shapes that resonate specifically with the practice of building and urban design. In exploring ways to challenge both the ideas and built practices of modernism, for example, radical architects looked to post-modernist theories, both from political economy and semiotics, to 're-discover' architecture as a form of communication and meaning-making. In what was termed deconstruction, this was developed further – and differently – through continuing interactions with linguistics, but also cultural studies, chaos theory and various other approaches which could articulate society as a complex, only partially coherent, fragmented and dynamic entity (Jameson 1991). More recently, theoretical work has moved away from this focus on cultural meaning and its representation, to a new concern with the non-representational (Thrift 2007), both in thinking about affect and examining social and spatial practices rather than 'readings'.

> **It is still not fashionable to be disabled.**
>
> (Goodley *et al.* 2012: 1)

Disability studies has persistently and critically reviewed these changing fashions in theory, in terms of the continuing marginalization and invisibility of disabled people – even in theories of 'other' minorities such as feminism, queer and post-colonial studies. At the same time it is also exploring its own (diverse) attitudes to the role of theory per se with the aim of establishing better theorizing around dis/ability and re-defining its relationship to activist campaigning that can improve the lives of disabled people. Here, then, I will take the opportunity to intersect architecture with different 'external' theories to the ones currently in circulation within the discipline – both disability studies and other recent approaches, particularly from science and technology studies.[1] I will explore some of these contemporary movements in ideas, to see what kinds of conceptualizations about the world can make dis/ability an integral part of design thinking and doing, and not just a problematic 'add-on'.

Re-thinking architecture

In the previous sections I have suggested that most architectural approaches and methods have some inherent flaws that actually prevent the inclusion of diverse occupancy and dis/ability, by locating disability as predominantly to be 'included as excludable'. Several abled everyday narratives and strategies maintain and perpetuate this positioning. First, ordinary commonsense makes it normal and 'storyable' for disabled people to be simultaneously part of the 'anyone' who uses buildings, and to be a separate case, requiring different and specialist treatment. Here is the first gap through which disability disappears. Second, articulating occupancy in building design is centred on a case-by-case and site-specific form of diagnostic investigation, meaning that disability comes to be considered only in its 'special case' locations, that is, on some occasions but not others rather than in every situation or through a set of explicit underlying attitudes. Third, occupancy more generally is often translated via metaphor into the 'body' (form) of the building and its circulation. The lack of a theory of, or method for, interrogating occupancies as integral to architecture means that unconsidered assumptions from the position of ableness continue to inform the discipline's own theory and practice. We have hardly begun to properly explore the inter-relationships between everyday social and spatial practices of dis/ability and building design.

In addition, there is a tendency to understand occupancy as particularly about people's relationship to the building as *architecture* (to be contemplated, experienced through movement and as functional support) rather than, say, architecture as one of many *devices* for enhancing people's everyday lives. This recognizes, but then displaces, the inter-connections between people, encounters, artefacts and spaces, performed through a dynamic and endless coming in and out of focus. Rather than investigating these as having enabling or

1 Science and technologies studies (STS) explore the inter-relationships between scientific research, technological innovation and society. STS starts from the belief that these are inseparable – that societal, cultural and political assumptions and values will affect how science and technology develop, and vice versa.

disabling effects, much architectural design is interested instead only in the specific patterns of distraction and intensity of our engagement with the built form. Finally, a series of thoughtless (that is, not thought about) binary oppositions, with built-in superior–inferior resonances, often artificially separate out experience/abstraction/formal from the function/practical/technical, and make the latter not only banal and trivial but also left to the end of the design process.

Some of these problems are prevalent in social theory and philosophy more generally. For example, definitions of the human subject remain predominantly – and unproblematically – assumed as 'rational', mobile, independent and autonomous. And theories tend to operate either at the level of the individual (as case study) or at the level of society (abstract structures), without any connecting conceptual framework, except a kind of vague circuit of interaction through association, which prevents the disconnect in methods from being obvious or open to critical analysis. At the same time, as I have already noted, the internal discourses of architecture in framing occupancy in general, and disability in particular, seem to operate in a parallel universe to theories from the social sciences (illustrated here by showing the value of existing methods from, for example, ethnomethodology that can offer ways of investigating everyday social and spatial practices, and their differential and discriminatory ways of framing disabled people). Importantly for the argument in this book, that disconnect is nonetheless powerfully reproduced through, and embedded in, existing architectural education and practice, in ways that make it hard to criticize (and as I have already suggested, anxious and defensive in response to a questioning through dis/ability). This has a surprisingly strong *silencing* effect. My initial, stumbling attempts to intersect specific architectural theories with dis/ability in Section II remain (to me) still inarticulate for this reason. When David Gissen juxtaposes what is 'storyable' as an architecture student and what is dis/ordinary in being disabled through his criticism of the Yale Architecture School (Text Box 9.1) he is well aware that such things are not easy to say, that they can be ignored or treated patronizingly as minor and unimportant 'access' issues; that as an insider to architectural discourses, he should not be challenging them through such a 'trivial' means. But he also knows that in intersecting disability and architecture we need to have forms of critique that go beyond an individual's 'difficulties', that can instead help us get at the unspoken assumptions about ableness within architectural theory and practice:

Text Box 9.1 David Gissen, 'Disability as architectural criticism – Yale/Rudolph', 3 October 2008

In 1996 a former architectural history professor of mine at Columbia asked me how I enjoyed being a student at the Yale School of Architecture, particularly how I enjoyed being an inhabitant of Paul Rudolph's

Architecture and Art Building. Like virtually all students who have been in that building, I think the building is an extraordinary feat of design and construction. The building was just renovated, expanded and renamed, and I can't wait to see it.

But as a disabled person my relationship to that building was peculiar, to say the least. It's not just that the building is set over many levels, and many levels on one floor. Navigating the interior spaces and the multiple floor changes and stairs was a pain. The 'floating stairs' everywhere, particularly in the entryway leading to the building's foyer, were particularly difficult to negotiate. What seemed like comedy to my friends, but really just a huge nuisance to me, was, my former professor argued, an avenue to architectural criticism. 'You should write about it,' she said, and now more than ten years later I am.

But it's not just the Rudolph building; I have literally rolled (in a wheelchair), limped and crutched in many 'masterworks' of modern architecture. Here is my not-so-brilliant critical assessment of disability in architecture: Anything that claims to have been inspired by some type of architectural heroism or any building in which someone might describe the architect as 'heroic' (as is virtually always the case with this particular work by Rudolph) will generally impart a bumpy ride for the disabled inhabitant. If I start an architectural tour and someone mentions one of these concepts as the inspiration behind the building, I generally brace myself for the inevitably intense walking experience.

And this is no accident. The Romanticist theory that lurks behind the concept of a heroic architecture contains a strong masochistic streak. After all, the Romanticist writers who inspired the call to 'experience' and 'heroics' in the late 18th and 19th century were people who wrote about the intense effects of tuberculosis, war and other horrific assaults on the body. In acknowledging this, we should seriously consider how many war-time and post-war-time architectural practices (Civil, Spanish American, WWI, WWII, Korean, think also Jameson/Vietnam/Bonaventure) often unleash spaces in which the body appears to be pressed to some type of physical limit – pressed, one might argue, into the position of hero. As I recall, it was the historian of Rudolph, Timothy Rohan (2014), who acknowledged a hyper-masculine and masochistic tenor to the spatial and material treatments of the Yale Architecture School. The space was about many things, including Rudolph overcoming his own subjectivity as a closeted homosexual man. But this heroic overcoming, articulated by Rohan, is certainly imparted to many of those (not just Rudolph) who navigate this space.

> I do not think the very act of struggling to move through a building can be read as an act of critique in and of itself. Do the struggles of a disabled person ever read as architectural criticism? The 'failures' of the body/space interaction here always falls back either on the 'disabled' person or the 'larger social' milieu in which disability appears. The disabled cannot seem to speak through disability against particular theories of architecture. What is demanded here is something that we might term 'performance critique' where the interface between disability and space is continuously repeated to uncover the (underlying) ideas . . . That is, through repetitive performance we see disability as an idea designed to be overcome in those spaces that appear inherently 'insensitive'. In the Yale Architecture School, by demanding repetition, we uncover the hidden image of overcoming the 'lesser body' that I really believe moves through the heroic theory of architecture.
>
> (Gissen 2008)

Gissen's critique, then, becomes not of a lack of accessibility but about a romanticized, heroic and, therefore, deliberately difficult spatial form (to which could be added Imrie's argument (1998) that modernism often used stepped level changes to enhance the visual contemplation of the architecture itself). I have similarly been exploring ways to challenge the invisibility in architecture's own discourses about itself around dis/ability. Zumthor's steps (Chapter 5), for example, have a different logic framed around what we are all assumed to share – the archetypical memories of a childhood where steps embody deep emotional feelings. Again the criticism is not that the steps can be inaccessible, but that Zumthor's 'anyone' is, in fact, a very specific kind of (meditative, country-living, traditional – even strangely isolated) individual.

With what has been called a 'material turn' that has been occurring over the last few years, across disciplines as diverse as cultural geography, critical sociology, anthropology, feminism, phenomenology and the philosophy of science (Latour 2007a, Miller 2009, Ingold 2011), much contemporary theory offers potentially valuable tools here. I will propose that these, when intersected with contemporary disability studies, can increase our ability to unravel and challenge the commonsense of everyday social and spatial practices – both as these are lived through material landscapes, and as performed in architectural theories and practices. Such theories are attempting to articulate more generative, embodied, process-based, complex and non-representational understandings of the lived world. Here, bodies and their encounters with each other, objects and spaces are seen not so much as networks or relationships that can be 'looked at' (as if from a great height) but as entanglements or meshworks which are enacted and performed.

What use, we can ask, is this to architects and other built environment professionals? Existing architectural theories are there to enable the innovative generation of approaches to, and methods of three-dimensional form-making. This is a powerful and potent internal aspect of architecture as a discipline, central to what it does, and how it sees itself. However, specific approaches take hold more popularly across the profession because of their resonance – aesthetically, intellectually, emotionally, socially, politically – to upcoming generations of architectural students and practitioners. The mainstreaming of particular attitudes and approaches, then, is not because of any orchestrated analysis of its actual value for other participants in the procurement, development, design, construction, management and occupancy of buildings (although this may have been taken into account in some aspects). It does not include much rigorous critical reflection on the responsibilities of architectural theories to their many clients and stakeholders. And it does not explicitly require a method for understanding how social and spatial practices *work*. *Doing Disability Differently* has argued that we cannot move on beyond discrimination against disabled people through building design, without being self-conscious of, and critical about, the relationships between architecture and its occupancy. Architectural theory therefore needs, whatever its approaches to form, a way of interpreting the relations between people, artefacts and spaces *applicable to every case*, which enables everyday design decision-making embedded in, and creatively engaging with, dis/ability, diversity and difference.

I will go further. Taking the architect's primary responsibility for duty of care, any theoretical framework in architecture should be centrally concerned with equality and social and spatial justice, whilst acknowledging the problematic and not always powerful location of architects and other built environment professionals in building development, design and occupation processes. Architecture has within it a strong social commitment that can get distorted, not just by the pressures of reality, but also by the very strategies and tactics through which the discipline theorizes relationships between the social and the architectural. This is not to say that many architectural practices from avant-garde to mainstream to community-based and art-related practice are not explicitly examining the social aspects of what they do, only that the dominant conceptual frameworks and procedures may no longer be fit for the job. What, then, would such a theory look like – not a theory of occupancy to inform architectural form and its generation, but of everyday social and spatial practices and its implications for designing?

On science and technology studies: ANT and the door-closer

As I have already outlined, central to contemporary social theory – in its many guises from post-humanism to new materialism to critical sociology – is a shared intention to not separate out human from non-human or non-matter from matter and to find methods for better understanding the world which articulate it as a process of continuous flows or assemblages, rather than as discrete entities (subjects/objects, people/animals, man/environment) which then interact:

> Instead a multitude of affective actants-in-relation take and hold their shape performatively, as precarious achievements whose durability and reach is spun between the potencies and frailties of more than human kinds.
>
> (Whatmore 2012: 251)

So when Bruno Latour, 'inventor' of Actor–Network Theory (ANT), for example, looks at architecture (Latour and Yaneva 2012) he immediately highlights the essential paradox of buildings: that whilst they appear as static objects par excellence, 'a fixed, stolid structure' (Latour and Yaneva 2012: 107), they are in fact an endlessly moving and contested process:

> Only by enlisting the movements of a building and accounting carefully for its 'tribulations' would one be able to state its existence: it would be equal to the building's extensive list of controversies and performances over time, i.e., it would be equal to what it does, to the way it resists attempts at transformation, allows certain visitors' actions and impedes others, bugs observers, challenges city authorities, and mobilizes different communities of actors.
>
> (Latour and Yaneva 2012: 112)

For Latour 'everyone knows – especially architects of course – that a building is not a static object but a moving project' (ibid.: 107). But he suggests that the historical development of single-point perspective in the western world, and its continuing impact on architectural forms of representation, has led to the 'normal' techniques for designing and communicating of Euclidean space to be mistaken for reality, as if these are an accurate understanding of 'how space works'. What is more, where other theorists, for instance phenomenologists, have critiqued this idea of neutral, objective space, they have done so by adding human subjective dimensions to an already pre-existing material world, '"human bodies" ambling through a "lived environment"' (ibid.: 108). As I have explored elsewhere in this book, even when the 'user' within architecture has been re-thought beyond the universal type, they are still conceived of as independent, interchangeable entities, who are not *already* shaped by ideas, encounters and contexts. I have shown how this makes disability invisible except as a functional 'problem'. Latour makes a more general point: that the individual–environment relationship not only reproduces the artificial split between the objective building as a material form, and its subjective experience through occupancy, but it also reduces all the processes through which architecture goes from production to existence to its one version as a drawn set of plans and elevations:

> [D]uring its flight, a building is never at rest and never in the shape of Euclidean space that was supposed to be its 'real material essence' to which one could then add its 'symbolic', 'human', 'subjective' or 'iconic' dimension.
>
> (Latour and Yaneva 2012: 111)

Latour proposes that we instead map buildings as a flow of transformations, what he has called elsewhere assemblages. As an example, he considers the design process, writing one of the best summaries of the experience that I have seen:

> The hundreds of models and drawings produced in design form an artistically created primal matter that simulates the haptic imagination, astonishes its creators instead of subserviently obeying them, and helps architects fix unfamiliar ideas, gain new knowledge about the build-to-come, and formulate new alternatives and 'options', new unforeseen scenarios of realization. To follow the evolution of drawings in an architectural studio is like witnessing a juggler who keeps adding more and more balls to his skillful acrobatic show. Every new technique of drawing and modeling serves to absorb a new difficulty and add it to the accumulation of elements necessary to entertain the possibility of building anything. It would be simply inappropriate to limit to three dimensions an activity that, by definition, means piling on more and more dimensions every time, so as eventually to 'obtain' a plausible building, a building that stands.
>
> (ibid .: 110)

This flow of assemblages, crucially, does not differentiate between humans and non-humans (that is, people, objects, spaces, technologies, texts and so on). Nor does it separate out 'context' as a kind of backdrop to activity; in fact context as such disappears. The same 'way of looking' can be used at any scale, to explore the design process, or a building in use, or forms of professional practice, or a single designed element. For example, Latour (under the guise of a pretend academic called Johnson) writes an extended investigation into a simple automatic door closer (Johnson 1988: 298). Here, the material door and its (usually working) closer is seen as being *delegated*, the work of differentiating between a particular inside and a more ambiguous outside, because

> the reversible door is the only way to irreversibly trap inside a differential accumulation of warm sociologists, knowledge, papers and also, alas, paperwork; the hinged door allows a selection of what gets in and what gets out so as to locally increase order or information.
>
> (ibid.: 299)

This, then, is a way of understanding the intersections of human and non-human actants – the latter perform a role as a substitute for what would otherwise be a much more complicated human activity (rebuilding the wall every time you want to go in or out; closing the door properly on each occasion, employing a doorman). This, for Latour, also gives a means of judging the relative value of the non-human replacement – 'every time you want to know what a non-human does, simply imagine what other humans or non-humans would have to do if this character was not present' (ibid.: 299). Such interactions are therefore expressed as a kind of balance sheet, weighing up shifts from major to minor efforts, through the passing backwards and forwards of agency across humans and non-humans. Matter becomes a kind of equal, interchangeable partner, not invisible (as it is in much sociology) or merely a tool 'added on' to human capabilities. What, then, are the alternatives, and their 'costs' compared to the door-closer? What about swapping it for a doorman? The problem here, though, is that it depends on human (un)reliability. In this case, Latour suggests that proper disciplining of a doorman 'is an enormous and costly task that only Hilton Hotels can tackle, and that for other reasons which have nothing to do with keeping the door properly closed' (ibid.: 300).

I will return to these 'other' reasons in a moment. First, let's look at how Latour articulates the diverse users of this, and other versions of, the door-closer:

> We have all experienced having a door with a powerful spring mechanism slam in our face. For sure, springs do the job of replacing grooms, but they play the role of a very rude, uneducated porter who obviously prefers the wall version of the door, to the hole version.
>
> (ibid.: 301)

Here, then, is another cost to be added to the minus side of the balance sheet, because in these cases, it is humans who have to adapt to the door. The problem for 'inventors' is to design a non-human character that delegates for humans, without demanding special or unexpected skills of its human users. He next considers the example of a hydraulic door-closer (noting appreciatively in passing the elegant solution of using people's own energy to power the door):

> This does not solve all the problems though. To be sure, the hydraulic door-closer does not bang the noses of those who are not aware of local conditions . . . but it still leaves aside segments of the human populations. Neither my nephews, nor my grandmother could get in unaided because our groom needed the force of an able-bodied person . . . because of this prescription these doors discriminate against very little and very old persons.

He suggests, however, that if you put aside maintenance issues, and the 'few sectors of society that are discriminated against' (ibid.: 302) the door-closer is an effective (inter-twined) non-human substitute. We do not need to make assumptions about what are human and non-human functions, or which works better than the other. This is an incredibly insightful and, I suggest, particularly for architects, useful conceptual framework for close looking at social, spatial and aesthetic entanglements. However, there are two big surprises in this work, given the extent to which Latour articulates such a powerfully resonant embodied and enmeshed world. First, his scientists and technologists (or architects and designers) appear to stand outside of the human and non-human entanglements he describes. They are like gods, looking down at their research analyses, old-fashioned Enlightenment-style rational and objective beings:

> As Elam has noted, there is something scriptural in the demeanor of Latour's writing that 'assumes a position outside of action, only to re-appear as science-in-action personified . . . [it is as though he] cannot help re-enacting the imperial ambitions that infuse the networks he charts.
>
> (Whatmore 2012: 251–2)

Whilst agency moves around, authoritative *problem-solving* remains with the experts. Second, what might be thought of as the core of a sociological understanding – ordinary social and spatial practices and the everyday powers and authority they reproduce – disappear, replaced instead with the scientist/engineer/technologist/architect/designer's 'rational' balance sheet comparing, associating, substituting different non-humans and then making 'sensible' decisions based on relative degrees of effort-saving and robustness 'from a provisional less reliable one to a longer-lasting more faithful one' (Johnson (Latour) 1988: 306). In a way, both of these difficulties with Latour's work are symptomatic of the same issue: his enmeshed world, rather than being already there, affecting our enactments within it from both where we are placed and how we place ourselves, remains, despite its dynamic complexity, an entity 'out there', on which scientists and researchers can 'look down' to make their analyses. This is odd given the amount of work in feminism, post-colonial studies and other parts of sociology, cultural theory and so on, that has already explored this (Button 1993, Law 1991, Law and Hassard 1999, Haraway 1994, 2003, 2007), another point to which I will return.

Finally, as many critics have pointed out, ANT is deeply problematic because it tends to stay with 'professional action' and within science and technology in the academy. This makes it less attentive to other actors, and sites of both resistance and creative transformation. Unlike the scientists who make analytical creative decisions and therefore *act on* the world, other actors only have freedom in how they *respond to* a scene, to behave differently to what the 'delegation' has expected, or to exempt themselves from, or 'happily acquiesce' (Johnson (Latour) 1988: 307) to a particular situation.

As sometimes happens with sustainability, concern is only about a kind of resource management, with no interest in how to enable social change; what Whatmore calls an 'apparent indifference to the witness of those living (and dying) at the sharp end of technoscientific re-orderings' (2012: 251). In the context of thinking and doing disability and architecture differently, I have already argued that it is both much more relevant and much more pressing to examine how:

> the stakes are thoroughly and promiscuously distributed through the messy attachments, skills, and intensities of differently embodied lives whose everyday conduct exceeds and perverts the designs of parliaments, corporations and laboratories.
>
> (Whatmore 2012: 252)

Going back to that door-closer: its 'inventor's' choices are not merely rational, but already inscribed with assumptions about what is *normal* in framing who goes in and out of a particular building, how that process is filtered, and how it can or should intersect with the other delegating procedures being performed by doors, such as energy performance, light, view, security and so on. As Latour hints, a Hilton hotel entrance performs relationships between its participants differently to a university *through* the deliberate expression of excessive effort (the doorman). And in his glancing reference to discriminating against less mobile entrants, Latour is merely reproducing exactly the commonsense everyday practices that put disability and diverse bodies a long way down the balance sheet. Human and non-human assemblages, then, are not just exchanges of agency evaluated against some abstract concept of durability, but include a tendency to delegate *towards* or *away* from particular bodies, technologies, spaces, functions, etc. This is what becomes worth unravelling. This is what can inform choices for designers, who are of course already working across and between the 'normal', the dis/ordinary and the 'transformational' (always within constraints) that might shift the enabling and disabling effects of one kind of door-closer or door over another, one spatial configuration over another, through opening up to investigation the kinds of relationships we can make between diverse human and non-human assemblages.

Taking on ANT from disability studies

Science and technology studies (STS), and ANT in particular, have also had an impact on disability theory, studies and activism. It has been fiercely contested, and resisted in many places, partly because as Galis notes, 'the first generation of STS scholars appeared to attempt to understand, explain and effectively reinforce the hegemony of science and scientists, rather than to question their bias' (2011: 829), thus supporting the medical model of disability. But Galis does believe that contemporary science and technology studies *can* inform disability studies and challenge medical and social models, by removing 'the focus from interpretative approaches to what disability is and shift(ing) the sociological analysis of how disability is created, through different interactive processes between the impaired body, the built environment and policy-making' (p. 825), to offer 'a political account of the enactment of disability in material and semiotic practices' (p. 829).

For him, this method can enable an unravelling of the intersecting potentials between articulating disability *as doing* (rather than just through its expressions and effects as a concept and stereotype) and a central concern of disability studies to inform activism; that is, 'all new associations between humans and non-humans that modify the collective; and deliberate problem solving by lay people in areas previously dominated by scientific experts' (Latour 2007b: 816–17). This emphasis on disability as doing is particularly relevant to architecture because it goes beyond the social model to integrate disability as impairment with, in and against the barriers model of the building and urban design, instead exploring 'the lived experience of impaired, gendered, ethnic bodies interacting with the configuration of the built environment and its materiality' (Galis 2011: 827). This becomes a means to address how disability experiences are articulated and come into being within specific practices, cultures and institutions, and on whose authority:

> Thus, using ANT does not involve the privileged study of either impaired bodies or socio-material constructions, but the analysis of situations where the interactions of bodies and materiality/culture produce action or inaction, ability or disability . . .
>
> Different bodily forms, abilities and disabilities are not independent of architecture, but are mutually constitutive such that 'produced space' also forms 'social norms'.
>
> (Galis 2011: 830–1)

Studying disability as enactment – 'to track down how we do disability' (p. 831) – becomes the study of multiple objects and domains. It starts from dis/ability but breaks with research centred on an assumed stable and already pre-existing disabled/abled divide, replacing this with a whole range of human to non-human relationships, enabling both engagements with diverse human bodies and their various delegations, whether – for instance – glasses, prescriptions, colostomy bags, hearing implants, houses, kitchen equipment, doors, steps, white canes, hip replacements, wheelchairs, toilets, reception desks or dogs. It can explore these relations across multiple scales and locations simultaneously, building up the kinds of interwoven registers that Sobchack characterized in doing/thinking with/about her prosthesis outlined in Chapter 6. And just as importantly, it can move beyond the 'normal' realms where disabled people are investigated (and, it should be added, designed *for*):

> Accordingly, the sociological analysis ought to study the ordering of disability and the experience of impairment in locations that are not merely socially constructed or medicalised by social policies, the media, special education, economics and rehabilitation (Moser 2005, 671). We have to also look at locations where the ordering of disability meets and enacts everyday life, governmental action to configure the built environment, scientific bodies to confront impaired bodies and so on.
>
> (Galis 2011: 832)

Galis also points out problems with ANT, including the blurring over issues of agency (Collins and Yearly 1992), a lack of interest in power asymmetries, an obsession with powerful actors, the difficulties of being able to record discriminations and exclusions, and the overlooking of the contribution of other participants beyond 'experts'. I have already noted how Actor–Network Theory fails to recognize already-built-in ordinary socio-spatial practices in which those in authority are as much immersed as everyone else. Galis adds another important consideration: the effects that non-experts have in transforming those practices by demanding shifts and enabling changes. He is therefore also interested in how ANT can map how ordinary disabled people have, individually and collectively, challenged and resisted 'normal' discriminatory practices. In addition, returning to Titchkosky, we need to unpick how authority is maintained through justificatory narratives and actions:

> [Examining] even washrooms – whose taken-for-granted status is almost necessary – is essential for gaining an understanding of how everyday embodied experiences are managed by discourses of competition for scarce resources, hetero-normative expectations, colonizing powers, and neoliberal demands. My analysis focuses on stories of justification for 'what is'; things said which present disability as something either to be explained by or subjugated to 'what is'. My analysis of justification narratives follows a fundamental assumption of interpretive social inquiry: how people justify 'what is', is an interpretive social act. The interpretive act of justification is intimately tied to collective understandings of the meaning of what is. As an interpretive social act, justification is not merely second order to the fact of exclusion; it is our 'facticity', it is a 'form of human life', it is how we *do* exclusion as well as *generate* its everyday sensibility (Gadamer 1991: 216, 220). This means that justifying 'what is' *governs* our ability to imaginatively relate to our lives as embodied beings.
>
> (Titchkosky 2008: 41, italics added)

Doing disability and architecture

How then do these kinds of articulation help us do architecture and disability better? First, I suggest, they are a means of looking at how disability and ability are delegated across the discipline of architecture and its related professions, and – crucially – what happens to it in those processes of delegation. It means moving beyond the artificial and opposed divisions between disability and ability to see them instead as ambiguous and relational, that 'criss-cross, connect and separate, and become present and absent for each other' (Schillmeier 2010: 127). This means opening up to view other kinds of enactments with material space which the disabled–abled divide obscures, most particularly terms not included in the binaries of active/passive, autonomous/dependent, mobile/immobile, competent/incompetent such as interdependencies, care, vulnerability and so on. Second, we need to unravel underlying patterns (assumptions, actualities, 'normal' practices) of what is permissible and what not, in what circumstances. This is in no way a simple 'balance sheet' enumerating relative degrees of agency and effort. It is an unravelling inspection, which asks how specific forms of encounter (between buildings, people, objects, actions), 'everyday' social and spatial practices (who should be where, when, with what kinds of material and spatial artefacts) and framing devices (in architecture as a discipline, in production and consumption procedures, in social, cultural and regulatory processes) come to be generally and repetitively made concrete in one form rather than another. As before, this is not to make building and urban design the only or causal effect of discrimination against disabled people, but it is to see it as a component having crucial impact on both the 'normal' articulation of disability and on the lived experiences of both disabled and abled people. Finally, it means examining just where and how architects, and others involved in the building design process, might review these delegations and permissions, so as to undo the discriminatory location of disability and take responsibility for ableism.

Conclusion: delegating towards dis/ability

How, then, is dis/ability delegated within architecture? Most immediately it is delegated to the regulatory and technical end of practice, to other expertise, organized through access consultants, audits and forums, and to a set of commonly used 'assistive' technologies such as ramps, platform lifts and specialist signage, repetitively reproduced and legitimized through the leaflets, brochures, websites and books that offer accessibility design guidance. But it is also to be found in the negotiations with particular clients case by case, in the diagramming procedures through which architects develop stable architectural forms from complex situations and problems, in the theories they develop to define attitudes and methods; and in the 'tradition and practices' of the built environment professions and their many clients. And, of course, it is not separate from the 'ordinary' talk or normal enactments that locate disability, from the point of view of the abled, in everyday life.

What, then, is permissible ('storyable') in these different types of delegation? In his guise as Jim Johnson in 'Mixing Humans and Non-Humans Together: The Story of a Door-Closer' (1988) Latour uses the term 'permissible' only once, in a glancing aside, probably to mean both allowable and doable. Here, though, I take it to mean, first, what is permissible in ordinary commonsense – just doing the usual/nothing much – through reproducing 'normal' social and spatial practices; and second, how this becomes filtered and translated through architectural decision-making, that is, choosing to design something this way rather than that. Permissibility for architects already includes what is allowable and doable, through such issues as resource constraints, client requirements and regulatory structures. What is interesting here is the extent to which, within what is allowable and doable, architects reproduce, adapt, challenge or transform normative social-spatial practices. This *is* a part of architectural practice, particularly amongst those who explicitly position themselves as socially committed (for example, in community-based practice, or inclusive design). But as I have already argued, in its intersections with other aspects of architectural discourse and practice, social engagement and its particular delegations into material form and space can become *peculiar*, distorted in the interstices between the parallel universes of architectural discourse and diverse experiences. I have also proposed that, in different ways, many if not most architectural delegations (from human to material or spatial device) act to *forget* the everyday work taken to be dis/abled, to maintain and perpetuate 'normal' socio-spatial practices, and fail to even notice the dis/ordinary. In fact, it is *through* many of these designed delegations – either by not attending to dis/ability or by framing it in limited and constraining ways – that it is enabled to invariably be included as excludable.

What is powerful about ANT is that, despite all its problems, it enables close looking at any of these different delegations across a variety of scales, from the local encounter, to the design process, to the regulatory regime; and at a number of different registers simultaneously, all within the same method. It also allows thought experiments; for example, in exploring what happens by changing delegations across human and non-human actions, or adjusting what is permissible. So, we can return to Latour's door-closer and look at how entrances deal with dis/ability in different contexts. What are the processes of delegating towards and away from dis/ability in a typical public entrance combination of revolving doors and automatically controlled 'accessible' openings (Figure 9.1)? Here, designers are making complex balances, delegating between and across energy efficiency, entry, view, security, etc. For participants going in or leaving a building, the resulting arrangement also offers choices. Even the most casual observation shows that, though these kinds of doorways are now quite common, there occurs a regular kind of 'stutter' at the moment of transition, as

Figure 9.1 Typical public building entrance, Angel Islington, London.

individuals decide if they 'count' as disabled, if they can be bothered to push the circular door, or wait for others using it, if they are willing to wait whilst the automatic door button (which needs to be hit quite firmly) does its job, if they and a friend can fit together in a single revolving section or must co-ordinate themselves into a mini-queue, if they can get through the automatic section before it (automatically) closes, and what other people are doing coming the other way. Wheelchair users need to have a strong hand for the button; people carrying parcels, with a guide dog, pushing a trolley, bicycle, buggy, etc., need to stop and juggle with their burdens.

In fact, this conventional 'accessible' solution exposes – if only we took time to notice – not only the ambiguities of what makes bodies dis/abled in different situations, but also how built spaces and devices work to enable and disable, albeit here in a relatively minor way (and with some explicit delegation towards wheelchair users). In fact, like some of Latour's door-closer examples, the revolving door delegates *against* any but the most abled, whilst the other doors are easier, but also slow and clumsy (marking them in everyday social practice, as with their associated signage, as only for the disabled). By separating out so clearly, and treating so differently, an 'abled' and a 'disabled' public entrance, also everyone (who lives in a much more blurry world) has – just for each moment of coming and going – to decide where they fit.

Finally, as I have said before, we also need to examine in much more detail the various architectural procedures from design through to discourse through which disability is delegated *away from* or delegated *towards*. What do I mean by away from or towards? Well, delegations away from disability might include an unconsidered reliance on accessibility design guidance; an unnoticed including as excludable of disabled people in a building project; an expressed frustration at the regulatory requirements and/or at the 'additional' costs, that is, at the 'burden' of disability for designers; designs for disabled people which take the 'easiest' option, even where that means complicated and separate entrances and routes, or wheelchair-accessible seating areas in a theatre with very poor sightlines; accessible design mainly at the level of appearances, so that regulatory demands can be 'seen' to be met; the unthinking associations of disability with practicalities that 'prevent' spatially and aesthetically good design: the avoidance of dis/ability as an issue in professional and theoretical discourses; and the use of justificatory narratives across architectural education and practice which not only accept the disabling effects of such delegations *away*, but agree with them.

> **Aesthetic judgments about the built environment remain unquestioned when architects make the case against accessible designs on the grounds that access produces ugly buildings, even though the buildings called beautiful are fashioned to suppress the disabled body from public view**.
>
> (Siebers 2003)

Delegations *towards* disability include taking notice of how disabled people explain their experiences; considering the everyday work for both disabled and abled people in living different lives, in their intersections with built space; recognizing the unnoticed assumptions of being abled; opening up to view what constitutes 'normal' social and spatial practices and creatively intervening towards enabling rather than disabling effects; challenging the lack of engagement with dis/ability in architectural theories and practices; and working towards conceptual frameworks and methods which critically and creatively inter-weave questions of form-making with better understandings of how the social and the spatial are entangled.

As I noted in the introduction, starting from disability does *not* lead to universal or simple design solutions. It does not provide any easy answers and will certainly not result in a built environment that is perfectly accessible to everyone, everywhere. But this is not a good reason for architects to continue delegating away from what should be the very centre of their practice – enhancing occupancies. In fact, in many ways, starting from dis/ability and a critical and creative engagement with everyday social and spatial practices is just like all the other 'normal' architectural design processes: operating exactly in the complex, messy and often contradictory spaces of our diverse and varying lives with others, artefacts and material form. Architecture *already* demands a response to many partial and often conflicting variables (social, material, financial, functional, cultural, etc.). It requires a complex set of interacting predictive actions, underlined by uncertainty. It operates in a wider context of decision-making where the designer may have little control and must always compromise; will never get everything right. Designs only come to fruition through complex negotiations across many, often conflicting interests. Dis/ability is not some accidental add-on to this process; it is at its heart. Imagine, then, a world where rather than having books on building typologies and technical detailing manuals to support them, architects have books on social and spatial practices, that map our diverse strategies and narratives for intersecting with the material landscape, laid out so as to open up their inherent ambiguity and partiality, but also to offer up gaps and opportunities for positive change. Where architecture diagramming not only analyses but also interweaves formal manipulations, spatial patterns and dis/ordinary practices. Where precedent study books are not just about famous architects' works but also capture a multiplicity of details across many buildings. Where we talk and argue over dis/ability as an essential and embedded aspect of architectural education and practice.

And ultimately, is it possible to say what the resulting – hopefully cool and avant-garde – architecture will be like? Crucially this has to go beyond either adding a disability aesthetic to an already existing set of architectural theories and practices, or merely proposing an oppositional alternative to those theories and practices that is only about better understanding everyday social and spatial practices. Rather, such a different kind of architecture needs to be built out of the critical and creative intersections *between* discourses about form-making and an embedded engagement with the social, both in its ordinary and dis/ordinary forms; it is only then that dis/ability and critical social and spatial practices finally can become completely enmeshed with the language of form itself.

Glossary of terms

Commissioned from disability writer and critic David Watson, with additional entries by Jos Boys and John Walker.

Ableism Whilst it has been increasingly possible to name particular situations and actions as sexist or racist, it just doesn't seem that easy to use the expression ableist. Which is a pity. And tells us quite a lot about the 'place' of disabled people in society.

Accessibility Accessibility is equality; the degree to which an environment, product, website or service is accessible or usable by people of all abilities. For disabled people this means not only equal physical access but access to the same tools, services, facilities and opportunities (social, political, financial, educational, employment) as non-disabled people.

Actor–network theory (ANT) This approach, popularized by Bruno Latour and developed by Michel Callon, John Law and others, often regrets its own name. This is because neither the term Actor nor Network capture the complex inter-weavings between humans and non-humans (whether other species or material spaces or inanimate objects) that ANT explores. It is best known for its insistence that both humans and non-humans act in networks, aiming to map their dynamic relationships backwards and forwards, rather than allocate cause and effect to one or the other.

Affect Throughout, this book has been concerned with exploring *practices* – that is how human–objects–space inter-relationships are performed or enacted. The concept of affect is also important here, because it not only expresses the idea of multiple, and cross-register entanglements between people and things, but also recognizes it as work. As Thrift writes: 'This unremitting work of active reaction imposes enormous evaluative demands, equally enormous demands on immediate memory, and similarly large demands on the general management of attention' (2007: 7). Whilst affect may not be consciously perceived in everyday life, it is a central mechanism through which we can learn to feel and act in particular ways rather than others.

Affirmation model Swain and French (2000) explain that this is 'essentially a non-tragic view of disability and impairment which encompasses positive social identities, both individual and collective, for disabled people grounded in the benefits of lifestyle and life experience of being impaired and disabled' (p. 569).

Archetypes It is easiest just to give the dictionary definition, which captures some of the interesting slippages in this concept:

1a very typical example of a certain person or thing: *he was the archetype of the old-style football club chairman*

1b an original which has been imitated; a prototype: *an instrument which was the archetype of the early flute*

2 *Psychoanalysis* (in Jungian theory) a primitive mental image inherited from the earliest human ancestors, and supposed to be present in the collective unconscious.

3a recurrent symbol or motif in literature, art, or mythology: *mythological archetypes of good and evil*

http://oxforddictionaries.com/definition/english/archetype

Assistive technologies This is a term that tends to be used specifically to describe supporting equipment for disabled people, rather than, for example, cars or computers which are also assistive, but also 'normal'. As Peter Anderberg puts it, 'The only absolute reason to define assistive technology is the funding people with disability can receive to obtain assistive devices' (2006b: 48). His argument, also followed here, is that all technologies can be enabling or disabling depending on the situation and context.

Blob architecture 'Its surface seems slick, perhaps reflective, often translucent, skinlike, visually viscous; its form appears curved, ballooned, bulging, segmental, warped, and twisted; . . . Its architect calls it a "blob", and compares it to a history of similar objects in nature that cultural theory since Georges Bataille has identified with the *informe*. The techniques of its design are drawn not from architecture but from animation software that generates its complex forms with the help of digital avatars that work, independent of the architect, to produce multiple iterations of possible combinations' (Vidler 2000).

Commonsense 'Commonsense' is often seen as an obvious and unproblematic view of the world that is shared by most people, so straightforward as not to require any discussion. Here, on the contrary, it is taken as crucially important that we take more careful notice of, and critically unpack, our commonsense beliefs, as a means of exposing how the everyday world, and people's assumed different places within it, come to be shaped in particular ways rather than others.

Crip humour If the abled express awkwardness around disability, many disabled people use this in response; and also to have a good laugh at the expense of both themselves and what would otherwise be the depressing and frustrating foibles of abled people.

Cyborgs The dictionary definition of a cyborg is 'a fictional or hypothetical person whose physical abilities become superhuman by mechanical elements built into the body' (*Webster*). But famously, for Donna Haraway – in her 'Cyborg Manifesto' (1991) – using the notion of the cyborg as a hybrid of machine and organism allows us to explore creatively and differently inter-relationships between social reality and fictions about that world; and she writes: 'I am making an argument for the cyborg as a fiction mapping our social and bodily reality and as an imaginative resource suggesting some very fruitful couplings' (Haraway 1991: 149).

Deafness and disability Many Deaf people, particularly those who use BSL (British Sign Language), argue that they are a linguistic minority with their own language and (Deaf) culture; and therefore do not define themselves as disabled. Often deaf people prefer to use Deaf with a capital D. As John Walker says, when you

> refer to deaf people who use signed languages; it would be correct to use an upper case as defined by Woodward (1975). It distinguishes from the biological condition of 'not hearing' and focus on the social construction of Deaf people's lives.
>
> I would argue that while Deaf culture inextricably linked to signed languages, it is the cultural norms that define the spaces, in my view. Signed languages have its own spaces that form syntactically on the hands and in front of the body; it represents the spaces as well as how deaf spaces are perceived. Ultimately, it is the visualness of spaces that is central to Deaf space, rather than the language.
>
> (personal email exchange 11 September 2013)

Deaf space Deaf space is an emerging concept in the relationship between Deaf people and their spaces and places. The visual nature of the Deaf community is central to this concept, and it questions how Deaf people, and their communities, embody their spaces. Deaf space gives ideas about the physical parameters of architecture, as well as how signing families shape their spaces and how the temporal international spaces, held at global Deaf events, form.

Evidence of Deaf spaces can be found in history where Deaf families and schools and churches for Deaf people, hold historical accounts of the relationships between Deaf people and Others, and are manifested in the design of Deaf places. It also looks at the syntactic and topographical spaces used in signed languages and how the space is represented linguistically and symbolically. Spaces are also defined by thinking in colonialism and how Deaf people have been 'controlled' to shape the world in pre-assigned ways (e.g. oralism), including their potential post-colonial responses. Primarily, Deaf spaces will embrace the visual nature of spaces, where 'seeing' is more important than any other sense or function.

Deconstruction Within architecture, the term deconstruction was a development of, and critical response to, post-modernism. It came to describe a method where the programme of a building was first 'deconstructed';

that is, broken into fragments, and then re-constructed, often bringing together distorted shapes and dislocated elements; and aiming to play with unpredictability and chaos in form-making.

Diagramming If modernist architects used the term 'brief' to describe the set of client requirements for a building project, more recently the concept 'programme' has become dominant. This is perhaps because it aims to articulate activities rather than 'needs' and frames space and what goes on in it as a dynamic and inter-relational process. In addition, the idea of 'diagramming' is taking hold, particularly through the influential work of Peter Eisenman (Vidler 2000, Eisenman 1999, Garcia 2010). Whilst architects have always used diagrams as a means of analysing situations, and sketching out and testing design ideas, the contemporary interest is in how diagramming can work as a conscious design act, through rigorously intersecting multiple variables, both obvious and unexpected.

Disability arts The problem for disabled artists is whether they 'come out' or not. Because disability arts is often assumed by 'normal' people to be a kind of therapy for the disabled – to keep them occupied – the very strong body of work being developed by disabled artists (informed by, but not only about their disability) continues to be marginalized. In addition many disabled artists do not want to be labelled, and would rather make their way successfully in the art world without mentioning their disability. See Disability Arts Online to keep up with the best disabled artists in the UK: www.disabilityartsonline.org.uk.

Disability and impairment Most disabled and Deaf people differentiate between a medical and social model of disability. The medical model focuses on the individual and their impairment; perceived as a problem that can be improved through medical intervention. The social model of disability argues instead that the problem is not with individuals but that it is the barriers, prejudice and exclusion by society (purposely or inadvertently) which are the ultimate factors in defining who is disabled and who is not in a particular society.

Disability Discrimination Act (DDA) The Disability Discrimination Act (DDA) is a UK parliamentary act which makes it unlawful to discriminate against disabled people in relation to employment, education, housing, transport, the provision of goods and services and access to the functions of public bodies. In addition, the Act places duties and responsibilities on employers and service providers to ensure that disabled people are not treated unfavourably in relation to their disabilities and requiring them to make 'reasonable adjustments' in order to make employment, services and premises accessible to disabled people. Sounds good, doesn't it? However, the Act is easily circumvented, permitting employers and service providers to justify unfavourable treatment and failure to make reasonable adjustments depending on whether or not the adjustments meet the needs of the disabled person, whether or not they are affordable and whether or not the adjustment will have a serious effect on other people.

Disability equality Disabled people are just like other people and deserve equal rights and treatment under the law to anyone else. Which is why the UK government is making good progress towards achieving its ambition of equality for disabled people by 2025. Seriously 2025. No word on which month yet.

Disability equality duty Since December 2006, it has been a legal duty for all public sector organizations to promote equality of opportunity for disabled people.

Disability impact assessment A disability impact assessment is a method by which organizations can examine their activities and services to ensure there is no potential for discrimination against disabled people.

Disablism The disability charity Scope defines disablism as 'discriminatory, oppressive or abusive behaviour arising from the belief that disabled people are inferior'. Whilst there are undoubtedly examples of hate crimes committed against disabled people (a worrying trend that appears to be on the increase) most 'disablism' is unconscious and grows out of society's widespread acceptance of the medical and charity models of disability; a belief that the problems faced by disabled people are not discriminatory in nature but private, medical problems that can be 'cured' through medical intervention or eased by charitable organizations or government benefits.

Duty of care A duty of care is a legal obligation placed on individuals and organizations to take reasonable care of a person who may be affected by their activities. And it is written into architectural practice.

Ethnomethodology Ethnomethodology is the study of the everyday methods that people use for the production and perpetuation of social order, and as a means of making sense of the world. It is problematic in some ways, because it has been predominantly used for mapping only 'normal' social and spatial practices, rather than offering critiques and challenges to those practices. However, it is used here because it is particularly good at unravelling the various mechanisms through which 'ordinariness' is maintained.

Inclusive design Inclusive design is a general approach to design where the designer ensures that their product or service addresses the needs of the widest possible audience regardless of their ability or age.

Lifetime homes Lifetime homes cater to changing needs over a person's lifetime by including a degree of adaptability within the design of the accommodation. The standards ensure this by including features such as a level threshold, entrance-level living space, potential for entrance-level bed-space and an entrance-level WC with potential for a shower to be installed. This helps cater for the changing needs of disabled and older people, including disabled visitors and people with a temporary impairment such as a broken leg.

Medical and social models Most disabled and Deaf people differentiate between a medical and social model of disability. The medical model focuses on the individual and their impairment; perceived as a problem that can be improved through medical intervention. The social model of disability argues instead that the problem is not with individuals but that it is the barriers, prejudice and exclusion by society (purposely or inadvertently) which are the ultimate factors in defining who is disabled and who is not in a particular society.

Modernism Modern architecture looked to simplify form and to avoid decoration. It wanted to 'strip' buildings of their artificial elements, and instead just express the function and meaning of a building through its form, preferably using modern materials such as steel and glass.

Normalcy The quality or condition of being normal. Creeping normalcy is a term often used to refer to the way a major change can be accepted as normality if it happens slowly, in unnoticed increments, when it would be regarded as objectionable if it took place in a single step or short period. Examples would be a change in job responsibilities, a change in a relationship or a change in a medical condition.

Otherness Otherness is the condition of being strange or different; of being something other than normal. Disabled people are often stigmatized by society's attitude towards them and made to feel like outcasts.

Phenomenology Phenomenology is the philosophical study of the structures of consciousness from a first-person perspective. In terms of architecture and design, phenomenology is the study and exploration of the physical experience of buildings, building materials and their sensory properties.

Post-humanism Post-humanism is a developing critical theory that has grown out of challenges to renaissance and modernist humanist thought, with its strict divides between minds and bodies, subjects and objects and humans and other species. Instead the post-human approach starts from trying to better understand the fluidity and ambiguity of inter-relationships, for example, between people, spaces, objects, animals and technologies. See Hayles (1999) and Wolfe (2009).

Post-modernism Post-modernism was a late twentieth-century architectural and design approach, which challenged modernist architecture by being jokey, brightly coloured and aiming to interconnect high and low cultural meanings.

Reasonable adjustments The Disability Discrimination Act requires employers to change the workplace environment or working arrangements if they make it very difficult for a disabled person to do their job. In some circumstances, it is appropriate to make adjustments as a general response to the needs of all disabled people (disability awareness training or taking accessibility into account when refurbishing). In other circumstances, the individual disabled person's needs should be taken into account. Adjustments can be as individual as the people who need them and the circumstances in which they are used.

Sensory design The design of an environment or landscape (often a garden) that offers a wide range of diverse sensory experiences and responses.

Sensory design encourages the user to physically interact with their environment, appealing to all five senses: touch, taste, sight, sound and smell.

The Slow Movement The Slow Movement is a cultural movement advocating the slowing down of life's pace in favour of a more enriched, less stressful lifestyle. Turn off the mobile, turn off the BlackBerry, turn off the laptop. Work less overtime, see your family, go for a walk. Smell the roses. Fight for your right to relax. Contrary to popular belief, however, it is not an excuse to be lazy but a cultural shift away from consumer culture. Not to be confused with constipation, which involves a less satisfying slow movement.

Spatial practices Go for a walk. Really.

Stereotypes A stereotype is a generalized, prejudicial label that stigmatizes a group or individual and is often based on superstition and myth with little or no basis in reality. Stereotyping negates a person's individuality and humanity. Disabled people are blessed with a diverse range of stereotypes. We can be inspirational. Tragic. Lazy. Evil. Pitiful. Pathetic. Twisted and bitter. A burden on society. An outcast. Special and brave. Stupid. Funny. Worthless. We're usually non-sexual, we often have a chip on our shoulder but just as often we triumph over 'adversity'. Obviously these stereotypes bear little resemblance to the reality of disability. However, if you catch a little person you can make them show you where they've hidden their pot of gold.

Toilets So vital, so relevant to everyone's lives and – the public and accessible ones – so badly designed and ugly.

Universal Design Universal Design approaches the design of products and environments from the point of view that they should be designed with everyone in mind, not just disabled people. It also places a greater emphasis on look and beauty than existing accessible design that is often purely functional.

Bibliography

Aaa-PEPRAV (ed.) (2007) *Urban Act: A Handbook for Alternative Practice*, Paris, France: aaa-PEPRAV.

Adams, R. (2013) 'Making a scene: a vivid genealogy of The Asclepius Machine', in *Scapegoat Journal: Architecture, Landscape, Political Economy: 0.4 Currency*, CreateSpace 054/02/2013. Online. Available HTTP: <http://www.scapegoatjournal.org/docs/04/04_Adams_MakingAScene.pdf> (accessed 24 October 2013).

Ahmed, S. (2000) *Strange Encounters: Embodied Others in Post-Coloniality*, London: Routledge.

Ahmed, S. (2006) *Queer Phenomenology: Orientations, Objects, Others*, Durham, NC: Duke University Press.

Ahmed, S. and Stacey, J. (eds) (2001) *Thinking through the Skin*, London: Routledge.

Akrich, M. and Latour, B. (1992) 'A summary of a convenient vocabulary for the semiotics of human and nonhuman assemblies', in W.E. Bijker and J. Law (eds), *Shaping Technology/Building Society: Studies in Sociotechnical Change*, Cambridge MA: MIT Press, pp. 259–64.

Albrecht, G.L., Seelman, K.D. and Bury, M. (eds) (2001) *Handbook of Disability Studies*, Thousand Oaks, CA: SAGE Publications.

Allen, L., Borden, I., O'Hare, N. and Spiller, N. (eds) (2009) *Bartlett Designs: Speculating with Architecture*, Chichester: John Wiley and Sons.

Anderberg, P. (2006a) 'Might and machines', in B. Jönsson (ed.) *Design Side by Side*, Lund, Sweden. Online. Available HTTP: <http://www.certec.lth.se/doc/designsidebyside> (accessed 28 September 2013).

Anderberg, P. (2006b) 'FACE: disabled people, technology and the internet', Doctoral Thesis for CERTEC Division of Rehabilitation Engineering Research, Department of Design Sciences, University of Lund. Online. Available HTTP: <http://www.arkiv.certec.lth.se/doc/face/face_final_version_5.pdf> (accessed 28 September 2013).

Bachelard, G. (1994) *Poetics of Space*, Boston, MA: Beacon Press.

Bayley, S. (2007) 'Now the South Bank's fit for a Festival again', *The Observer*, 20 May. Online. Available HTTP: <http://www.theguardian.com/artanddesign/2007/may/20/architecture.communities> (accessed 7 February 2014).

Bêka, I. and Lemoine, L. (2013) *Koolhaas Houselife*, BêkaPartners. Online. Available HTTP: <http://www.living-architectures.com/Koolhaas_houselife.php> (accessed 28 September 2013).

Benjamin, W. (2008) *The Work of Art in an Age of Mechanical Reproduction*, London: Penguin.

Bennett, J. (2010) *Vibrant Matter: A Political Ecology of Things*, Durham, NC: Duke University Press.

Bhabha, H. (1989) *The Location of Culture*, London: Routledge.

Bloomer, K.C. and Moore, C.W. (1977) *Body, Memory Architecture*, New Haven, CT: Yale University Press.

Blundell Jones, P., Petrescu, D. and Till, J. (eds) (2006) *Architecture and Participation*, London and New York: Spon Press.

Booker, C. and Lycett Green, C. (1973) *Goodbye London: An Illustrated Guide to Threatened Buildings*, London: Fontana.

Borden, I. (ed.) (2009) *Bartlett Designs: Speculating with Architecture*, Chichester: John Wiley and Sons.

Borden, I., Penner, B. and Rendell, J. (eds) (1999) *Gender, Space, Architecture: An Interdisciplinary Introduction*, London: Routledge.

Boys, J. (2007) *Making Discursive Spaces: A Collaboration between Deaf and Disabled Artists and Interior Architecture Students*. Online. Available HTTP <http://www.discursivespaces.co.uk/domains/discursivespaces.co.uk/local/media/downloads/Discursive_Spaces.pdf> (accessed 28 September 2013).

Boys, J. (2008) 'Between unsafe spaces and the comfort zone? Exploring the impact of learning environments on "doing" learning', paper at SOLSTICE conference, Edge Hill University, 5 June 2008.

Brueggemann, B.J. *et al.* (eds) (2002) *Disturbing Discourses: A Disability Studies Source*, New York: Modern Language Association (MLA) Press.

Buchanan, I. and Lambert, G. (eds) (2005) *Deleuze and Space*, Edinburgh: Edinburgh University Press.

Bunting, M. (2007) 'We need an attentiveness to nature to understand our own humanity' 'Comment is free', *The Guardian*, 30 July. Online. Available HTTP: <http://www.theguardian.com/commentisfree/2007/jul/30/comment.bookscomment> (accessed 10 February 2014).

Butler, J. (1993) *Bodies That Matter*, London: Routledge.

Butler, R. and Bowlby, S. (1997) 'Bodies and spaces: an exploration of disabled people's experiences of public space', *Environment and Planning D: Society and Space* 15(4): 411–33.

Butler, R. and Parr, H. (1999) *Mind and Body Spaces: Geographies of Illness, Impairment and Disability*, London: Routledge.

Button, G. (1993) 'The curious case of vanishing technology', in G. Button (ed.) *Technology in Working Order: Studies of Work, Interaction and Technology*, London: Routledge, pp. 10–28.

Byrd, T. (2007) Deaf Space *Gallaudet Today: The Magazine*, Spring. Online. Available HTTP: <http://www.gallaudet.edu/communications_and_public_relations/gallaudet_today_magazine/deaf_space_spring_2007.html> (accessed 29 September 2013).

Caruso, A. (2009) *The Feeling of Things*, Barcelona, Spain: Ediciones Poligrafa.

Cassara, S. (ed.) (2006) *Peter Eisenman: Feints*, Milan, Italy: Skira Editore.

Cavanagh, S. and Ware, V. (1990) *At Women's Convenience: Handbook on the Design of Women's Public Toilets*, London: Women's Design Service.

CEBE Special Interest Group (2002) *Building and Sustaining a Learning Environment for Inclusive Design*. Online. Available HTTP: <http://www.cebe.heacademy.ac.uk/learning/sig/inclusive/report.php> (accessed 28 September 2013).

Chaillou, T. 'Interview with Ryan Gander', *The White Review*. Online. Available HTTP: <http://www.thewhitereview.org/art/interview-with-ryan-gander/> (accessed 28 September 2013).

Chandler, E. (2011) 'The space of disability as geographic containment', Society for Disability Studies (SDS) Conference, Denver 2011.

Colletti, M. (1999) 'DigiTales', *Marjan Colletti* (blog). Online. Available HTTP: <http://marjan-colletti.blogspot.co.uk/1999/05/digitales.html> (accessed 6 February 2014).

Colletti, M. (2008) 'CyberBaroque and other DigiTales', OS1: LSBU Lecture Series 2007/08, London South Bank University UK, *Marjan Colletti* (blog). Online. Available HTTP: <http://marjan-colletti.blogspot.co.uk/2009/10/cyberbaroque-and-other-digitales-marjan.html> (accessed 6 February 2014).

Colletti, M. (2009) 'CyberBaroque architectural design', in K. Thorsen, U. Ender and P. Cernusca (eds), *Nordic Talking: 4 1/2 Years in Studio with Kjetil Thorsen*, New York: SpringerWien.

Collins, H.M. and Yearly, S. (1992) 'Epistemological chicken', in A. Pickering (ed.) *Science as Practice and Culture*, Chicago and London: University of Chicago Press.

Colomina, B. (ed.) (1996) *Sexuality and Space*, New York: Princeton Architectural Press.

Cook, P. (2008) *Drawing: The Motive Force of Architecture*, Chichester: John Wiley and Sons.

Corker, M. (1999) 'Differences, conflations and foundations: the limits to the "accurate" theoretical representation of disabled people's experiences', *Disability and Society* 14(4): 627–42.

Corker, M. and French, S. (eds) (1999) *Disability Discourse*, Buckingham: Open University Press.

Cousins, M. (1998) 'Building an architect', in J. Hill (ed.) *Occupying Architecture*, London: Routledge.

Cousins, M. (2011) 'Technology and prosthesis', *Hurly-Burly, The International Lacanian Journal of Psychoanalysis* 5 (March): 191–9.

Creal, L.D. (2006). 'The "disability of thinking" the "disabled" body course paper for ambiguous bodies', Studies in Contemporary Sexuality course paper, York University, Toronto, Canada. Online. Available HTTP: <http://www.broadreachtraining.com/advocacy/artcreal.htm> (accessed 10 February 2014).

Crow, L. (1996) 'Including all our lives', in J. Morris (ed.) *Encounters with Strangers: Feminism and Disability*, London: The Women's Press, pp. 206–26.

Crow, L. (2013) 'Lying down anyhow: an autoethnography', *Qualitative Inquiry*, 18 June 2013.

Crutchfield, S. and Epstein, M. (eds) (2000) *Points of Contact: Disability, Art and Culture*, Ann Arbor, MI: University of Michigan Press.

Cruz, M. (2008) 'Cyborgian interfaces', in M. Cruz and S. Pike (eds) *Architectural Design Special Issue: Neoplasmatic Design* 78(6) (November/December): 56–9.

Cruz, M. (2013) *The Bartlett Book*, London: Bartlett School of Architecture.

Cruz, M. (2014) 'Research interests', *NeoArch: The Blog of Marcos Cruz*. Online. Available HTTP: <http://marcoscruzarchitect.blogspot.co.uk/2009/11/research-interests-my-research-is.html> (accessed 6 February 2014).

Cruz, M. and Colletti, C. (2005) *MarcosandMarjan Interfaces/Intrafaces: 2* (Consequence Book Series on Fresh Architecture), Berlin: Springer Verlag.

Cupers, K. (ed.) (2013) *Use Matters: An Alternative History of Architecture*, London: Routledge.

Davis, L.J. (1995) *Enforcing Normalcy: Disability, Deafness, and the Body*, London: Verso.

Davis, L.J. (ed.) (1997) *The Disability Studies Reader*, London: Routledge.

Davis, L.J. (2002) *Bending Over Backwards: Disability, Dismodernism and Other Difficult Positions*, New York and London: New York University Press.

Davis, L.J. and Smith, M. (eds) (2006) 'Stumbling blocks: disability-visuality', *Journal of Visual Culture* 5(2).

De Cauwer, P., Clement, M., Buelens, H. and Heylighen, A. (2009) 'Four reasons not to teach inclusive design', conference proceedings, 'Include', Helen Hamlyn Centre, Royal College of Art, UK, 5–8 April 2009.

De Certeau, M. (2011) *The Practice of Everyday Life*, Berkeley, CA: University of California Press.

Dezeen (2013) 'Dyslexic Objects win New Designer of the Year Award 2013', *Dezeen Magazine*, 4 July. Online. Available HTTP: <http://www.dezeen.com/2013/07/04/dyslexic-products-by-henry-franks-win-new-designer-of-the-year-2013> (accessed 7 February 2014).

Dodd, J., Sandell, R., Delin, A. and Gay, J. (2002) 'Buried in the footnotes: the representation of disabled people in museums and galleries', Leicester University Department of Museum Studies. Online. Available HTTP: <https://lra.le.ac.uk/handle/2381/33> (accessed 28 September 2013).

Dunham-Jones, E. (2013) 'The irrational exuberance of Rem Koolhaas', *Design Observer*, 4 February. Online. Available HTTP: <http://places.designobserver.com/feature/rem-koolhaas-irrational-exuberance/37767/> (accessed 28 September 2013).

Dunne, A. (2008) *Hertzian Tales: Electronic Products, Aesthetic Experience and Critical Design*, Cambridge, MA: MIT Press.

Dunne, A. and Raby, F. (2013) *Speculative Everything: Design, Fiction and Social Dreaming*, Cambridge, MA: MIT Press.

Dutton, T.A. and Hurst Mann, L. (eds) (1996) *Reconstructing Architecture: Critical Discourses and Social Practices*, Minneapolis, MN: University of Minnesota Press.

Eisenman, P. (1999) *Diagram Diaries* (Universe Architecture Series), London: Thames and Hudson.

Elam, M. (1991) 'Living dangerously with Bruno Latour in a hybrid world', *Theory, Culture and Society* 16(4): 21.

Erevelles, N. (1997) 'Re-constituting the "disabled" other: historical materialism and the politics of schooling', paper presented at Annual Meeting of the American Research Association Chicago, 24 March 1997.

Evans, R., Johnston, P. and Mostafavi, M. (eds) (1996) *Translations from Drawing to Building and Other Essays*, London: AA Publications.

Ferre, A., Kubo, M. and Prat, R. (eds) (2002) *Verb Natures*, Barcelona: Actar.

Fitzsimons, K.J. (2012) 'Seeing motion otherwise: architectural design and the differently sensing and mobile', *Space and Culture* 15: 239, originally published online 16 August. Online. Available HTTP: <http://sac.sagepub.com/content/15/3/239> (accessed 28 September 2013).

Fox, A., Fox, J. and Ridley, P. (2008) *Overalls: A Blank Canvas*, Brighton: Access to Art/CUPP University of Brighton.

French, S. (1999) 'The wind gets in my way', in M. Corker and S. French (eds) *Disability Discourse*, Buckingham: Open University Press, pp. 21–7.

Fries, K. (1997) *Staring Back: The Disability Experience from the Inside Out*, New York: Plume.

Froyen, H., Herssens, J. and Heylighen, A. (2008) 'Buildings revis(it)ed', *A+ Belgisch Tijdschrift voor Architectuur* 210: 82–5.

Gabel, S. and Peters, S. (2004) 'Presage of a paradigm shift? Beyond the social model of disability toward a resistance theory of disability', *Disability and Society* 19(6): 571–96.

Gadamer, H. (1991) 'The conflict of interpretations: debate with Hans-Georg Gadamer', in M.J. Valdés (ed.) *A Ricoeur Reader*, Toronto, Canada: University of Toronto Press, pp. 216–41.

Galis, V. (2011) 'Enacting disability: how can science and technology studies inform disability studies?' *Disability and Society* 26(7) (December): 825–38.

Gallaudet University (2009) 'Making connections: DeafSpace concept goes to national architecture conference'. Online. Available HTTP: <http://www.gallaudet.edu/news/making_connections_deafspace_concept_goes_to_national_architecture_conference.html> (accessed 7 February 2014).

Garcia, M. (2010) *The Diagrams of Architecture: AD Reader*, Hoboken, NJ: Wiley.

Garfinkel, H. (1967) *Studies in Ethnomethodology*, Upper Saddle River, NJ: Prentice Hall.

Garland Thomson, R.G. (1997a) *Extraordinary Bodies: Figuring Physical Disability in American Culture and Literature*, New York: Columbia University Press.

Garland Thomson, R.G. (1997b) *Freakery: Cultural Spectacles of the Extraordinary Body*, New York: New York University Press.

Garland Thomson, R. (2009) *Staring: How We Look*, Oxford: Oxford University Press.

Ghirardo, D. (ed.) (1991) *Out of Site: A Social Criticism of Architecture*, Seattle: Bay Press.

Gill, C.J. (1995) 'A psychological view of disability culture', *Disability Studies Quarterly* 15(4).

Gissen, D. (2000) *Subnature: Architecture's Other Environments*, Princeton, NJ: Princeton University Press.

Gissen, D. (2008) 'Disability as architectural criticism – Yale/Rudolph', *HTC Experiments*, 3 October. Online. Available HTTP: <http://htcexperiments.org/2008/10/03/disability-as-architectural-criticism-yale-1996> (accessed 7 February 2014).

Gissen, D. (2013) 'New project: disability and historical reconstruction', *HTC Experiments*, 14 February. Online. Available HTTP: <http://htcexperiments.org/2013/02/14/new-project-disability-and-historical-reconstruction> (accessed 7 February 2014).

Goggin, G. and Newell, C. (2003) *Digital Disability: The Social Construction of Disability in New Media*, Lanham, MD: Rowman and Littlefield.

Goldsmith, S. (1997) *Designing for the Disabled: The New Paradigm*, Oxford: Architectural Press.

Goldsmith, S. (2000) *Universal Design*, Oxford: Architectural Press.

Goodley, D. (2011) *Disability Studies: An Interdisciplinary Introduction*, London: Sage.

Goodley, D., Hughes, B. and Davies, L. (eds) (2012) *Disability and Social Theory: New Developments and Directions*, Basingstoke: Palgrave Macmillan.

Goodman, C. (2011) *Lifetimes Homes Design Guide*, Watford: IHS BRE Press.

Grandin, T. (1995) *Thinking in Pictures: And Other Reports from My Life with Autism*, London: Vintage Books.

Grandin, T. (2005) *The Unwritten Rules of Social Relationships*, Arlington, TX: Future Horizons Inc.

Gregg, M. and Seigworth, G.J. (eds) (2010) *The Affect Theory Reader*, Durham, NC: Duke University Press.

Grosz, E. (1995) *Space Time and Perversion*, London: Routledge.

Grosz, E. (2001) *Architecture from the Outside*, Cambridge, MA: MIT Press.

Hagan, A. (1999) 'Carving out a space to act: acquired impairment and contested identity', in M. Corker and S. French (eds) *Disability Discourse*, Buckingham: Open University Press.

Hamraie, A. (2012) 'Universal design research as a new materialist practice', *Disability Studies Quarterly* 32(4).

Hamraie, A. (2013) 'Designing collective access: a feminist disability theory of universal design', *Disability Studies Quarterly* 33(4). Online. Available HTTP: <http://dsq-sds.org/article/view/3871/3411> (accessed 10 February 2014).

Handler, S. (2010) 'Resistant sitting: the pensioner's alternative street furniture guide', Project Report RIBA/ICE McAslan Bursary. Online. Available HTTP: <http://www.architecture.com/Files/RIBAProfessionalServices/Education/Awards/2010/SophieHandlerReport.pdf>. See also <http://www.ageing-facilities.net/projects/#post-49> (both accessed 10 February 2014).

Haraway, D. (1985) 'A cyborg manifesto: science, technology, and socialist-feminism in the late twentieth century', *Socialist Review* 80 S: 65–108.

Haraway, D. (1991) *Simians, Cyborgs and Women: The Reinvention of Nature*, London: Routledge.

Haraway, D. (1994) 'A game of cat's cradle: science studies, feminist theory, cultural studies', *Configurations* 2(1): 59–71.

Haraway, D. (1997) *Modest_Witness@Second_Millennium.FemaleMan©Meets_OncoMouse™: Feminism and Technoscience*, London: Routledge.

Haraway, D. (1998) 'The persistence of vision', in N. Mizoeff (ed.) *The Visual Culture Reader*, London: Routledge.

Haraway, D. (2003) *The Companion Species Manifesto: Dogs, People, and Significant Otherness*, Cambridge: Prickly Paradigm Press.

Haraway, D. (2007) *When Species Meet*, Minneapolis, MN: University of Minnesota Press.

Harrison, A.L. (ed.) (2012) *Architectural Theories of the Environment: Posthuman Territory*, London: Routledge.

Hayles, K.N. (1999) *How We Became Posthuman: Virtual Bodies in Cybernetics, Literature and Informatics*, Chicago, IL: University of Chicago Press.

Heidingsfelder, M. and Tesch, M. (directors) (2008) *Rem Koolhaas: A Kind of Architect*, Arthouse Films.

Hensel, M., Menges, A. and Hight, C. (2009) *Space Reader: Hetrogeneous Space in Architecture (AD Reader)*, Chichester: John Wiley and Sons.

Hensel, M., Menges, A. and Weinstock, M. (eds) (2004) *Emergence: Morphogenetic Design Strategies* (Architectural Design), Hoboken, NJ: Wiley.

Hertzberger, H. (2009) *Lessons for Students in Architecture*, 2nd revised edn, Rotterdam: 010 Uitgeverij.

Hetherington, K. (2003) 'Accountability and disposal: visual impairment and the museum', *Museum and Society* 1(2) (June): 104–15.

Heylighen, A., Herssens, J. and Froyen, H. (2009) 'Architecture criticism blindfolded', conference paper presented at 'Include' Conference 'Inclusive design into innovation: transforming practice in design, research and business', Royal College of Art, London, 5–8 April 2009.

Hill, J. (ed.) (1998) *Occupying Architecture: Between the Architect and the User*, London: Routledge.

Hill, J. (2003) *Actions of Architecture: Architects and Creative Users*, London: Routledge.

Holl, S. (2000) *Parallax*, Princeton, NJ: Princeton University Press.

Holl, S., Pallasmaa, J. and Perez-Gomez, A. (eds) (2006) *Questions of Perception: Phenomenology of Architecture*, 3rd edn, San Francisco, CA: William Stout.

Holmer Nadesan, M. (2005) *Constructing Autism: Unravelling the 'Truth' and Understanding the Social*, London: Routledge.

Howes, D. (ed.) (1991) *The Varieties of Sensory Experience: A Sourcebook in the Anthropology of the Senses*, Toronto: University of Toronto Press.

Hunt, P. (1996) 'A critical condition', in P. Hunt (ed.) *Stigma: The Experience of Disability*, London: Geoffrey Chapman. Online. Available HTTP: <http://disability-studies.leeds.ac.uk/files/library/Hunt-critical-condition.pdf> (accessed 28 September 2013).

Husserl, E. (1969) *Ideas: General Introduction to Pure Phenomenology*, St Leonards, Australia: Allen and Unwin.

Imrie, R. (1996) *Disability and the City*, London: Paul Chapman.

Imrie, R. (1998) 'Oppression, disability and access in the built environment', in T. Shakespeare (ed.) *The Disability Reader: Social Science Perspectives*, London: Cassell, pp. 129–46.

Imrie, R. (2003) 'Architects' conceptions of the human body', *Environment and Planning D: Society and Space* 21(1): 47–65.

Imrie, R. and Hall, P. (2001) *Inclusive Design: Designing and Developing Accessible Environments*, London and New York: Spon Press.

Ingold, T. (2011) *Being Alive: Essays on Movement, Knowledge and Description*, London: Routledge.

Jacobs, J. (1961) *The Death and Life of the Great American Cities*, London: Vintage.

Jain, S.S. (1999) 'The prosthetic imagination: enabling and disabling the prosthetic trope', *Science, Technologies and Human Values* 24(1).

Jameson, F. (1991) *Postmodernism or the Cultural Logic of Late Capitalism*, Durham, NC: Duke University Press.

'Johnson, J.' (Bruno Latour) (1988) 'Mixing humans and nonhumans together: the sociology of a door-closer', *Social Problems* 35(3), Special Issue: The Sociology of Science and Technology (June): 298–310. Online. Available HTTP: <http://links.jstor.org/sici?sici=0037-7791%28198806%2935%3A3%3C298%3AMHANTT%3E2.0.CO%3B2-U> (accessed 28 September 2013).

Jönsson, B. (ed.) 'Design side by side', *Certec*. Online. Available HTTP: <http://www.arkiv.certec.lth.se/doc/designsidebyside/> (accessed 28 September 2013).

Jönsson, B. and Anderberg, P. (1999) 'Rehabilitation engineering and design research: theory and method', Lund, Sweden: Lund University, LTH, *Certec*. Online. Available HTTP: <http://www.english.certec.lth.se/theory.html> (accessed 10 February 2014).

Kajita, M. (2013) 'Spatial dimensions of accessibility', PhD thesis, Institute of Planning, the Royal Danish Academy of Fine Arts, School of Architecture, Design and Conservation (unpublished).

Keidan, L. and Mitchell, C.J. (eds) (2012) *Access All Areas: Live Art and Disability*, London: Live Art Development Agency.

Keith, L. (1996) 'Encounters with strangers', in J. Morris (ed.) *Encounters with Strangers: Feminism and Disability*, London: The Women's Press, pp. 69–88.

Kimmelman, M. (2011) 'The ascension of Peter Zumthor', *New York Times*, 13 March. Online. Available HTTP: <http://www.nytimes.com/2011/03/13/magazine/mag-13zumthor-t.html> (accessed 28 September 2013).

Knevitt, C. and Wates, N. (2013) *Community Architecture: How People Are Creating Their Own Environments*, London: Routledge Revivals (orig. pub. 1987).

Knight, G. and Bichard, J. (2011) *Publically Accessible Toilets: An Inclusive Design Guide*, London: Helen Hamyln Centre for Design, Royal College of Art.

Knox, P.L. (2005) 'Creating ordinary places: slow cities in a fast world', *Journal of Urban Design* 10(1) (February): 1–11.

Koolhaas, R. (1994) *Delirious New York*, New York: Monacelli Press.

Koolhaas, R. (1998) *OMA/Rem Koolhaas: Living, Vivre, Leben*, Basel: Arc en Rêve Centre D'architecture and Birkhäuser.

Koolhaas, R. (1999) 'Transformations'. Van Dyck Laboratorium Antwerpen, Lecture, 25 June.

Koolhaas, R. (2004) *Content*, Cologne: Taschen.

Koolhaas, R. and Mau, B. (1995) *S, M, L, XL*, New York: Monacelli Press.

Koolhaas, R. and Obrist, H.U. (2007) *The Conversation Series 4*, Cologne: Walther König.

Kurtzman, S.L. (2011) 'Presence and prosthesis: a response to Nelson and Wright', *Cultural Anthropology* 16(3).

Latour, B. (1992) 'Where are the missing masses? The sociology of a few mundane artifacts', in W.E. Bijker and J. Law (eds) *Shaping Technology/Building Society: Studies in Sociotechnical Change*, Cambridge, MA and London: MIT Press.

Latour, B. (2007a) *Reassembling the Social: An Introduction to Actor–Network Theory*, Oxford: Oxford University Press.

Latour, B. (2007b) 'Turning around politics: a note on Gerard de Vries' paper', *Social Studies of Science* 37(5): 811–20.

Latour, B. and Yaneva, A. (2012) 'Give me a gun and I will make all buildings move: an ANT's view of architecture', in A.L. Harrison (ed.) *Architectural Theories of the Environment: Posthuman Territory*, London: Routledge, pp. 107–14.

Laurier, E. (2005) 'Searching for a parking space', *Intellectica* 2–3(41–42): 1010–15.

Law, J. (1991) 'Introduction: monsters, machines and sociotechnical relations', in J. Law (ed.) *A Sociology of Monsters? Essays on Power, Technology and Domination*, London: Routledge, pp 1–23.

Law, J. and Hassard, J. (eds) (1999) *Actor Network Theory and After*, Oxford and Keele: Blackwell and the Sociological Review.

Leach, N., Turnbull, D. and Williams, C. (eds) (2004) *Digital Tectonics*, Lagos, Nigeria: Academy Press.

Lellis, J.C. (2011) 'Silence on the stomping grounds: a case study of public communication about disability in the 1990s', *Disability and Society* 26(7): 809–23. Online. Available HTTP: <http://dx.doi.org/10.1080/09687599.2011.618734> (accessed 1 March 2013).

Lewinson, A. (2005) 'At the Guggenheim Grozny', *Hayden's Ferry Review*, 36 (Spring/Summer). Online. Available HTTP: <http://www.asu.edu/piper/publications/haydensferryreview/issue36/fiction/pdfs/guggenheim_grozny.pdf> (accessed 6 February 2014).

Lifchez, R. (1986) *Rethinking Architecture: Design Students And Physically Disabled People*, Berkeley, CA: University of California Press.

Linton, S. (2002) *Claiming Disability: Knowledge and Identity*, New York: New York University Press.

Lokko, L. (ed.) (1999) *White Papers, Black Marks: Architecture, Race, Culture*, London: Continuum.

Lynn, G. (2011) *Animate Form*, Princeton, NJ: Princeton University Press.

MacPherson, H. (2012) 'Guiding visually impaired walking groups: intercorporeal experiences and ethical sensibilities', in M. Paterson and M. Dodge (eds) *Touching Space, Placing Touch*, Farnham: Ashgate.

Mairs, N. (1996) *Waist-High in the World: A Life Among the Nondisabled*, Boston, MA: Beacon Press.

Manley, S., de Graft-Johnson, A. and Lucking, K. (2011) *Disabled Architects: Unlocking the Potential for Practice*. Project Report. London: Royal Institute of British Architects (RIBA).

Matrix (1984) *Making Space: Women and the Man-Made Environment*, London: Pluto Press.

McCorquodale, D., Wigglesworth, S. and Ruedi, K. (eds) (2001) *Desiring Practices: Architecture, Gender and the Interdisciplinary*, London: Black Dog.

McDonough, W. and Partners (1992) *The Hannover Principles: Design for Sustainability*, Charlottesville, VA: William McDonough & Partners. Online. Available HTTP: <http://www.mcdonough.com/wp-content/uploads/2013/03/Hannover-Principles-1992.pdf> (accessed 28 September 2013).

Melhuish, C. (2005) 'Concrete as the conduit of experience', in K. Lloyd Thomas (ed.) *Material Matters*, London: Routledge.

Merleau-Ponty, M. (2013) *Phenomenology of Perception*, London: Routledge (orig. pub. 1945).

Michalko, R. (1998) *The Two in One: Walking with Smokie, Walking with Blindness*, Philadelphia, PA: Temple University Press.

Michalko, R. (2002) 'Estranged-familiarity', in M. Corker and T. Shakespeare (eds) *Disability/Postmodernity: Embodying Disability Theory*, London: Continuum.

Miller, D. (ed.) (2009) *Anthropology and the Individual: A Material Culture Perspective*, Oxford: Berg.

Minter, S.B. (2007) *Unruly Bodies: Life Writing by Women with Disabilities*, Chapel Hill, NC: University of North Carolina Press.

Mol, A. (2008) *The Logic of Care: Health and the Problem of Patient Choice*, London: Routledge.

Mol, A., Moser, I. and Pols, J. (eds) (2010) *Care in Practice: On Tinkering in Clinics, Homes and Farms*, Bielefeld, Germany: transcript Verlag.

Morris, J. (ed.) (1996) *Encounters with Strangers: Feminism and Disability*, London: The Women's Press.

Morrow, R. (1999) 'One step forward, two steps back: how the process of thinking and evaluation can undermine inclusive design in schools of architecture', *Journal of the European Institute of Design and Disability* 5: 61–3.

Morrow, R. (2000) 'Architectural assumptions and environmental discrimination: the case for more inclusive design in schools of architecture', in D. Nicol and S. Pilling (eds) *Changing Architectural Education Towards a New Professionalism*, London and New York: Taylor & Francis, pp. 43–8.

Morrow, R. and Moore, K. (2004) 'An inclusive design dialogue on ethics and aesthetics', conference proceedings, Open Space international conference on inclusive environments, Edinburgh, 27–9 October. Online. Available HTTP: <http://www.openspace.eca.ac.uk/conference/proceedings/summary/MooreK.htm> (accessed 28 September 2013).

Morrow, R., Parnell, R. and Torrington, J. (2004) 'Reality versus creativity?' *CEBE Transactions* 1(2) (December): 91–9. Online. Available HTTP: <http://cebe.cf.ac.uk/transactions/pdf/RuthMorrow.pdf> (accessed 28 September 2013).

Moser, I. (2005) 'On becoming disabled and articulating alternatives: the multiple modes of ordering disability and their interferences', *Cultural Studies* 19(6): 667–700.

Moser, I. and Law, J. (1999) 'Good passages, bad passages', in J. Law and J. Hassard (eds) *Actor–Network Theory and After*, Oxford: The Sociological Review and Blackwell, pp. 196–219.

Moser, I. and Law, J. (2003) '"Making voices": new media technologies, disabilities, and articulation', in G. Liestøl, T. Rasmussen and A. Morrison (eds) *Innovation: Media, Methods and Theories*, Cambridge, MA: MIT Press, pp. 491–520.

Norberg-Schulz, C. (1980) *Genius Loci Towards a Phenomenology of Architecture*, New York: Rizzoli International Publications.

Novak, M. (1991) 'Liquid architectures in cyberspace', in M. Benedikt (ed.) *Cyberspace: First Steps*, Cambridge MA: MIT Press.

Oliver, M. (1992) 'Changing the social relations of research production?' *Disability, Handicap and Society* 7(2): 101–14.

Oliver, M. (1996) *Understanding Disability: From Theory to Practice*, Basingstoke: Macmillan.

O'Neill, J. (1995) *The Poverty of Postmodernism*, London: Routledge.

Östlund, B. (2004) 'Social science research on technology and the elderly: does it exist?', *Science Studies* 17(2): 44–62.

Pallasmaa, J. (2005) *The Eyes of the Skin: Architecture and the Senses*, Chichester: John Wiley and Sons.

Pallasmaa, J. (2009) *The Thinking Hand*, Chichester: John Wiley and Sons.

Partington-Sollinger, Z. (2008a) 'The seven strengths of Inside Out', Architecture-InsideOut. Online. Available HTTP: <http://www.architecture-insideout.co.uk/?location_id=28> (accessed 28 September 2013).

Partington-Sollinger, Z. (2008b) *Naked Space*, CABE Scholarship report. Unpublished.

Payne G.C. (1976) 'Making a lesson happen: an ethnomethodolgical analysis', in M. Hammersley and P. Woods (eds) *The Process of Schooling*, London: Routledge.

Penner, B. (2013) *Bathroom*, London: Reaktion Press.

Petrescu, D. (ed.) (2006) *Altering Practices: Feminist Politics and Poetics of Space*, London: Routledge.

Price, M. (2009) 'Access imagined: the construction of disability in conference policy documents', *Disability Studies Quarterly* 29(1).

Pullin, G. (2009) *Design Meets Disability*, Cambridge MA: MIT Press.

Rashid, H. and Couture, L.A. (1995) *Asymptote: Architecture at the Interval*, New York: Rizzoli International Publications.

Rasmussen, S.E. (1964) *Experiencing Architecture*, Cambridge, MA: MIT Press.

Reiser, J. and Umemoto, N. (2006) *The Atlas of Novel Tectonics*, Princeton, NJ: Princeton University Press.

Ridell, A. and Watson, N. (eds) (2003) *Disability, Culture and Identity*, Harlow: Pearson.

Roets, G. and Braidotti, R. (2012) 'Nomadology and subjectivity: Deleuze, Guattari and critical disability studies', in D. Goodley, B. Hughes and L. Davies (eds) *Disability and Social Theory: New Developments and Directions*, Basingstoke: Palgrave Macmillan.

Rohan, T.M. (2014) *The Architecture of Paul Rudolph*, New Haven, CT: Yale University Press.

Rose, S. (2007) 'The perforated palace', *The Guardian*, 19 November. Online. Available HTTP: <http://www.theguardian.com/world/2007/nov/19/germany.architecture> (accessed 28 September 2013).

Rudosky, B. (1987) *Architecture without Architects*, Albuquerque, NM: University of New Mexico Press.

Ryave, A.L. and Schenkein, J.N. (1974) 'Notes on the art of walking', in R. Turner (ed.) *Ethnomethodoloy*, London: Penguin.

Sacks, H. (1984) 'On doing "being ordinary"', in J.M. Atkinson and J. Heritage (eds) *Structures of Social Action: Studies in Conversation Analysis*, Cambridge: Cambridge University Press.

Samuels, E. (2002) 'Critical divides: Judith Butler's body theory and the question of disability', *National Women's Studies Association Journal* 14(3) (Fall).

Sargent, E. (ed.) (2012) *Superhuman: Exploring Human Enhancement from 600BCE to 2050*, Wellcome Collection exhibition catalogue (19 July–16 October).

Schillmeier, M. (2010) *Rethinking Disability: Bodies, Senses and Things*, London: Routledge.

Scott, J.W. (1988) 'Deconstructing equality-versus-difference: or, the uses of post-structuralist theory for feminism', *Feminist Studies* 14(1): 32–50.

Searle, A. (2011) 'Ryan Gander: Locked Room Scenario – review', *The Guardian*, 25 August. Online. Available HTTP: <http://www.theguardian.com/artanddesign/2011/aug/25/ryan-gander-locked-room-scenario-review> (accessed 6 February 2014).

Shakespeare, T. (ed.) (1998) *The Disability Reader: Social Sciences Perspectives*, London: Cassell.

Shakespeare, T. (2000) *Help (Imagining Welfare)*, New York: Venture Press.

Shakespeare, T. and Corker, M. (eds) (2002) *Disability/Postmodernity: Embodying Disability Theory*, London: Continuum.

Sheldon, A. (2004) 'Changing technology', in J. Swain, S. French, C. Barnes and C. Thomas (eds) *Disabling Barriers, Enabling Environments*, London: Sage.

Shildrick, M. (1997) *Leaky Bodies and Boundaries: Feminism, Postmodernism and (Bio)ethics*, London: Routledge.

Shildrick, M. (2001) *Embodying the Monster: Encounters with the Vulnerable Self*, London: Sage.

Shildrick, M. (2012) *Dangerous Discourses of Disability, Subjectivity and Sexuality*, Basingstoke: Palgrave Macmillan.

Shonfield, K. (2000) *Walls Have Feelings: Architecture, Film and the City*, London: Routledge.

Shove, E. (2003a) 'Converging conventions of comfort, cleanliness and convenience', *Journal of Consumer Policy* 26: 395–418. Online. Available HTTP: <http://seedconsortium.pbworks.com/w/file/fetch/45925154/shovecomfort.pdf> (accessed 10 February 2014).

Shove, E. (2003b) 'Rushing around: coordination, mobility and inequality', published by the Department of Sociology, Lancaster University, Lancaster. Online. Available HTTP: <http://www.lancaster.ac.uk/sociology/research/publications/papers/shove-rushing-around.pdf> (accessed 10 February 2014).

Siebers, T. (2003) 'Disability aesthetics and the built environment', Lecture at Penn State University, 5 December 2003. Online. Available HTTP: <http://rockethics.psu.edu/events/disability-aesthetics-and-the-built-environment> (accessed 28 September 2013).

Siebers, T. (2008) *Disability Theory*, Ann Arbor, MI: University of Michigan Press.

Siebers, T. (2010a) *Disability Aesthetics*, Ann Arbor, MI: University of Michigan Press.

Siebers, T. (2010b) 'The art of disability: an interview with Tobin Siebers by Mike Levin', *Disability Studies Quarterly* 30(2).

Singer, J. (1999) 'Why can't you be normal for once in your life?', in M. Corker and S. French (eds) *Disability Discourse*, Buckingham: Open University Press, p. 64.

Slack, S. (1999) 'I am more than my wheels', in M. Corker and S. French (eds) *Disability Discourse*, Buckingham: Open University Press, p. 33.

Smith, K. (2002) 'Evaluating an "unhealthy" seminar', *Universal Design Education*. Online. Available HTTP: <http://www.udeducation.org/techniques/98.html> (accessed 6 February 2014).

Snyder, S.L. and Mitchell, D.T. (eds) *Cultural Locations of Disability*, Chicago, IL: University of Chicago Press.

Snyder, S.L., Brueggemann, B.J. and Garland-Thomson, R. (eds) (2002) *Disability Studies: Enabling the Humanities*, New York: MLA Press.

Sobchack, V. (1995) 'Beating the meat/surviving the text, or how to get out of the century alive', in M. Featherstone and R. Burrows (eds) *Cyberspace/Cyberbodies/Cyberpunk: Cultures of Technological Embodiment*, London: Sage, pp. 205–14.

Sobchack, V. (2004) 'Abstract for the Art, Technology and Culture Colloquium', UC Berkeley's Centre for New Media, 15 March 2004. Online. Available HTTP: <http://atc.berkeley.edu/bio/Vivian_Sobchack> (accessed 28 September 2013).

Sobchack, V. (2006) 'A leg to stand on: prosthetics, metaphor, and materiality', in M. Smith and J. Morra (eds) *The Prosthetic Impulse: From a Posthuman Present to a Biocultural Future*, Cambridge, MA: MIT Press.

Sontag, S. (2004) *Regarding the Pain of Others*, London: Penguin.

Spiller, N. (1998) *Digital Dreams: Architecture and Cyberspace*, London: Ellipsis.

Stengers, I. (2000) *The Invention of Modern Science*, Minneapolis, MN: University of Minnesota Press.

Strickfaden, M. and Heylighen, A. (2009) 'Who are they? Student voices about "the other"', conference proceedings, 'Include', Helen Hamlyn Centre, Royal College of Art, UK, 5–8 April 2009.

Strickfaden, M., Devlieger, P. and Heylighen, A. (2009) 'Building empathy through dialogue', 8th European Academy of Design Conference – 1–3 April 2009, The Robert Gordon University, Aberdeen, Scotland. Online. Available HTTP: <https://lirias.kuleuven.be/bitstream/123456789/198821/2/Strickfaden+et+al2009Building+empathy+through+dialogue.pdf accessed> (accessed 28 September 2013).

Studio H (2010) 'Architectural precedent studies', 8 October. Online. Available HTTP: <http://www.studio-h.org/architectural-precedent-studies> (accessed 7 February 2014).

Swain, J. and French, S. (2000) 'Towards an affirmative model of disability', *Disability and Society* 15(4): 569–85.

Swain, J., Finkelstein, V., French, S. and Oliver, M. (1993) *Disabling Barriers: Enabling Environments*, London: Sage.

Thomas, C. (1999a) 'Narrative identity and the disabled self', in M. Corker and S. French (eds) *Disability Discourse*, Buckingham: Open University Press.

Thomas, C. (1999b) *Female Forms: Experiencing and Understanding Disability*, Buckingham: Open University Press.

Thrift, N. (2007) *Non-Representational Theory: Space, Politics, Affect*, London: Routledge.

Till, J. (2009) *Architecture Depends*, Cambridge, MA: MIT Press.

Titchkosky, T. (2002) 'Cultural maps: which way to disability?', in M. Corker and

T. Shakespeare (eds) *Disability/Postmodernity: Embodying Disability Theory*, London: Continuum.

Titchkosky, T. (2003) *Disability, Self and Society*, Toronto: University of Toronto Press.

Titchkosky, T. (2007) *Reading and Writing Disability Differently*, Toronto: University of Toronto Press.

Titchkosky, T. (2008) '"To pee or not to pee?" Ordinary talk about extraordinary exclusions in a university environment', *Canadian Journal of Sociology/Cahiers canadiens de sociologie* 33(1).

Titchkosky, T. (2011) *The Question of Access: Disability, Space, Meaning*, Toronto: University of Toronto Press.

Titchkosky, T. and Michalko, R. (eds) (2009) *Re-thinking Normalcy: A Disability Studies Reader*, Toronto: Canadian Scholars' Press Inc.

Tschumi, B. (1996) *Architecture and Disjunction*, Cambridge, MA: MIT Press.

University of Brighton (2008) 'Overalls research', Faculty of Arts, University of Brighton. Online. Available HTTP: <http://arts.brighton.ac.uk/study/fine-art/maiap/projects/overalls-research2> (accessed 7 February 2014).

UPIAS (Union of the Physically Impaired Against Segregation) (1975) *Fundamental Principles of Disability*. London: Union of Physically Impaired Against Segregation. Online. Available at: <http://disability-studies.leeds.ac.uk/files/library/UPIAS-fundamental-principles.pdf> (accessed 10 February 2014).

Vidler, A. (2000) 'Diagrams of diagrams: architectural abstraction and modern representation', *Representations* 72 (Autumn): 1–20. Online. Available HTTP: <http://links.jstor.org/sici?sici=0734-6018%28200023%290%3A72%3C1%3ADODAAA%3E2.0.CO%3B2-G> (accessed on 28 September 2013).

VocalEyes (2007) 'Case study – VocalEyes architecture tours: engaging with our built environment'. Online. Available HTTP: <www.vocaleyes.co.uk/core/core_picker/download.asp?id=343> (accessed 28 September 2013).

Wates, N. (1976) *The Battle for Tolmers Square*, London: Routledge and Kegan Paul.

Weiss, G. (2003) 'The body as a narrative horizon', in J. Cohen and G. Weiss (eds) *Thinking the Limits of the Body*, New York: State University of New York Press, pp. 25–38.

Wendell, S. (1996) *The Rejected Body: Feminist Philosophical Reflections on Disability*, London: Routledge.

Whatmore, S. (2012) 'Hybrid cartographies for a relational ethics', in A.L. Harrison (ed.) *Architectural Theories of the Environment: Posthuman Territory*, London: Routledge, pp. 249–57.

Wigley, M. (1991) 'Prosthetic theory: the disciplining of architecture', *Assemblage* 15 (August): 6–29. Online. Available HTTP: <http://www.jstor.org/stable/3171122> (accessed 8 February 2014).

Wigley, M. (1996) 'Untitled: the housing of gender', in B. Colomina (ed.) *Sexuality and Space*, New York: Princeton Architectural Press.

Williamson, A. (2010) 'Disability and new artistic models: a study room guide to live art and disability', *This is Live Art*. Online. Available HTTP: <http://www.thisisliveart.co.uk/uploads/documents/SRG_aaron_williamson_2010.pdf> (accessed 10 February 2014).

Wilson, J.C. (2000) 'Making disability visible: how disability studies might transform the medical and science writing', *Technical Communication Quarterly* 9: 149–61.

Wilson, J.C. and Lewiecki-Wilson, C. (eds) (2001) *Embodied Rhetorics: Disability in Language and Culture*, Carbondale, IL: Southern Illinois University Press.

Winance, M. (2006) 'Trying out the wheelchair', *Science, Technology, and Human Values* 31(1): 52–72.

Wolfe, C. (2009) *What is Posthumanism?* Minneapolis, MN: University of Minnesota Press.

Woodward, J. (1975) 'Variation in American sign language syntax: agent–beneficiary directionality', in R.W. Fasold and R.W. Shuy (eds) *Analyzing Variation in Language*, Washington DC: Georgetown University Press, pp. 303–11.

Zola, I.K. (1993) 'Self, identity and the naming question: reflections on the language of disability', *Social Science and Medicine* 36(2): 167–73.

Zumthor, P. (1999) *Thinking Architecture*, Berlin: Birkhauser.

Zumthor, P. (2010) *Atmospheres: Architectural Environments – Surrounding Objects*, Berlin: Birkhauser.

Index

Note: Page numbers in **bold** refer to the Glossary/terminology. Numbers followed by 'n' refer to footnotes.